PROBLEMS OF
HISTORICAL PSYCHOLOGY

Problems of

Historical Psychology

by

Zevedei Barbu

GROVE PRESS, INC.   NEW YORK

To
LUCIAN
who taught me humility
by bearing so lightly
the burden of his greatness

CONTENTS

Contents

PREFACE

This study is rooted in the conviction that a close co-operation between the disciplines of psychology and history opens new and fruitful perspectives for the understanding of both fields. Though presented in the idiom of psychology, the problems with which this book is concerned, appeal to historian and psychologist alike. Of course, research in the combined disciplines is not an easy task. My aim, therefore, was to do no more than to present a few selected examples which should illustrate, on the one hand, the application of historical concepts and methods to the study of the human mind, and on the other, the use to the historian of some of the conceptual tools of contemporary psychology. I say 'illustrate' since I am aware, as the reader will be, that all the problems tackled here need to be followed up by more detailed investigation.

There is something else which this study tries to illustrate, namely, a single-handed inter-disciplinary approach. Though this may appear as easy rationalization, I have to confess to a certain dislike of the idea of 'team work' so frequently used in the field of the social sciences. Admittedly, the 'team approach' presents certain advantages, such as a more detailed and accurate account of the facts bearing on a specific problem, but it seldom produces what is supposed to produce, namely, the feeling of unity. The impression which such an approach gives is often that of a series of 'themes' running in parallel, of a wrongly counterpointed polyphony.

I cannot close this preface without acknowledging my warmest gratitude to Professor W. J. H. Sprott who read the manuscript and made a number of fruitful criticisms. I owe very much, too, to Professor R. W. Pickford, Professor N. Davis, Professor R. G. Smith, Mr. H. O. Chalk, and Dr. A. Wasserstein who took the trouble to read and discuss with me various parts of the manuscript.

In the editing of the book I relied on the kind help of many friends. I wish to express my indebtedness in particular to

Miss I. Coventry, and Mr. J. M. Rillie. I would also like to thank my wife for her constant assistance.

One last word for the reader. As English is a relatively recent acquisition of mine, I apologise for all the unpleasant feelings which my clumsy use of the language may arouse in him.

Z. B.

I

INTRODUCTION

PSYCHOLOGY AND HISTORY

OF all living creatures man alone is truly historical, and this is because he has a mind by which he can create new conditions of life which absorb and transform the previous ones. Of all civilizations, Western civilization is the most historical in character. In spite of this, one of the main aims of modern psychology has been to model itself on the pattern of the natural sciences; its main ambition has been to formulate concepts, descriptive and explicative, which can be applied generally. Thus time and even space are considered as abstractions; they do not affect either the nature, or the norms of psychological phenomena. Various attempts have been made to build up 'mathematical' models of behaviour. Even Freud, who was more aware than any other modern psychologist of the basically irrational character of the human mind, was obsessed with the idea of an almost mechanical determinism in the field of psychological phenomena. It was this idea that fostered in him the belief in the universal validity of the basic concepts of his system. The knowledge of the statistical nature of the norms governing psychological phenomena did not temper this ambition of modern psychology. As in other scientific disciplines, probability has easily been turned into a new form of determinism.

A certain change in this situation has been brought about by the recent development of a psychologically-oriented anthropology, and of a social psychology in particular. This has increased the psychologist's awareness of the fact that the validity of his concepts is relative to a specific socio-cultural system. The 'personality-culture' theory is one manifestation of this spirit of relativity in modern psychology. If the analogy with the development of the natural sciences can be stretched, one could say that in psychology too space has ceased to be an abstraction; in its concrete form of social space it has become an important dimension of psychological phenomena. Thus an individual act of perception, of memory, or imagination, a feeling, an attitude, or a specific mental structure can adequately be understood only within a surrounding social space.

But these perspectives opened by social psychology and anthropology have as yet had little effect on the development of present-day psychology. The psychologists—social psychologists included—are consciously, or unconsciously, reluctant to face all the implications which the idea of the socio-cultural relativity of mental phenomena has for the constitution of their discipline as a science. They are particularly reluctant to admit that any socio-cultural relativity entails historical relativity, that a culturally-conditioned is at the same time an historically-conditioned phenomenon.

To mention two typical methodological trends in present-day psychology will illustrate this. Curiously enough these seem to be more characteristic of social psychology than of other branches of modern psychology. The first can be briefly described as a 'situational' approach to the study of mental phenomena. The term 'situational' is used here in a broader sense than that assigned to it by Lewin, for the simple reason that the kind of attitude which it suggests cannot be confined to a specific school in present-day psychology. It denotes a tendency widespread among psychologists to determine and explain any mental phenomenon in terms of a limited number of elements existing in a given situation contemporaneously with the phenomenon itself. In other words, it denotes the psychologist's unwillingness, or incapacity, to include in his model of explanation conditions which do not belong to a manipulable present. The tendency is to make '*hic et nunc*' decisive for the determination of any mental event. Obviously, by such an attitude the psychologist minimizes, or ignores altogether the importance which past experiences, individual or collective, might have upon the determination of a specific mental phenomenon. In other words, *time,* individual or historical, is not considered as a dimension of the human mind.

Even more symptomatic is the tendency to *predict* behaviour.

This is more than just a tendency, it is an ambition, an aspiration so often voiced by psychologists that one might well think that the whole future of psychology depended on it. I do not wish to discuss here the legitimacy of such an attitude. I would like, however, to stress as much as possible the fact that such an attitude is based on the assumption, or leads to the conclusion, that mental phenomena are anhistorical in their nature. Thus the part played by concrete time in the determination of these phenomena is deliberately suppressed. Such an attitude would make no sense unless accompanied in the mind of the psychologist by the belief that a specific mental reaction can be isolated from its concrete circumstances, from the living system of an individual's mind, and repeated as if nothing has happened between its first and its second occurrence; as if the reactor's experiences, or his development within this interval of time did not take place. Moreover, on the basis of this attitude, the psychologist acts as if the behavioural structure or, what one usually calls the mind, of an individual can be conceived in a vacuum, as if it were not—as I believe it to be—in an essential way part of a socio-cultural structure. It obviously follows that since a socio-cultural structure is normally submitted to historical changes, the structure of the mind itself is changeable in a historical sense.

ANTHROPOLOGY AND HISTORICAL PSYCHOLOGY

It is in fact contemporary anthropology that has made the psychologist aware in a dramatic way of the close inter-connection between the social relations and institutions formed in a community, and the characteristic mental development of individual members of this community. If the empirical material presented by some recent anthropological studies, and the conclusions drawn from it, are to be taken at their face value, the influence of society upon the mental development of the individual can hardly be overestimated. This influence touches not only various functions of the individual's mind, such as perception, imagination, memory, or thinking, but it also affects the structural character of the mind. This influence is not confined to the contents of the individual's consciousness, but it goes deep into the unconscious motivational aspect of the mind. The anthropologists speak, for instance, about modes of social reactions and organization which determine in the individual a specific mental structure based on the feeling of guilt, or on the feeling of shame. Moreover, they are ready to admit that there are societies and cultures which create a schizoid (Bali), or paranoid (Dobu, or Nazi) mental structure. Thus most anthropologists and sociologists support through their work the idea of the sociological relativity of mental phenomena. Moreover, many of them feel that one of their main tasks is to provide the psychologist with evidence by which he can prove how a specific cultural structure leads to a specific mental structure.

The same idea can be supported by historical evidence also. In this case the psychologist can use data furnished by history to demonstrate how dependent the individual's mental structure is upon the historical circumstances of his community. Here again, the point should be made clear that the historical development of a community, or of a culture, has not merely a superficial but a deep structural effect on the individual's mind. Thus, one can speak about a personality structure characteristic of the archaic or of the classical era of Greek society, or about a medieval or modern personality structure. Similarly one can speak—as D. Riesman does—about an 'other-directed' and an 'inner-directed' personality structure characteristic of the present-day and of an earlier stage of American culture respectively. All this points to the idea that the human mind is a social phenomenon in the sense of being determined in its structure by the historical development of a specific society. Thus historical psychology opens a new perspective to the study of the human mind. As a branch of psychology its task is to study the human mind as an historical phenomenon.

Though both historical psychology and contemporary anthropology regard the human mind as a social phenomenon, the differences between them are more important than their common ground. They differ firstly in their methods of research. The anthropologist can readily demonstrate, for instance, that the mental structure of the Balinese is different from that of the present-day American. He can take his evidence by observing, analysing, and even measuring actual pieces of behaviour displayed by the members of these groups. This is not the case with the historical psychologist. He cannot observe actual behaviour; he can only infer it from, or 'construct' it out of indirect and normally incomplete evidence made available to him by historical sources. Consequently his evidence about the social nature of the human mind

4

is of a more indirect character than that provided by the anthropologist.

A more fundamental difference between historical psychology and anthropology is the nature of their approach to the study of the human mind. Anthropology is concerned with the variations of the human mind on a horizontal line, i.e. with the differences between mental structures characteristic of groups of individuals; anthropology is concerned with inter-cultural, and historical psychology, on the other hand, studies the variations of the human mind on a vertical line, or, the changes which have occurred in the mental structure of groups of individuals as a result of the development in time of their culture as a whole. In other words, anthroplogy is concerned with inter-cultural, and historical psychology with intra-cultural differences in the structure of the mind. Consequently, while anthropology works with simple differential concepts, historical psychology works with evolutionary, or developmental concepts. It is, therefore, obvious that not only the methods, but also the body of hypotheses and the general frame of reference used by historical psychology is different from those used by anthropology.

DIFFERENTIAL, HISTORICAL AND EVOLUTIONARY CONCEPTS

Many psychocultural phenomena described or explained by present-day anthropology receive a new significance when looked at in the light of historical psychology. For instance, the anthropologists normally connect the formation of the personality structure based on the feeling of shame, and that based on the feeling of guilt, with two entirely different societies and cultures. In fact these personality structures may also be expressions at a psychological level of two stages in the historical development of a society. This is precisely what I have tried to show in Chapter IV of this study. The ancient Greeks, particularly in Attica, seem to present a typical example of a community moving in its historical evolution from a culture and character structure based on 'shame' to one based on 'guilt'. The specific meaning of this process will be discussed at a later stage. For the moment it will be enough to mention that between the archaic and the classical eras of Greek civilization one can notice an increasing process leading to the internalizing by the individual of the social and moral code of his community. This allows me to treat 'shame' and 'guilt' as historical-evolutionary rather than simple differential concepts. I have treated in a similar manner other psychological concepts such as 'perception', 'emotionality', 'personality', and 'national character'.

That the structure of the individual's perceptual field depends to a considerable extent on the structure of his culture is a fact sufficiently demonstrated by a series of recent investigations into the field of social perception. In the present study I have tried, however, to go a step further, by showing that the structure of the perceptual field changes with the historical evolution of a given community. This is the sense in which I say, for instance, that the sixteenth-century Frenchman had a different perceptional field from that of the Frenchman living at a later period. The influence of the historical process upon human emotionality, or upon a specific national character is too complex a problem to be treated briefly here. Most characteristic and more challenging in this respect, is the concept of personality. I have become convinced that this concept too can be treated historically. The organization of the human mind under the form of 'personality', that is to say, a harmonious integration of the individual within himself (presupposing a high degree of self-awareness), and at the same time, an integration of the individual with his culture (presupposing a high degree of rationalization of his behaviour) takes place only in a specific historical context, and requires a certain historical development of a community. The view advocated in this study is that the Athenian Community of the fifth and fourth centuries B.C. provided almost ideal conditions for such a mental development.

For further understanding of the theoretical basis of historical psychology, it is necessary to distinguish between historical and evolutionary concepts. A historical event is in essence a cultural event; a phenomenon that induces a definite change in the socio-cultural structure of a community of people. It follows that the concepts used by historical psychology refer normally to group phenomena; they describe or explain mental changes produced in a group of individuals, or in an individual as a result of the development in time of their culture and society. On the other hand evolutionary concepts refer to individual psychology; they describe or explain the mental development of an individual as determined by the process of growth. Heinz Werner has formulated the norms of this process as a development from a low to a high degree of differentiation and articulation in the individual's mental structure. Freud also outlines some evolutionary norms when he describes various necessary stages in the erotic development of an individual.

There are two ways in which the historical psychologist can look at the evolutionary concepts mentioned above. Firstly, he can consider them as historical in their nature. Thus the kind of mental evolution outlined by Werner or Freud is characteristic only of individuals of certain cultures or in certain periods of a culture. Secondly, he can use these concepts as 'analogues' of his own concepts and hypotheses. In this study I have more than once resorted to analogies between what I called 'historical' development of the human mind and the mental evolution of an individual. For instance, I have compared the historical development of the ancient Athenian community from a 'shame' to a 'guilt' stage in its culture and personality organization with the transition from a 'heterogeneous' to an 'autonomous' morality, two stages, according to Piaget, in the mental evolution of an individual in modern Western culture. Moreover, I am inclined to think that this type of historical development of the mind has a more general character than would appear at first sight. Many communities have given signs of such development. It seems to me that the mental development from a 'shame' to a 'guilt' stage, from a heteronomous to an autonomous morality, is closely connected with the historical development of a community from a patriarchal to a more democratic organization, from a pre-individualized to an individualized social order. This is obviously a frequent mode of historical development.

However, I did not go beyond the terms of an analogy. I do not know whether there is a determining relation between the norms of mental evolution of an individual and the psycho-historical development of a community of people. Even if such a relation exists, it is beyond the scope of the present study to demonstrate it. One thing should, however, be made clear: the analogy between the individual's mental evolution and psycho-historical processes has nothing to do with the famous parallel between ontogenesis and phylogenesis.

7

Introduction

PURPOSES AND PROBLEMS

The book which one begins to write is seldom the book which is actually written. However, I cannot speak here about my failures and frustrations, for the simple reason that they are too numerous. Instead, I can say a few words about some of the intentions, problems, and purposes which were in my mind while writing this study.

My main intention was to make a rapprochement between psychology and history. I have been made aware of the necessity of such a step by my own contact with historical studies in general, and with the writings of some psychologically-minded historians in particular. Historians such as Tocqueville, Dilthey, Toynbee, Marc Bloch, and above all Lucien Febvre have considerably contributed to my interest in such problems. Of course, I have included in this study only a limited number of problems in the selection of which a certain amount of arbitrariness was inevitable. In a study dealing with the relationship between psychological and historical phenomena, it may be regarded as a gross error that the problem of the personality of the historian has not been treated separately. I decided to leave this problem out partly because of its complexity, but chiefly because it would make a complete study in itself.

The central problem which the present study sets out to answer is: how, and to what extent, is the human mind influenced by the process of history? As I have said, the topics for discussion provide a general survey and illustration of this problem. The discussion centres round the following three points:
1. *Historical development and various specific mental functions*;
2. *Historical development and the mental organization of the individual*;
3. *Historical development and collective mental structures*. As an illustration of the first point I have chosen the problem of perception, insisting on the changes in the perceptional field of the individual in modern Western society. The reason for this choice is mainly technical. Firstly, perception is a relatively well-studied phenomenon from the psycho-cultural point of view. Secondly this is a field in which there is a certain amount of historical material available. Febvre's and Franactel's studies are of a particular importance in this respect. To illustrate the second point I discuss the individual of ancient Greek civilization for the obvious

8

reason that few other communities have displayed a higher degree of historical devlopment than the ancient Greeks. This is proved beyond doubt by the political, social, and cultural differences between the Homeric period and third-century Athens. My purpose therefore has been to follow the changes in the mental structure of an individual within the framework of a culture with a rapid and wide historical development. As an illustration of the third point, I have chosen the problem of the English national character. Here my concern is with the historical origins of a collective mental formation.

I have to admit that many important problems of historical psychology have for one reason or another been left out of this book. Febvre's cry for a history of human 'sensibility', i.e. the history of the feeling of love, fear, or death, is one of them. Fragments of this aspect of human behaviour were discussed in the second chapter dealing with perception and particularly in the third chapter bearing the title 'History and Emotional Climates'. But, my main concern in the third chapter was methodological. I wanted to demonstrate in the simplest manner possible how, and to what extent, certain collective emotional states are dependent on historical circumstances, and to what extent such states may, in their turn, create new historical circumstances. I must confess that a more systematic treatment of this subject, namely, the history of certain feelings within a given civilization, lies far outside my competence. I wonder, indeed, whether such problems can ever be tackled by a psychologist alone. In this area of historical psychology, as in most others, a close co-operation between psychologists and historians seems to be imperative.

The chief purpose of this study, however, is not that of presenting the reader with a systematic account of the historical development of the human mind within a given civilization. For the present this aim would be unrealistic. Conscious of this, I have restricted my main objective to a point of principle: I wanted to investigate as thoroughly as possible what I believe to be a constitutive element of mental life: its historicity. Mind in all its manifestations is never only what it is, but also what it was; it is a system which has depth. Freud has applied this assumption on the individual plane. What I have endeavoured to do in this study is to apply it on a collective and cultural plane. If the analogy can be stretched, I would say that the past—the historical past—is a dynamic structure, and therefore, makes itself present in any mental act. The nearest I could get to the formulation of this idea is in the chapter dealing with the historical origins of the English national character. The psycho-historical situation of the sixteenth century was, in my opinion, decisive in this respect. It was a psycho-historical focus. The rise and development of the modern English character—which I defined as a prevailing personality structure—can be understood as a reaction to, and from that situation. One of the main tasks of the historical psychologist is to detect and define such psycho-historical focuses within a given civilization. In this way he will trace the origin of a series of enduring mental dispositions which lie at the basis of the main aspects in the behaviour of a group of individuals, i.e. at the basis of their emotional pattern, of their perception, of their way of thinking, and of their specific way of organizing the environment. I do not assume—as a Freudian does—that these underlying dispositions are anhistorical. On the contrary, they are affected by the historical process. However, within a given historical period they can be considered as the main generators of human behaviour.

I can never stress enough the idea that my main concern has been with the origins of some important traits in the modern English character and not with the development of the character throughout the modern era. It is obvious that a full account of the English character had to include other traits which emerged at a later historical stage, and which strengthened, counterbalanced, or contradicted the traits discussed in the present study. This point has to be made clear at this introductory stage, for some readers might easily feel that I presented a one-sided, or even unfair picture of the modern English character. If there is any one-sidedness in this study, it is methodological. I have deliberately isolated certain traits which could be traced down to a specific psycho-historical condition of the English community, and which seem to me important for the formation and development of the English national character.

I am only too aware that my approach, with its search for 'origins', or for 'psycho-historical focuses', has often constrained me to over-simplify the problem. When I deal, for instance, with the mechanisms of affect-displacement and rationalization as characteristic of the English personality structure, I might have insisted too much on the idea that their origin can be found in the psycho-historical conditions of the sixteenth century. It is obvious that these mechanisms, and the place they occupy in the English personality structure were determined also by a series of other factors lying outside the psycho-historical situation of the sixteenth century such as climate, industrialization, to mention only a few. However, this does not invalidate the fact which I try to prove in this study, that during the period mentioned above these mechanisms were greatly intensified. It is this fact which gave me the clue to the origins of some important traits in the modern English character.

HISTORICAL AND PSYCHOLOGICAL PHENOMENA

Some of the points in the previous section require further elucidation. First of all, what is meant in this study by the term 'historical', and to what extent can this term be applied to psychological phenomena?

A historical event is—to use one of Febvre's favourite formulas—'*un fait de civilisation*'. As such, 'historical' is an attribute which can be assigned to an event, or group of events which have marked a change in the way of life of a community of people. The events can be in their nature political, economic, cultural, psychological, and even physical. But this does not entirely tally with a more or less traditional view, still well-represented among present-day historians, according to which the term 'historical' has primarily, if not exclusively, a social content. The assumption lying at the basis of such a view is that the development of a community of people within a period of time is best reflected by the political, economic and, generally speaking, by the social events of that period. Consequently history connotes the study of the political, economic, and sometimes technical development of a community of people.

In the present study the terms 'history' and 'historical' have a more comprehensive meaning than this. When I speak about the historical circumstances of a community of people I do not confine myself to the political, economic, or technical conditions prevailing in that community within a given period of time. I include here also a series of psycho-cultural conditions, such as current ideas and ideologies as well as dominant values and beliefs.

No less important is a group of phenomena of a purely psychological nature which in this study are covered by the term 'collective emotionality'. This consists of dominant feelings, or collective emotional states characterizing a group of people—a nation, a social class, a political party, or a religious sect—at a specific stage in their historical development. Such are the feelings of collective fear and insecurity, of aggression, of confidence, of suspicion, or of apathy.

Far be it from me to suggest that the psycho-cultural phenomena mentioned above have always been neglected by those interested in the study of history. After all, there were such historians as Lamprecht, Tocqueville, Dilthey, not to mention L. Febvre and M. Bloch. Even the dry and positivistic Ranke was ready to admit that 'the main source of human action—he meant by this historical action—'is to be found inside the human being'. Nevertheless, one can hardly fail to notice that most writers of technical history are too easily inclined to regard the psycho-cultural events of the past as being of a derivative order. Thus, a body of ideas, a system of values and beliefs, a collective emotional state, are too often considered dependent upon, moreover, reducible to certain specific social or economic circumstances of life. I cannot discuss here whether, or to what extent, this is true or false. The fact is that this 'reductionist' attitude has lowered the status of such events in the field of historical knowledge far too much with the inevitable result that we have today a 'political' history, an 'economic' history, and even a history of ideas, but no psychological history, i.e. no systematic account of the historical development of the human mind within a given civilization.

There is nothing more alien to the spirit of this study than a 'reductionist' attitude towards psycho-cultural phenomena. On the contrary, one can say that its chief aim is to demonstrate the importance which the study of such phenomena has for the understanding of the historical past. Moreover, in the opinion held in this book, phenomena such as prevailing beliefs and values as well as the predominant collective emotional states are important determining factors for the historical development of a community.

The above point is vital to the reader's understanding of this study; perhaps I might enlarge upon it here by summarizing the approach I have used in the chapter on historical aspects of human perception: I started by establishing a series of differences existing between the structure of the perceptual field of the sixteenth-century French individual and that of the nineteenth-or twentieth-century French individual. But, needless to say, a change undergone by a psychological function within a given period of time does not necessarily mean that it is historical in its character. That is why, in the second stage of my argument, I have tried to identify a series of events, or generally speaking, a series of factors to which such a change can be attributed, or simply related. At this stage, some hypotheses put forward by a series of recent researches in the field of social perception proved to be useful. It has emerged from these researches that the individual's system of beliefs and values constitutes one of the determining factors of his perceptual field. Consequently I have tried to describe and explain the structure of the perceptual field characteristic of the sixteenth-century French in terms of their dominant beliefs, values and ideas. This enterprise led me to the following conclusions: (a) the individual's perceptual field can be regarded as a historical phenomenon, i.e. it changes in some of its main aspects with the historical development of his community; (b) the change in the perceptual field can be understood in terms of the change taking place in the system of beliefs, values and general ideas; (c) it is, therefore, reasonable to assume that the historical character of man's perceptual field is dependent upon the historical character of his basic beliefs, values and ideas. Whether I was right or wrong in drawing such conclusions is for the reader to judge.

Of course I am aware of the difficulties involved in this procedure. Firstly, it is possible that by isolating the system of beliefs and values from the complexity of historical circumstances I have over-simplified the process of historical causation. Secondly, the objection may easily be raised that the system of beliefs, values, and ideas is a reflection at the psycho-cultural level of some more fundamental factors of a social or economic nature, in other words, cannot be considered as an autonomous factor in the field of historical development. This obviously implies that I have not gone deeply enough into my projected task of offering an explanation of the historical character of human perceptual functions. This may be true. I must confess, however, that throughout the present study I have avoided as much as I could, letting myself be caught in the labyrinth of historical causation. In order to prevent any possible misunderstanding I should like to throw more light on this point.

The present study sets out to criticize and refute both the spirit of 'fixism' and that of 'reductionism' in psychology. The former is manifested in all those general conceptions of, and attitudes towards the human mind which stress its anhistorical character. McDougall with his list of propensities characteristic of all men in all societies and historical times, or Freud with his claim to the universal character of the Oedipus Complex are typical examples of this. Less typical, but not less important in this respect are many other trends in modern psychology. Briefly speaking, the spirit of 'fixism' makes itself conspicuous in all those attempts to construct a universal model of the human mind as this was defined at an earlier stage in this Introduction. As against this, the present study stresses the historical character of the human mind.

What does the statement 'the human mind is historical in character' mean? My impression is that the first reaction most social scientists have to such a question is this: the mind is historical to the extent, or because it is affected by the development of the economic, political, or social circumstances of life. Now, before accepting or refuting this attitude, it would be advisable to point out some of its implications. Firstly, it implies that the historical process lies outside the realm of mental phenomena, thus it is propelled by non-mental factors. This leads to the conclusion that the mind plays a passive role in the historical process. One need hardly go any further to find out that the source of all this lies in a reductionist attitude by which any development of the mind is explicable in terms of non-mental factors.

The basic conviction of this study is that the human mind is a historical phenomenon in a more complex manner than that suggested above. The mind is an integral part of the historical process. This means that it is determined by, and at the same time, determines this process. In its simplest form this is expressed by the concept of *psycho-social cycles* in history which has been frequently used in the present study. I mean by this that the historical development of a community can be viewed as being alternatively propelled by social and psychological conditions. In other words historical causation moves in a circle from psychological to non-psychological factors. A set of external circumstances, social, economic, cultural, or physical characteristic of a community of people stimulate specific mental developments, such as specific attitudes, specific emotional states, specific personality types or specific social characters. These mental conditions have a feed-back effect; they react upon the external circumstances, and thus change their original character. The transformed external circumstances in their turn lead to new mental developments. Thus the historical process moves round the psycho-social cycle.

Though this idea is amply demonstrated in this study, I should like to illustrate it here with an example taken from more recent history, namely the rise and development of Nazism in Germany. The example presents the unique advantage of having been the object of a series of recent psychological studies. The starting-point in the search for the determining conditions of this historical event can be a psychological one, namely the analysis of Hitler's personality. Once the paranoid disposition of this personality is established, one can infer from this some basic traits in the Nazi movement, such as group grandomania, compulsive aggression, delusional behaviour displayed as a collective readiness to believe in myths. Therefore Hitler shaped a political and social organization according to some basic features of his personality. This amounts to saying that a structure of psychological conditions led to a structure of social conditions. However, Hitler's personality cannot be considered as a spontaneous phenomenon. Its paranoid disposition has its origins in certain social conditions. This time one has to consider a series of phenomena, such as the economic crises, the collapse of the old social institutions, the political and spiritual chaos which followed the defeat of 1918. All these economic, social and political phenomena constitute sources of frustration, insecurity and suspicion which lead to paranoid behaviour in the individual. Moreover, these phenomena are but aspects of a psycho-cultural climate which favours the formation of a paranoid type of personality. Thus, Hitler's personality, and that of many other individual members of the German community during the period under consideration, were in their turn conditioned by factors which were not psychological in their nature.

One could move still further round the psycho-social cycle.

Once paranoid personalities become frequent in a community, they react as a group upon their social environment by intensifying those aspects of it which support their paranoid type of behaviour; they create a rigid social organization based on power, in which suspicion, aggression and strong in-group feelings become necessary forms of adjustment. Thus, any attempt to establish the determining conditions of a historical event—in this case the rise of Nazism—takes one round in a circle in which psychological and non-psychological factors follow each other in a chain of cause and effect.

It would, however, be erroneous to conclude that the psychological and cultural factors describe a sterile circle in history. The continuous movement from one to another leads up in a spiral. Thus the same movement takes place at different levels. One starts, for instance, with the 'socio-genesis' of Hitler's personality, that is to say, with the social field of his formative period. This leads to a psychological factor, i.e. to the paranoid structure of his personality. But this new factor is not simply a product; it becomes creative at a new level. Hitler acts upon a different environment from that which conditioned the formation of his personality. He becomes a leader and as such determines the social conditions of the whole German group. The circular movement now goes round at a new level. The social and political conditions which he determines for the German group lead to the formation of paranoid behaviour, individual and collective. This determines in its turn new social and political conditions in the whole of Europe. Thus Hitler's personality becomes a source of historical events, i.e. a psychological factor in itself becomes a '*fait de civilisation*'. This shows the inadequacy of any reductionist attitude in history.

METHODS

The methods of historical psychology are those of history in general, namely, the interpretation of various kinds of traces left by past events. The historical psychologist construes a psycho-historical event; or a structure of events out of what he considers to be symptomatic fragments. In this respect his proceeding is not qualitatively different from that of any kind of psychologist who construes a mental phenomenon such as a feeling, an attitude, a character structure, out of fragmentary mental reactions. The problem of the historical psychologist, however, is made more difficult by the fact that he investigates mental phenomena of the past. The first question he has to answer is what are the adequate sources he can consult for this purpose? This is complicated by another question, namely, what are the enduring expressions of mental phenomena? In other words, what are the documents of the past which preserve in themselves the emotions, the attitudes, the beliefs, and on the whole the mental structure of the individual to which they refer? Frankly speaking the historical psychologist has a poor choice in this respect. Since psychology is a young discipline, he can seldom, if ever, use systematic and technical information—such as made available in a present-day survey—about people's feelings or attitudes in the past. Most of the time the historical psychologist has the hard task of interpreting sources of evidence of a very indirect character. A few examples will illustrate this methodological problem. In trying to follow the main mental changes in individuals belonging to ancient Greek civilization, I have resorted to the psychological analysis of the evolution of their language, as well as of their culture, as this was expressed in their religious beliefs and practices, political organizations, philosophy, literature, etc. Since the socio-cultural aspect of their history is more or less known, I have tried to base on this my investigation into the psychological field of their historical development. The inter-relation between these two aspects of their historical development is a complex matter, the principles of which were outlined in the previous section. I can only repeat here that I have never assumed a simple causal determination between these two aspects.

Perhaps even more illustrative in this respect is the chapter about the historical evolution of perception. Following Febvre, I took the written language as a main mode of expression of the perceptual field of a community of people. I have, however, broadened my sources of information on this point by analysing concurrently the changes in the perceptual field and in the system of beliefs as well as in various modes of artistic expression which took place in a community of people within a specific historical period. In doing so I have naturally assumed that the system of beliefs has something to do with the perceptual field of an individual, and that artistic vision is not merely a 'concept', but also a 'percept', i.e. a mirror of the individual's perception of the world. Though in some ways debatable, these assumptions seem to me sound on the whole, particularly if one bears in mind some recent developments in the study of social perception. I realize the weaknesses of such methods of investigation into the historical aspect of the human mind. Yet I have not tried to make virtue out of necessity. The sources of evidence are scarce, and the methods of investigation are lacking in precision but the importance of the subject is such as to make the present enterprise worth while.

II

HISTORY AND PERCEPTION

It has been by custom and law determined
for the eye, what it is supposed to see and not to see,
for the ear, what it is supposed to hear and not to hear,
for the tongue, what it is supposed to say and not to say,
for the hand, what it is supposed to do and not to do,
for the foot, whither it is supposed to proceed and not to
    proceed,
for the heart, what it is supposed to want and not to want.

ANTIPHON

INTRODUCTION

THE simplest way of investigating the historical character of the human mind would be to treat it analytically. This would mean research into the historical aspects of various mental functions and processes, such as perception, memory, imagination, and intelligence. The same kind of research can be applied to various emotional aspects of behaviour. Does the part played by various mental functions in the process of adjustment change with the historical evolution of a community, or, does the relative position occupied by a specific function in the structure of personality vary from one historical period to another? This is the kind of question with which this part of historical psychology is concerned.

For various reasons, however, the most important being lack of adequate information, the discussion in this chapter will be confined to one mental process only, that of perception. The same considerations have played a part in the selection of the historical periods covered.

HISTORICAL VARIABLES IN THE FIELD OF PERCEPTION

Though the interest in, and the study of perceptual processes are at least as old as psychology itself, psychologists are still much in the dark with regard to the nature of the determining factors of such processes. The physiological approach is still holding its ground in this field. Thus, perception is often explained entirely in terms of the specific organization of the sense organs, on the one hand, and of the nature of the stimulus, on the other. Lately, however, a different approach, a more comprehensive one, has developed side by side with the physiological one. The way in which the individual perceives his world is seen more and more in the function of his basic interests, beliefs and values, or even of some unconscious structures and mechanisms. Thus, perception has come to be regarded as a personality factor, i.e., as a mode of reaction reflecting not only the bio-physiological make-up of an individual, but also the specific organization of his mind within a given socio-cultural setting. In any perceptual process the individual selects from the multitude of stimuli presented to him; he organizes the field of perception by emphasizing some aspects and rejecting others. In any such process, the personality of the individual is an active factor of the first rank. If, for instance, someone is presented with a number of written words at a certain distance, he perceives more quickly and more distinctly those which appeal to his own interests and values. Though the size of a coin and that of a metal disc is objectively the same, the former is normally perceived as being bigger than the latter.[1] Furthermore, one often speaks about defence mechanisms operating in the field of perception. M. Gilbert, for instance, speaks about the 'obviating', 'diverting' and 'constricting' functions of beliefs and prejudices in the individual's perceptual field. The members of the Nazi group perceived more readily events and phenomena which supported their basic beliefs and values, obviating, at the same time, those which contradicted these beliefs and values.[2] The degree of articulation of the individual's inner life is another factor interfering with the structure of the perceptual field. Recent experimental and clinical researches have

[1] Bruner, J. S. 'An Approach to Social Perception.' In *Current Trends in Soc. Psychol.* 1949.
[2] *The Psychology of Dictatorship.* N.Y. 1950.

demonstrated that the development of the 'self', and of the 'ego-feelings' have a direct bearing upon the individual's perception of the external world. People with a low level of development in this sense, such as children under the age of thirteen and individuals suffering from certain mental disorders, show in their perceptions a pronounced dependence upon the structure of the external field; their perception of the world is less articulated and less differentiated than that of a normally developed person.[1]

This illustrates clearly the need, as well as the usefulness, of an historical approach to the problem of perception. For, if perception depends on the individual's interests, beliefs and values, then it is an historical phenomenon. This is expressed by one of the basic ideas of present-day anthropology, according to which the individual's interests, beliefs and values, and, one can add here the degree of articulation of his inner life, depend to a considerable extent upon the type of his civilization, as well as upon the historical level of his civilization. Thus, in order to study the specific way in which a group of individuals perceive their world, one has to take into account their current interests, beliefs and values, as well as the type of mental organization characteristic of their historical period. In other words, a complete study of human perception has to deal also with the historical variables of this mode of behaviour.

Here the first difficulty arises. From the empirical point of view, the main question is one of method. How can one assess the historical variables of human perception? The question can be answered indirectly by trying to analyse from this specific point of view the behaviour of a community of people of various historical periods. Fortunately, a significant start in this direction has been made by some psychologically-orientated historians. In his studies of the sixteenth century in France, Lucien Febvre deals also with the 'specific' way in which individuals belonging to this period perceived their world. His remarks on this point can be used to illustrate the main thesis of this chapter.[2]

There is, according to Febvre, a remarkable difference between the perceptual world of the sixteenth, and that of the twentieth

---

[1] Witkin, H. A. and others: *Personality Through Perception*. N.Y. Particularly relevent are chapters 7, 17 and 21.

[2] Particularly important in this respect is his: *Le Problème de l'Incroyance au XVIe Siecle: La Religion de Rabelais*. Paris. 1947.

century Frenchman. Firstly, the perception of the world was much more 'vivid', and at the same time, inconsistent, in the sixteenth century than it is today. The main reason for this is that the perception of the sixteenth-century Frenchman was more influenced by emotional factors than that of the twentieth-century Frenchman. On this point Febvre often refers to two psychological traits of the late Middle Ages as formulated by J. Huizinga, namely, to 'the violent tenor of life', and to the 'high-strung personality'.[1] The reflection of these traits in the field of perception can be seen in the people's preference for primitive, vivid and contrasting colours, a fact which is demonstrated by the manner of dressing, and particularly by the art of the period. Secondly, the sixteenth-century Frenchman reacted to his environment in a manner which suggests that the constellation of his perceptual functions was somehow different from that of the Frenchman living in the centuries which followed. His olfactory, tactile and auditory functions were relatively more developed than his sight; he was guided, or motivated more often by the former senses than by sight.

Febvre draws his main evidence from the analysis of the written language of the period. Considering the frequency of various types of images in the poetry of the period, he concludes that this poetry was anything but '*la poesie du visuel*'. In Ronsard, for instance, even a kiss is, as in a radio play, suggested by auditory elements. Things and situations which are for us primarily visual, are described by sixteenth-century writers in tactile, olfactory and auditory terms. Bouchet in his description of a house, Jean Goujon in his 'Silhouettes', du Bellay in his description of France made predominant use of auditory and olfactory terms. The appeal of nature, through the medium of the eye was not discovered, or was not exploited. It was more interesting, and perhaps more profitable to call an hotel 'l'Homme Sauvage', or 'Le Lion d'Or', rather than 'Bellevue' or 'Beau Site'. Few, if any sixteenth-century writers used visual terms for descriptive purposes. When Rabelais occasionally did so, his intention was to offend rather than to describe the persons to whom he referred. We do not know how Marguerite de Navarre looked, says Febvre alarmingly.

Now, Febvre certainly does not believe that sixteenth-century

[1] *The Waning of the Middle Ages.*

man did not have good sight. It is only that, in his relation to his environment, he used his ears more, and his eyes less than we normally do. It is primarily on this account that Febvre characterizes the sixteenth-century Frenchman as suffering from 'visual backwardness', (*le retard de la vue*). Moreover, he refers to the sixteenth-century perceptual world as a world of hearing, mentioning the rise of modern music as another proof of this. As compared with this, the seventeenth- and particularly the twentieth-century perceptual world is the world of the visual, with which is closely related the rise of modern science.

The explanation offered by Febvre for the phenomena mentioned above can be formulated in psycho-social terms. He identifies one determining factor as cultural conditioning. Teaching, learning, and many other forms of inter-communication were, during this period, mainly oral. The second conditioning factor is closely connected with the physical environment of the sixteenth-century Frenchmen, but it involves, at the same time, certain technical aspects of the civilization of the period. Owing to the scarcity of artificial light, the periods of darkness were, in the sixteenth century, considerably longer than today. Hence the relative predominance of hearing over seeing in the process of adjustment.

Febvre offers, however, a better clue to the understanding of the perceptual field of the members of the sixteenth-century French community when he describes in some detail the main psycho-cultural traits of this period. This was a pre-rationalistic period dominated by animistic and magic beliefs. From the perceptual point of view, the world had a high degree of fluidity. In his colourful manner, Febvre speaks about 'fluidité d'un monde ou rien n'est strictement délimité, ou les êtres eux-mêmes, perdant leur frontières, changent en un clin d'oeil, sans provoquer autrement d'objection de forme, d'aspect, de dimension, voire de règne'.[1] This was a world in which things did not preserve their separatedness and their identity; stones could turn into living beings, animals could behave like humans. A pig which killed a man was tried by professional judges and hanged according to the law. One could be in two different places at the same time . . . This was a world in which the barriers between objective and subjective, between real and imaginary, between natural and supernatural were flexible, or non-existent. It was generally

[1] Op. cit. pp. 473–4.

believed that a decapitated man could run away holding his own head in his arms. Everybody believed in ghosts; encounters with them were part of their everyday lives. Ronsard, while on his way to his mistress, saw '*dans l'air la* CHASSE INFERNALE'. In such a world of magic beliefs, man's interests—and his sensory functions too—were stimulated by what lay 'behind' things, i.e. by the world of beliefs, rather than by things themselves. Thus, the shape and character of things and events were greatly determined by emotional factors.

This poses the main question of this section: what is the connection between the prevailing system of beliefs and the relative predominance of auditory, olfactory, and tactile functions in the behaviour of these people? These questions can tentatively be answered in two main ways:

Firstly, touch, smell, and hearing have often been described as 'affective senses' because they are more closely connected than sight with the sources of emotional life. Consequently, the individual adjusts himself to an environment organized by emotional factors, such as fears, desires, hopes, beliefs, more successfully through his hearing, smell, and touch than through his sight. This is because the contact with his environment mediated by these sensory functions is more indefinite and diffuse than that mediated by sight. Thus, the former three senses support to a higher degree than the eye the individual's beliefs in the fluid character of the world of objects.

But the argument outlined above can be considered from a different angle. The same basic attitudes and beliefs which stimulate and emphasize auditory and olfactory functions in the perceptual field of the individual can, at the same time, weaken and repress his visual functions. Visual perceptions may, by their articulate character, and particularly by the light they throw on the individual character of things, weaken these basic beliefs. This might explain partly the 'visual backwardness' of sixteenth-century man; a highly visualized perceptual field, that is, a perceptual field dominated by visual factors, would have threatened his emotional system of security.[1] For, needless to say, in a pre-

---

[1] It is inadequate to refer to visual perception as an isolated sensory function. Most human perceptions are based on a co-ordinated activity of many sensory functions. Thus, visual perception means in fact visualized perception, that is, the dominance of the eye in the perceptual field.

scientific age, spirits, angels, or demons were explanatory agencies as well as symbols of order in an otherwise capricious and incomprehensible universe. Transposing this into the key of depth psychology, one could say that sixteenth-century man was in the position of Rousseau's Vicaire Savoyard who '*aime mieux de se tromper que de ne rien croire*'. His 'visual backwardness' was deeply motivated.

At this point, the following question arises: if hearing and smelling are closely associated with an emotional relation between man and his environment, is sight different from this point of view? In other words, does sight play a more important part than other senses in an intellectualized, or rationalized environment? The analysis, however superficial, of the intrinsic qualities of visualized perceptions suggests that the answer to these questions can be in the affirmative. First of all, visualized perceptions are more plastic than any other perception. In the visual field things and situations emerge as differentiated and independent units; they grow from the neutral background of the environment as pointers in the direction of the perceiver. This differentiation in the perceptual field constitutes a strong stimulus for observation, and, needless to say, observation as a primarily visual activity lies at the basis of modern science, that is, of a rational picture of the world.

The plastic, differentiated, and individualized character of visualized perceptions suggests in many ways the origins of an intellectualized, scientific relation between man and his environment. The notions of dimension, of form, of movement, and even that of quantitative variation have their roots in a visualized perception. Perhaps based on such, or similar considerations, Abel Rey tries to demonstrate that the plastic quality—*intuition plastique*—of the Greek mind, obviously a visual function determined mainly by the geographical setting, had led to the rise of Greek geometry. Moreover, he is inclined to think that the root of Greek mathematics lies in the same trait. Therefore, Rey relates the basis of any scientific approach to the environment, viz. geometry and mathematics, to the function of the eye.[1] The same idea is developed in a different manner

[1] '*L'imagination grecque est surtout visuelle et remarquablement visuelle,*' says Rey in his: *La Jeunesse de la Science Grecque.* Paris, p. 27. This '*imagination visuelle*' is a structural quality of Greek culture: '*Dans les récits grecs de la cosmogonie, l'histoire, l'ordre des changements composent une ascension vers la clarte, une dialectique de la lumiere.*' Op. cit. p. 28.

by Febvre. The gradual decline of religious beliefs and super-
stitions, and the rise of secular rationalism following the close
of the sixteenth century was, according to him, associated with
the reorganization of the human perceptual field. He speaks in
this context about the gradual development, within Western
civilization, of an intellectualized, as opposed to an emotionalized,
contact between the individual and his environment. The central
trend of this large process consists in the growth of the modern
scientific frame of mind. Like Abel Rey, Febvre thinks that a
scientific attitude implies a visualized type of perception; like
Abel Rey, he describes sight as an 'intellectual and scientific
sense'.

PERCEPTION AND THE SYSTEM OF INNER SECURITY

Febvre starts by observing a series of historical coincidences regarding the development of human visual functions and that of a
rational scientific attitude in life. These coincidences took place in
the French community round the beginning of the modern era.
Then, in the second stage, he construes the logical connection between these two psycho-historical phenomena by pointing to a
series of analogies between the functions of the eye, and a scientific
explanation of the world. In fact, the true nature of this connection is psychological rather than logical; it can more adequately
be disclosed by the analysis of the deep irrational motivation of
human behaviour. For this purpose one has to widen the historical horizon of the present investigation. One has, in the first
place, to start with the phenomenon often regarded as one of the
chief characteristics of the Renaissance, namely, the decline of
religious faith, and the consequent secularization of life. Though
it is not easy to reconstruct the psychological aspect of this complex phenomenon, it seems, nevertheless, appropriate to start by
describing it as a process of displacement and reorientation of
human emotionality. One should, however, bear in mind that
this was a long process, and that the individuals belonging to
various communities of the Renaissance were affected by it in
various ways and degrees. But, in a general manner, one can
formulate it as follows: man's emotionality was withdrawn from
the symbols and objects of a transcendental order of life and
directed primarily towards himself. This accounts for the spurt of

man's awareness of himself as an individual which is the seed of modern humanistic and individualistic civilization. Civilization means, in this context, adjustment, that is, a new equilibrium between man and his environment. Now, it was the establishment of this new equilibrium that led to the development of both (a) a rational scientific organization of the environment, and (b) a visualized type of perception. This idea should be further illustrated.

The belief in the transcendental order of life lay at the basis of the system of emotional security of pre-Renaissance man. As this belief became gradually weaker, man's search for security was directed towards himself and his environment. He discovered new sources of security in the logical principles of his mind, in the norms and conventions of his society, and in the 'intrinsic' order of nature. Needless to say, the emergence of these new sources of security and order did not take place spontaneously. During the Renaissance, and even after, the order of the human mind and of society, as well as the order of nature, were regarded as emanations of the divine order. But the ever-growing tendency was to divorce them from any supernatural intervention, and to regard them as three aspects of an autonomous source of order and security. Thus, immanent reason forms the core of modern man's system of security which can be called the secular, as opposed to the transcendental system of security, the latter being characteristic of medieval man.

The three main sources of modern man's system of security can be described as individualized reason, secular morality and natural reason. Security is experienced by modern man through self-knowledge and self-realization as a rational being, through the recognition—or through the construction—of the rational order of his society, and finally, through the recognition of the rational order of nature. Any superficial analysis of the main trends of Western civilization can prove this.

The eagerness with which modern man turned to the analysis of thought processes constitutes the main proof of the first point, security through self-knowledge. It seems that, at the beginning of the modern era, clear thinking, or thinking according to well-established principles, was more than a philosophical concern; it was a vital necessity. '*Cogito ergo sum*' becomes particularly relevant in this respect, if one took the trouble to uncover the emotional background of such a highly rationalized intuition. In the psycho-cultural climate created by the withdrawal of the transcendental order, the individual's capacity to think, as well as to become aware of the general rules of his thinking, was a safe guide in life; it was a remedy—the only remedy, according to Descartes—for doubt, that is, for insecurity.

Secular morality was motivated by the same situation. An outstanding Protestant theologian of today hits the nail on the head when he writes about the moral effects of the Reformation as follows: 'The destruction of the Catholic ideal of saintliness and the emphasis on the transcendence of God leave a vacuum which is occupied by the humanistic idea, the emotional motive of which is the appeal to obedience and to law, and the actual character of which is '*conformity to bourgeois conventions*'.[1] In this 'emotional motive' lies the source of modern man's inclination to rationalize his social environment. Though this has advanced at a slower pace than the rationalization of the inner life, it is, nevertheless, obvious that, since the Renaissance, Western man has steadily worked himself into believing that the structure, as well as the purpose of his society actually fit, or can be made to fit, into a stable universal order. The deep motivation of this process lies in the need for guidance and security of a man who could no longer believe in the divine purpose of life. Consequently, a secular code of behaviour—commercial ethics, for instance—and a rationally organized society, according to the socialist or communist model, have gradually become basic aspects in the system of emotional security of modern man.

There remains little to be said about the third aspect of modern man's system of security, the rationalization of nature. This process was basically motivated by the need to establish order in a physical environment from which the agencies of divine reason were expelled. Hence the search for the laws governing natural phenomena. This brings into focus the main point of the present section, which is the rise of modern science as a central feature in modern man's system of security.

For a better understanding of the motivation of the process of rationalization it would be useful to distinguish between the normal attitude taken towards this process by contemporary man,

[1] Tillich, Paul: *The Religious Situation.* Eng. Trans. by R. Niebuhr. 1956. p. 202. Italics mine.

and that taken by seventeenth- or eighteenth-century man. While the former speaks about 'rational models' applied by him to nature and society, the latter believed in cosmic, or immanent reason; he believed in the intrinsic rationality of society and nature. This belief was a compensation for the withdrawal of transcendental reason, and consequently grew *pari passu* with the weakening of religious faith. At the conscious rational level, this process expressed itself as a struggle between science and religion which has been a central cultural theme of the modern era. As early as the fifteenth century, Jean Buridan tried to soothe his contemporaries' fears of chaos by telling them that his (scientific) explanation of nature could dispense with the intervention of divine agencies. Four centuries later, this process of displacement and compensation seemed to have reached a peak. 'In the history of natural science,' writes Engels, "God is treated by his defenders as Frederik Wilhelm II was by his generals and servants in the campaign of Jena. Little by little the whole army capitulated: the fortresses one after another fall in front of the advance of science which ends by conquering the infinite domain of nature with no place for the Creator's refuge."[1]

At this stage one can renew the attempt to elucidate the relationship between human visual functions and the rise of the scientific mind in the modern world. Since the contention of this section is that both phenomena have a common motivation, one can ask now what the relation is between man's perceptual field and what has been described so far as the secular system of security.

It has previously been mentioned that one of the main effects of the emotional displacement that started during the Renaissance consisted in the growth of the individual's self-awareness. It is precisely this growth of the self that explains, at least partly, the gradual increase in the importance of visual functions in the perceptual field of individuals of the Renaissance and post-Renaissance period. For, the growth of the self means the emergence of an inner centre of psychic energy which determines the individual's emergence from his environment as an autonomous unit. In other words, the growth of the individual's self-awareness is bound to increase the tension between himself and his environment, or as Dilthey rightly remarked, the feeling about the reality of the external world is closely related to the resistance

[1] Engels F.: *Dialectics of Nature*. pp. 264–5.

encountered by the outwardly directed energy of our impulses and desires.[1] All this points to the fact that the external world became more 'real' for Renaissance man, a fact attested in so many ways by the culture of the period. Psychologically, 'more real' means increased resistance to the newly released impulses, and the rapid growth of self-awareness in the man of the Renaissance period. And increased introspection goes hand in hand with increased observation of the external world. More 'real' means also more plastic and differentiated, that is, appealing more and more to vision, the most differentiated perceptual function of man.

An analogy with certain aspects in the development of the child's perception might be useful for the understanding of this process. The physical environment—his room, for instance—of a newly born child is visually diffuse. At this early stage he himself is submerged in his environment. In the process of adjustment, however, which is largely determined by a succession of clashes with the external world, the child gradually emerges from the 'sameness' of his existence by forming the feeling of his own unity, bodily and mental. The stronger and more differentiated the feeling of himself, the stronger and more differentiated the impression of the external world. Gradually the 'sameness-character' of his surroundings subsides. At this stage, the visual functions of the child are strongly stimulated. The environment is perceived in higher and higher degrees of differentiation, first, as having an existence of its own, then, as having various dimensions and as being made up of well-defined units, things and persons. This amounts to saying that the child's perceptual field has gradually been 'visualized'. To stress even more the meaning of this analogy, one has to bear in mind that visual functions develop ontogenetically—and perhaps, phylogenetically—later than other sensory functions.[2] In this lies yet another proof that they become necessary at the more differentiated stage, and particularly at a higher degree of tension in the individual's relation with his environment. The growth of the individual's self leads towards this stage.[3]

---

[1] Dilthey, W.: *Die Geistige Welt: Gesammelte Schriften.* Band 5. Leipzig. p. 98.

[2] The predominance of terms referring to smell and taste in the vocabulary of some primitive groups can be adduced as evidence.

[3] The connection between the feeling of the self and perception has also been revealed by recent studies of the perceptual field of schizophrenics: the disintegration of the self seems to be related to the deterioration of the perception of form, i.e. of the most visual element in the perceptual field.

We should examine once more the terms of the above analogy, of the development of the child to the development of Renaissance man. In both cases there is a rapid growth of self-awareness, or an intense process of individuation. The emergence of the individual from the web of collective-sacred medieval order was a slow and tortuous process; it started with the Renaissance, which was a period extending over more than two centuries, and went on throughout the modern era. As already mentioned, Febvre notices an intensification of visual functions in the individuals of the French community towards the end of the sixteenth and the beginning of the seventeenth centuries. This only means that the process of individuation had reached a particular degree of intensity during this period. On the other hand, Febvre specifies that sixteenth-century France still belonged to the Middle Ages. In other parts of Western Europe, arrival at this stage varied, being either earlier or later.

SKETCH FOR A HISTORY OF PERCEPTION

Suggestive ideas about the historical development of the perceptual field of individuals and groups of Western civilization can be found in a great variety of studies concerned with various types of artistic vision and hearing characteristic of this civilization. The following considerations are confined to three psychologically-oriented studies which, though differing widely in their formulations, seem to have a great deal in common both in their assumptions and in their conclusions. They can be taken as three illustrative examples.

Worringer, in his *Abstraction and Empathy*, published some forty years ago, distinguishes between two general attitudes of mind which express themselves in two types of artistic perception and style. The first attitude, characterized by the term *empathy* implies a positive participation into the organic world, the second, covered by the term *abstraction*, indicates, on the contrary, an escape from the bewilderment and instability of the organic into the regularity of the world of the inert. The former lies at the basis of 'naturalistic' art, while the latter, at the basis of 'abstract' art. The full significance of this idea becomes apparent when one takes into account that, according to Worringer, classical traditionalist art offers the best example of naturalistic style while abstract style is best represented by primitive and Byzantine art. But modern art too is considered by Worringer as a typical example of abstract style, and this is the very point in his study which throws open the doors to a historical interpretation of human perception. This point requires a more detailed consideration.

The first thing to be noted is that Worringer attempts to express in psychological terms the difference between two historical stages in Western visual art. More precisely, he tries to understand the transition from classical to modern art in terms of some basic attitude—feelings about the world, as he says—arising from the relation between the individual and his environment, physical and social. In other words, from the classical to the modern periods in Western art, this relation has changed its character from an 'empathetic' to an 'abstract' one. Now, on the basis of this central idea it is possible to advance two hypotheses with regard to the development of the perceptual field of modern man. But before discussing them, it would be useful to mention that the reason for this multiple, and sometimes contradictory interpretation consists not so much in the general and imprecise meaning of the key concepts in Worringer's study, as in the complex and indefinite nature of the phenomena to which these concepts refer. 'Modern art' normally includes more than one specific mode of artistic perception. Consequently, there must have been more than one important line of psycho-historical development from the period of classical, to that of modern art. What follows is an attempt to scrutinize this field of development.

The first possibility of a psycho-historical interpretation of Worringer's study arises when the author establishes a close association between 'naturalistic' art and a general attitude of confidence in the external world, on the one hand, and between 'abstract' art and an attitude of mistrust and withdrawal—at least from one aspect of the external world—on the other. In this context, an 'empathetic' relation between man and his environment implies—apart from an attitude of participation—a strong feeling of security. On the other hand, the development towards an 'abstract' relation with the external world involves the diminution of such feeling. The relevance of this to historical evolution becomes apparent if one bears in mind that the individual's feelings of security and confidence in the external world, as well as their opposite, insecurity and withdrawal, are to a considerable extent social and cultural products. A high degree of social integration and stability creates in the individual security and confidence in the external world, while instability creates insecurity and mistrust. It follows from this that the transition of Western visual art from a classical to an abstract style can be seen in terms of a certain type of historical development characteristic of the Western world, which is *a development from a higher to a lower degree of social integration and stability*. It remains only to show that this kind of social development has a certain influence on the individual's perception of the world in a sense which might explain, at least partly, the evolution of Western visual art. Two points have a particular significance in this respect:

The first refers to what one may call the 'introvert' or 'introjective' aspects of modern art. Modern artistic perception discloses an obvious tendency to subordinate the 'objective' world of external reality to an inner world of emotions and symbols of the unconscious mind which, needless to say, has little to do with the world of common perception, or with a rational organization of human experience. The dissolution of *form* is an outstanding characteristic of modern painting. Form-qualities become dominated by colour-qualities: 'One draws with colour,' says Cézanne. Physical space itself tends more and more to become psychological space, i.e. symbolic interpretation of mental states in the artist. From Goya to Chagall artistic perception became increasingly inner-oriented. '*La peinture est la couleur de la personnalité*', says Chagall.[1]

The second point reveals an even closer relation between perception and the feeling of insecurity which, as just mentioned, resulted from an increasing social instability in the modern world. It refers to the 'abstract' character of perception. Since Worringer does not speak about perceptual schemes in general, but about artistic perception, it is necessary to bring additional proof that insecurity in the individual determines in fact certain abstract, detached, and cold qualities in his perception of the world. The analysis of the perceptual field of individuals living under conditions of stress—prisons and war situations—yields such evidence abundantly. Ego, or libido withdrawal, depersonalization are usual terms which describe such change in the field of

[1] Jacques Lassaigne: *Chagall*. Paris. 1957. p. 33.

perception.[1] For a better understanding of this point it is necessary to discuss the second developmental hypothesis suggested by Worringer's study.

Certain aspects in the development of artistic perception in the period between the Renaissance and the present time can be understood in terms of the degree of organization and articulation of the individual's inner life. In this sense, an 'empathetic' relation with the environment can be taken as a symptom of a diffuse inner structure, partly emerged in the structure of the external world, in other words, of a relatively low stage in the development of the 'self'. An 'abstract' relation implies, on the other hand, a highly developed inner structure, a strong 'self' which dominates the external structure of the environment.[2]

To see the relevance of this to the psycho-historical understanding of perception it is necessary to go back to an idea borne out by some recent experimental studies mentioned at the beginning of this chapter, namely, that the extent to which the individual depends in his perception of the world upon the structure of the external field varies according to the degree of mental integration he has reached, and according to the growth and the strength of the 'self' in particular. In this sense, the child's mode of perception is more dependent than that of an adult upon the structure of the external field. In Worringer's terms, one could say that the individual's perception of the world develops from one based on an 'empathetic' to one based on an 'abstract' relation between him and the environment.

[1] Shonberg, S.: 'Disorders of the Ego in War Times,' *Brit. J. of Med. Psychol.* February, 1949.

[2] It is obvious that this interpretation of Worringer's thesis clashes in certain points with that expounded previously. However, I do not claim to have put forward a unique and coherent view of the historical development of modern artistic perception. Moreover, I am under the impression that the contradiction revealed here lies in the nature of the historical process. It seems that there were two lines of psycho-historical development between the Renaissance and our time, one leading to a high degree of inner integration, to a strong ego-structure, the other, to a weak ego-structure. With a remarkable insight, Chagall seizes upon this contradiction as it manifests itself in contemporary painting. He distinguishes two trends in the visual art of his time. The first, which he terms '*Illogisme plastique*' can paradoxically be defined as an anti-logical organization of perception (figuration anti-logique). This is, in his view, opposed to Cubism which can, by analogy, be described as a super-logical organization of perception. The former insists on colour-qualities, while the latter on formal qualities in the field of perception. The former is, in my view, a sympton of a weak ego-structure, while the latter, of strong ego-structure. Op. cit. pp. 25 and 33.

Now, the same kind of developmental scheme can, by analogy, be applied to the historical period between the rise of classical style and that of modern style in the evolution of Western visual art. Thus, if one has to describe briefly the central trend in the psycho-historical process of this period, one would say that this consists in a gradual increase of self-awareness in the individuals belonging to Western civilization. As mentioned elsewhere, the Renaissance itself constituted a remarkable spurt in this direction. Moreover, since then, up to the present time the whole pattern of life has become more and more individualized. In this specific context, this means more and more dependent upon the 'self' as a reflective—self-conscious—structure in the individual's mind. Thus, throughout this period, the individual has become more and more detached, more and more 'abstract' in his relations with the external world. The development of the scientific spirit is the main proof of this. It remains only to say that perception being part of this general psycho-historical development has become itself more and more detached and abstract. Worringer's chief merit consists in having pointed to this process as reflected in the evolution of artistic perception. One has, however, to specify that this kind of interpretation of Worringer's thesis applies mainly, if not exclusively, to that aspect of modern art in which the geometrical spirit dominates the representational element, in which a schematic abstract mode of representation and an ideographical sign are superimposed on common perception. 'Cubism' and 'Surrealism' can be cited as an illustration of this. As just mentioned, the psycho-historical development at the basis of such a mode of perception is akin to that at the basis of modern science. Both scientific and modern artistic perception are symptoms of a highly developed 'self'. Both demonstrate the manner in which a highly integrated rational self imposes its schemes upon the structure of the external environment.

A more systematic and comprehensive approach to the historical development of the perceptual field of modern man is made by Pierre Francastel in *Peinture et Société*. This study is concerned with the radical change in the perception of space as this had been demonstrated by the evolution of visual art from *Quattrocento* to the present time. Within this period there took place both the destruction of an old, and the creation of a new perception of space. From the very beginning, Francastel places his investigation within a historical context: 'Contrary to Wölfflin who tends to consider visual function independently from other mental functions, I believe it necessary to study it in relation with the whole human activity in a given historical period'. Thus, the hypothesis he sets out to test is that perception of space is related to a series of historical factors, such as intellectual attitudes, general conceptions, system of beliefs and values, techniques, briefly, the hypothesis that space perception is *un fait de civilisation*.

In the first part of his study, Francastel deals with the development in the visual art of the *Quattrocento* of a particular manner of space representation for the description of which he uses various terms, such as 'linear', 'scenographic', 'cubic', all of them pointing to the introduction of perspective in the field of visual perception. He distinguishes two sets of factors which, in his view, are connected with such a psycho-historical event. Firstly, he speaks about the 'cult of number' characteristic of the time, and about the introduction in society of the methods of solid geometry. These are, however, considered as merely tools which explain only the technical aspect of the new mode of space representation. On this point Francastel writes suggestively: 'On admittait que le nouvel espace avait la figure d'un cube: que toutes les lignes de fuite se rassemblaient en un point unique situé á l'interieur du tableau et correspondant á un point de vue unique de l'oeil humain; on admettait que la representation des objects par leur valuers colorés devait co-incider avec la représentation par la ligne' (p. 135). But how can one account for the source of these 'suppositions', or 'conventions' on which, admittedly, the Quattrocento mode of space representation was based? In order to answer this question, Francastel brings into the picture some important 'emotional elements' characteristic of the period. The fifteenth century was a period of a remarkable change in the system of general beliefs and values; it was, in fact, the time of the crystallization of *modern anthropocentric conception of the universe*.[1] This psycho-historical event occupies a key position in Francastel's argument. He is inclined to think that it was primarily the growth of such a conception that motivated *the revolutionary*

[1] In this context, Francastel refers to Piaget's hypothesis regarding the onto-genetic evolution of space perception, i.e. the transition from a 'topographical' to a 'projective' and, finally, to a 'geometrical' perception of space. He, very cautiously, uses this only to illustrate his general idea of the existence of various modes of space experience and representation.

change in the perception of space introduced and articulated by the painters of the Quattrocento. As compared with the pre-Renaissance theocentric world, in which the artist situated all objects at the same level, i.e. as being the same distance from God, the Renaissance world acquired depth. In Francastel's words, this means that the man of the Renaissance began to perceive the world as a stage for himself—not for God—or rather as a 'scenographic cube' in which things were placed at various (measurable) distances from a central point. Moreover, the man of the Renaissance believed in the stable, objective and permanent character of the external world; he lived within a universe created once and for ever. It was, therefore, this specific mental climate, this new relation between man and the world that stimulated in the artist of the *Quattrocento* the *perception of perspective*, i.e. the mental habit of seeing various aspects of the external world on a line of decreasing size and clarity starting from the eye.

This is not the place to go into a detailed critical analysis of this crucial point in Francastel's thesis. Even if one finds it difficult to agree with the manner in which he formulates it, the hard historical fact still remains that the development of perspective as a representational mode is closely connected with a humanistic anthropocentric civilization. At any rate, Francastel considers this as a solid enough foundation for further development of his argument. Thus, in the second part of his study, he tries to reveal the connection between the decline of the Renaissance conception of the world and the gradual destruction of the classical mode of space representation. The central trend in this complex process is the decline of the belief in the stable, objective and permanent character of the external world resulting from the growing rate of change in modern society as well as from the development of modern science. Its influence on the evolution of space representation in modern painting can be seen in the Romantics' 'predilection for adjusting the classical style to the emotional tenor of the subject', in the Impressionists' revolt against the supremacy of form over colour, in Cézanne's struggle for complete freedom in the treatment of the subject, in van Gogh's ambition to represent perspective by colour. All this leads to 'the disarticulation of Alberti's cube', that is, the symmetrical scenographic vision. The main line of this development goes towards the substitution for a mode of space representation based on the 'objective' norms of perception by another mode of representation adjustable to various conditions, conscious or unconscious, of the inner life, in a word, towards the substitution of a psychological for a geometrical space.

In the last part of his study, Francastel deals with the development of a new space vision in contemporary painting. He analyses from this specific point of view various contemporary techniques and conceptions of visualizing space, such as 'near vision', 'analytical vision', 'camera vision', pointing to the part they have played both in the dissolution of the formal qualities of perception and in the articulation of a new pictural space, a 'discontinuous', 'curved', 'open' space. The decline of the belief in the stable character of the external world is particularly relevant here. Space is no longer visualized as a static container of things, but rather as a 'field of innumerable forces' in which things are permanently created and re-created in their shape and significance.

This new mode of space representation is, according to Francastel, the expression of a new stage in the historical development of Western civilization. It expresses in the first place a specific scientific and technical advance, i.e. the perception of man familiar with the experience of flying, of filming and photographing, of a man who can bring to the very threshold of reason the complexity of his unconscious. The same new mode of space representation expresses the experience of a man in more immediate and varied contact with his environment than the man of the Renaissance. While the Renaissance was the age of a 'visual exploration of the universe', the new age is that of a 'polysensory exploration'. While the aspirations and values of the Renaissance age went towards stability, objectivity, and permanence, those of the present age go towards speed, rhythm, plasticity, deformation, transformation, mutation. Finally, the space representation of contemporary artists expresses a new conception of the universe, and a new relation between man and the world. 'The Renaissance,' Francastel writes, 'created the picture of Nature distinct from man, but on man's measure. Contemporary art shows that we are advancing towards a new world in which man ceases to be the model and the centre of things. In this new world it is Nature that serves as a model for man, and not man as a model for Nature. Contemporary man, enriched by his complex and detailed contact with his surroundings and with himself visualizes space on the measure of his experience, techniques and inner life' (p. 267). The new 'elastic', 'protean' space, in the representation of which *movement* plays a dominant part, is the reflex of a new collective attitude towards the world, of a new mathematical conception of matter, and a new scale of values.

Space perception is therefore a historical phenomenon in the sense that it is an expression of a specific type of relation between man and his environment which varies with historical periods. On this point Francastel is the exponent of a radical historical relativism: 'Space,' he writes, 'is not a reality in itself, varying only in its expression from one period to another; space is man's experience itself,' that is, part of an adjustment of a human group to the external world in a specific historical period. This points to the more general idea according to which the manner in which individuals and groups perceive their environment is a function of the global process of adjustment, i.e. of the satisfaction of their basic needs, interests, beliefs and values. In other words, a balanced adjustment, individual or collective, requires the presence in the field of perception of certain selecting, emphasizing, and eliminating processes for the purpose of soothing, or avoiding tensions and conflicts which may arise between the individual's interests, beliefs and values and various factors in his environment.

A third approach to the problem of the historical evolution of modern man's perceptual field is illustrated by A. Ehrenzweig's study: '*The Psycho-Analysis of Artistic Vision and Hearing*'. If such a complex, and sometimes nebulous study can briefly be described one would say that one of its main aims is to demonstrate the dependence of human perception upon a complex of psycho-cultural factors. The author's Freudian convictions, though a departing point for this study, need not retain us here. It is enough to say that he insists on the repressing and releasing function which such complexes have in the field of perception with the purpose of creating in the individual what one might call, after Francastel, a vital equilibrium. An example will make this idea clear.

A central point in Ehrenzweig's argument concerns the perception of depth. Ehrenzweig, even more than Francastel, is convinced that perspective vision is an element introduced in the field of perception during the Renaissance. This is, however, a point which deserves closer consideration than one can give it here. What is important for the present purpose is the fact that Ehrenzweig explains this psycho-historical phenomenon by the function of a repressing mechanism in the field of perception. Thus, based on evidence furnished by both Gestalt and Depth psychology, he demonstrates how certain aspects in the individual's sensory contact with the environment fail to be integrated into his actual conscious perceptual field. On this point, much of his argument rests on a rigorous distinction between an unconscious and a conscious mode of perception. He then reasonably assumes that those aspects in the individual's sensory contacts with the environment which are unnecessary, or harmful to his practical adjustment, that is to his interests, beliefs, and values, are repressed. The perception of depth, or perspective, is meant to illustrate this. For, perceiving an object in depth is, according to Ehrenzweig, not only unnecessary for practical-rational adjustment, but even complicates the *recognition*, and *identification* of the object. However, the important fact is that, during the Renaissance, previously repressed aspects of the perception of objects, such as perspective, were released from the unconscious, and articulated into the field of conscious perception. *Why did this happen during the Renaissance?* As a true Freudian, Ehrenzweig speaks about the emotional disturbances and stresses of this period, and about their weakening effect upon the mechanism of repression.

Admittedly, Ehrenzweig's thesis cannot easily be summarized. He speaks, for instance, about the evolution of artistic hearing from the five, to the seven, and finally to the chromatic scale, and explains it by the same mechanism of repression which operates differently at various historical levels. One general idea does, however, emerge from this study, particularly if one looks at it from a sociological point of view. It can be formulated as follows: Firstly, the perceptual world of a group of individuals within a society varies with the historical evolution of that society. Secondly, this variation can be spoken of in terms of repressions and accentuations operating within the perceptual field of the individual. Thirdly, these processes of repression and accentuation are connected with the effects upon the individual's behaviour of certain broad historical events, such as changes in social structure, in social stability, in fundamental beliefs and conceptions. In conclusion, one could say that a great variety of perceptual possibilities which exist diffusely in the individual's unconscious, are actualized and articulated differently in various historical contexts. The creative artist plays an important part in this process. This is why the history of perception is closely related to the history of artistic representation.

Though penetrating and full of possibilities, Ehrenzweig's study suffers from a too-narrow Freudian approach. Its author is almost exclusively concerned with the intra-psychic aspects of the process of human adjustment, individual and collective. For instance, he rightly describes the Renaissance as a period of emotional tension which, corroborating psycho-analytical theory, contributed to the breaking-up of the old established patterns of behaviour, perceptual behaviour included. But this hardly explains the nature of the historical process, that is, the appearance of new phenomena in place of existing ones. This point has to be considered more closely.

The model of explanation offered by Ehrenzweig rests too much, if not entirely, on the dynamic character of the unconscious mind. The key concept in his explanation of the historical development of human perception is that of unconscious perception—unconscious vision, or hearing—which is a diffuse, form-free and object-free perception, and as such, full of developmental potentiality. When he comes to the point of explaining various historical stages in the field of perception, his main concern is with successive 'releases', or explosions of unconscious modes of perception. It is mainly on this account that he fails to open a clear historical perspective to artistic perception, and human perception in general. As just mentioned, the gradual release of unconscious factors—which in a true Freudian sense are anhistorical—cannot in itself determine historical development. The occasional invasion of the consciously articulated field of perception by unconscious modes of perception can explain only the destruction and disarticulation of certain established perceptual schemes, and not the formation of new schemes. In other words, it cannot explain historical development in this field. That is why it is necessary to modify Ehrenzweig's views in this point in accordance with Francastel's. This may provide us with, at least, some basic elements of a theory concerning the historical evolution of perception within modern Western civilization. Thus, the changes and developments displayed by various aspects of perception—visual, auditory and others—can be, or are in fact motivated by the gradual realization of a certain unconscious symbolism, or by the unconscious perceptual possibilities in general. But the rise and the development of new modes of perception can only adequately be understood in socio-cultural terms. The techniques, ideologies, beliefs and values of a period constitute the proper formative climate of the individual's modes of perception. It is mainly owing to this fundamental fact that human perception evolves in a true historical sense.

III

HISTORY AND EMOTIONAL CLIMATES

A history of opinions would really be the key to the history
of deeds. HERDER

INTRODUCTION

THE term emotional climate connotes a complex of
feelings, or a pattern of emotional dispositions and attitudes characteristic of a group of individuals in a given
historical situation. Collective emotional states, or simply, collective emotionality are expressions which can often be used in the
same context. The rise and spread of a religious creed, of a type of
art, or the role played by an ideology at a given historical time
are all phenomena which cannot be properly understood without
resorting, in one way or another, to such a concept. It is, therefore, little wonder that in recent years one notices a growing
interest in this direction among historians. 'The reader of
technical history,' writes H. Butterfield, 'learns too little from
it of the hopes and fears of the majority of men, too little of their
joy in nature or art, their feelings of love, their family affection,
their spiritual questings, and their ultimate vision of things.'[1]

The complaint is legitimate. One wonders, however, whether,
and to what extent the plaintiff is aware of the difficulty involved
in his case. To what extent can this exploration into the mind of
men become a useful enterprise for historical knowledge? Even
after surmounting the difficulty of collecting the relevant evidence, he has to struggle with yet another important difficulty.
The mental phenomena included in the concept of emotional

[1] *Man on his Past.* 1955.

43

climate are often hidden in the unconscious mind of the people. This implies that the historian concerned with the study of such phenomena ought to be aware that he has to leave the shore of rationality. However, it is only fair to say that some historians know this instinctively.

The aim of this chapter is to extend the historical approach, as previously defined, to human emotional behaviour. For reasons lying in the very nature of the historical process, the focus of attention is directed towards collective emotional states, therefore this chapter deals with a specific problem of group psychology. Since emotionality is on the whole a more dynamic motivational factor than perception, the difficult problem of the relationship between socio-cultural and psychological factors poses itself this time under a new form, and with renewed intensity. This makes it necessary to state from the very outset that the study of emotional climate from a historical standpoint can be approached from two main angles: firstly, one can regard an emotional climate as an 'effect', as an expression of various social and cultural factors. In this case the attention is focused on the changes taking place within such a climate as a result of the various historical circumstances in which a community finds itself. Secondly, an emotional climate can be regarded as a dynamic factor; the question now is how, and to what extent it determines historical events. This latter aspect constitutes an important problem of historical psychology, not encountered in the previous chapter.

To introduce the subject in general terms, it is important to realize that one has to deal with irrational phenomena, that is to say, with phenomena directed mainly by the unconscious mind. Such phenomena tend to have diffuse and 'generalized' effect upon human behaviour. A feeling, or an emotional attitude aroused in a group by a specific stimulus, and in a specific circumstance of life, may subsequently determine the behaviour of that group in all spheres of life; it may even persist for a long time, historically speaking, after the specific situation has disappeared. It has often been said that feelings, and even more so, collective feelings, work according to the 'all-or-none' principle. This formula sheds light on a series of irrational processes, such as *displacement, compensation* and *regression* which operate within the sphere of collective emotionality. In the first place, an emotional attitude created in a specific situation can be manifested in other situations with no specific stimulus for it, or plainly speaking, for no apparent logical reason. A state of aggression, or insecurity, created in a group by specific economic conditions can be displaced in the religious or political fields. Regarding the second tendency, one can briefly say that some collective feelings often appear under a compensatory opposite form. Thus, deeply rooted fear and insecurity in a social group may be manifested as aggression, bravery and even an exaggerated self-importance on the part of the group. Finally, an intensive collective emotional state can induce a reversion to forms of behaviour characteristic of earlier stages in the life of the group, or even of earlier stages in the mental development of the individual members of the group.

It is hoped that further elucidation of the terms outlined above will result from their subsequent application to concrete historical cases. For the time being, a word of warning is necessary. The frequent use of terms such as displacement, compensation, regression and ambivalence should not induce anyone to believe that this is psycho-analytical study of collective emotionality. The use made by such terms here is by no means 'orthodox'. On the contrary, the view held in this study is that such terms become useful conceptual tools for the study of social and historical phenomena only after the Freudian spirits lying in them have been exorcised.

CULTURAL STRUCTURES AND DISPLACED EMOTIONALITY

'It is an established fact,' writes Marc Bloch, 'that from the twelfth century until at least the Reformation the communities of textile workers were one of the favourite breeding-grounds of heresies.'[1] The analysis of this relatively simple case of displaced feelings may throw light on some rules regarding the inter-relation between socio-cultural structures and emotional climates. At an objective factual level, one is concerned here with specific social groups—mainly from Flanders and the Upper Rhine Valley—consisting of poor townsfolk and uprooted peasants of a first generation. The textile industry of the time, like most industries in most times, underwent recurrent crises which provoked insecurity and resentment in the groups of textile workers. Therefore, the formula covering the facts mentioned so far is: privations

[1] *The Historian's Craft.* Engl. Transl. by P. Putnam. Manchester. 1954. p. 153.

45

in the economic field aroused insecurity, resentment and aggression in the groups of textile workers. But, one hastens to add, this is not exactly, at least not all, that the historian wants to say. He presents us with two sets of facts, one pertaining to an economic, the other to a religious order, which have no apparent logical relation to each other. Nevertheless, he consciously or unconsciously assumes that there is a connection. Briefly, he assumes that in this case economic discontent became religious heresy.

But assuming is one thing, and explaining another. Why were the feelings aroused in the economic field displaced in the religious field? Obviously there is no simple answer to such a question. To start with, the conflict aroused in the minds of the textile workers between their 'inhuman' economic condition and their expectations rooted in the belief in the Christian ethics of brotherhood was certainly a spring-source of their non-conformist attitude in the religious field. The degree of enlightenment which was slightly higher in urban than in rural areas, may also be mentioned as an additional fact. One can also suggest the possibility of a certain association in the mind of these workers between economic and religious authority. In a society dominated by religion this seems to be not only possible, but probable. A detailed examination of facts may prove that certain industrial settlements were run and owned by the Church. All these facts—to which others can be added—are relevant for the case in point. Nevertheless, they cannot entirely account for the recurrent outbursts of rebellious attitudes in the religious field among the communities of textile workers referred to above, unless and until the factual rational analysis is completed by a psychological analysis. The phenomenon mentioned by Bloch is at least partly irrational and can only be properly understood if one takes into account the diffuse and 'generalized' effects of emotional climate. Owing to their intensity, the resentment and aggression aroused in the economic field were gradually extended to other fields, and ultimately to the social order as a whole. Therefore, the case thus presented is one of generalized resentment and aggression in a specific social group.

A more specific question arises at this stage: why did the textile workers manifest their resentment and aggression in the form of religious rebellion? Since the answer to this question lies in the very structure of their society as a whole, the analysis of the objective historical circumstances becomes necessary again. The social order to which the communities of textile workers belonged was based on religion. Rebellion against religious authority, against the symbol of order in itself, represented, therefore, the most suitable and satisfying expression of a generalized resentment and aggression. The workers' attack was indirectly aimed at the very foundation of society. It was in this (irrational) way that economic discontent led to religious heresy.

One can easily object that all this refers to a specific historical case, and that frustration and resentment aroused in the economic field do not necessarily lead to rebellious attitudes in the religious field; indeed, they may not lead to displaced aggression at all. This is an important point which has to be clarified in stages for it reaches the core of the problem concerning the inter-relation between the emotional climate and the socio-cultural structure of a community. All one can say at this stage is that emotional attitudes formed in a specific field of social life can be displaced in other fields. But, and this is the main point, the direction taken by the process of displacement is dependent to a large extent upon the structure of the cultural field as a whole. Any attempt to explain a specific case of displacement in the field of emotionality has to take into account all the main factors determining the socio-cultural structure of the group under consideration, such as the prevailing system of beliefs and values, political organization and the system of leadership, dominant ideologies and propaganda processes, etc.

This amounts to saying that collective emotional states have a 'structural' character from a cultural point of view, i.e. they stimulate in the individual the perception of his socio-cultural environment as a basically organized whole. The rationale of this process is this: an emotional state of mind formed in a confined situation containing a specific stimulus for it extends to other situations until the whole socio-cultural field becomes imbued by it. At this stage, such an emotional state leads to 'totalitarian' attitudes, i.e. to the perception of the whole society and the whole world in its own terms. The rise of the workers' movements in Western Europe offers a typical example of this. The insecurity and aggression aroused in industrial workers by a specific stimulus situation such as workers' relations with their employers, had been quickly generalized; by the mid-nineteenth century, the

47

whole social setting became in the eyes of industrial workers a stimulus of insecurity and aggression. The anarchic moods dominating the early professional organizations of the industrial workers is a proof of this. The uprising of the silk workers in Lyons—1830 for example—was a desperate rebellion compared by a journalist of the time with the barbarian invasions which destroyed Roman civilization (Saint-Marc Girardin). These moods of generalized insecurity and aggression formed the mental breeding-ground of modern communist movements.

This sheds more light on the "structural" character of an emotional climate. In the case of the nineteenth-century industrial workers, the insecurity and resentment aroused by specific economic conditions were finally displaced, not in the religious field, as in the case of the late Middle Ages textile workers, but in the political field. This becomes understandable only in terms of the cultural structure of nineteenth-century societies. For this purpose one has to take into account a number of contributory factors, such as the prevailing democratic ideologies with their cult of the masses, the prevailing scale of values, the educational status of the industrial workers, and particularly the rise of science and the decline of religion. All this had contributed to the damming up of the workers' insecurity and aggression in a political sense.

One can therefore conclude that the process of displacement, though unconscious and irrational in itself, is in many important ways dependent upon objective factors pertaining to the social and cultural structure of a community; it is in fact a component of a psycho-cultural field. If conceived in this manner the concept of displacement becomes a useful tool in the hands of social scientists, be they social psychologists, anthropologists, sociologists or historians. J. Monnerot's use of the concept of '*le déplacement du sacré*' is a good example of this.[1] According to him, the absolutist sacred character of communist leadership, and the dogmatic character of communist philosophy, are the product of the displacement of certain emotional attitudes from the religious to the political fields of life. The factor mainly responsible for this lies in the development of modern science which had a repressing effect on the religious feelings of contemporary man.

The only point of criticism which can be raised against Mon-

[1] J. Monnerot: *La Sociologie du Communisme.* 1949.

nerot's thesis is that it is too narrow both in its foundation and its application. In fact the displacement of religious sensibility was a much more general process which affected many aspects of the historical development of modern society. The secularization, starting with the Renaissance, the rationalist way of thinking in general, and the development of science in particular had all, in the long run, repressing effects on the religious feelings of modern man; they have all minimized the importance of religious symbols in human life. The result of this was that individuals in modern societies had to look elsewhere for the satisfaction of their frustrated need for security and sacredness in life. This started a long process of displacement of religious feelings which explains the great variety as well as the importance of secular myths, or secular religions in the modern world. In this way, men transferred their need for sacredness in life, their need for absolute trust and belief to various secular aspects of life. The myth of 'man' and of humanity lying at the centre of modern humanism, the myth of 'nation', of race, of the proletariat, of the providential leader, of science, and many other forms of absolute beliefs are all examples of the displaced religious sensibility in modern man.

At this stage one can glance at another aspect of the relationship between collective emotionality and the historical conditions of a specific social group. As the last example shows, the collective emotional states created by specific historical conditions can in turn themselves become active factors in the historical development of a community. Thus, the repressed religious feelings became important determining factors in the development of new attitudes in life, of new structures of beliefs (secular myths), and finally of a new social order represented by the communist societies of today. A specific aspect of an emotional climate changes its role from a 'product' into a producer within the historical process. This point will be taken up at a later stage.

FORMS OF COMPENSATORY FEELINGS

The insecurity and defiance of authority aroused in a group by its specific economic conditions are not always displaced in other spheres of social life. They may not be expressed directly at all except in the form of compensatory feelings. For example, under the domination of Ptolemy and Rome, many Egyptian peasants crushed by taxes and tolls, left their village and went into the desert, or hid themselves in another village. They led the life of 'outlaws'. Now, it is believed that this socio-economic phenomenon was connected with the early Christian anchoretic movements; a certain number of fellaheen became anchorites in imitation of St. Anthony.

The case presents a more complex manifestation of collective emotionality which in its last stage involves a strong process of compensation. The insecurity and resentment created in a social group—the fellaheen —by economic frustrations and political oppression led in the first place to a form of 'anomia' which is obviously one and the same thing as what was previously described as generalized aggression. This became apparent in the anarchic behaviour of the outlaws. But it seems that the same emotional states gave rise to a sort of pacifist and retreatist attitude. Emotionality underwent, in this case, a process of compensation, in the sense that the world of religious beliefs presented for some peasants a relief from their frustration and insecurity. This motivated their flight from this world and their retirement to the inner world of their beliefs. Various social and cultural aspects of the situation contribute to this form of collective emotional behaviour. Firstly, there was the specific nature of the frustrating and repressing elements, i.e. the oppressive measures imposed by a strong autocratic ruler upon a group of individuals belonging to the lower classes, which ruled out the possibility of overt organized aggression. (This was partly compensated for by a diffuse form of aggression manifested by the outlaws.) Secondly, there was the place occupied by religious beliefs in the Egyptian community of the time, and particularly the value placed on the salvation of the soul. Lastly, one should not overlook the important cultural phenomenon of that period, anchoreticism which was practised by the fathers of the desert, not only as a simple religious technique but as a way of life. All this contributed to the new direction and form of the peasants' frustration in the manner shown above.

A similar constellation of socio-psychological factors explains another compensatory form of collective emotionality, the messianic feelings and attitudes of a group. The feelings of insecurity and inferiority created in a social group as a result of economic frustration and political oppression often lead by compensation to an exaggerated feeling of self-importance. In some cases, these feelings reach a stage at which the group is invested by its members with supernatural powers; the group becomes the saviour of humanity. The rise of the messianic idea among the ancient Jews, among the members of modern working classes, and more recently, among the German people, are typical examples of this kind. The well-known formula 'oppressed people, elect people' applies in all these cases. Naturally, this does not imply that these messianic movements are identical in their content. The way in which a social group works out its messianic aspirations depends to a considerable extent on its cultural structure. The system of beliefs and values is of paramount importance. In this respect it is enough to mention the difference between the Jewish messianism imbued with religious spiritual elements, and the scientific, realistic, messianic calling of the communist movements of today.

As just suggested, the compensatory feelings of a group are not always displayed in terms of everyday reality. Compensation can take the road of imagination in the field of religion, philosophy, art or literature. This is a well-known psychological process which is mentioned here for the light it throws on a particular aspect of the relationship between an emotional climate, as a psychological factor, and various social and cultural conditions of a group. As such it can be given as an example of the manner in which a social scientist, particularly an historical psychologist, can use the data furnished by artistic and ideological creations for the understanding of a specific historical period.

It often happens that the feelings expressed by the literary and artistic creations of a period cannot be attributed to the people living in the period; moreover they stand in opposition to the prevailing feelings of the people. Thus, the feelings of piety and serenity expressed in the art of a period can often be interpreted as a need in the people of that period to compensate for the cruelty and violence which dominated their everyday life. The Troubadours were most successful with their poetry of heroism and chivalry in a period when these virtues were in decline, and when the pleasures of a quiet sedentary life took hold of the members of the aristocracy. The historian of our period would certainly not take the revival of poetical drama as a sign of strong romantic feelings in modern industrial societies.

It is often a feeling which is dying in the hearts of men that reverberates vigorously in their cultural products. We are inclined to attribute to the people of the romantic period of Europe, of the first half of the nineteenth century in particular, a strong sense of the past. This was expressed with particular force in that doctrine typical of German romanticism, called historicism. There are, however, good grounds for wondering whether the romantic sense of the past was not in fact a yearning for the past, that is to say, a compensation for the moribund value of a traditional patriarchal social order. Thus the feeling about the past, gradually weakened by the advance of democratic society, had been inflated at the cultural level. There are times in which this inflation takes on unusual proportions; it may amount to conscious or unconscious falsification of historical documents regarding the value of the past. In one of these 'mythomanic' epochs some pseudo-Celtic poems were attributed to Ossian; Chesterton discovered 'Old English' in epic poems and ballads, and the allegedly medieval poetry of Clothilde of Surville aroused great enthusiasm. The defeated social past invaded human consciousness in an inflated form.

REGRESSIVE-REVOLUTIONARY EMOTIONALITY

Sometimes the escape into the past takes on the form of regressive behaviour. This happens when a collective emotional state provokes by its intensity a reversion to forms of behaviour characteristic of earlier stages in the life of a community, or even of earlier stages in the mental development of individual members of the community. The feeling of insecurity created among the members of a group by wars, political oppression, and calamities of various sorts usually leads to such behaviour.

Revivalism can sometimes be taken as a symptom of incipient regression in the life of a community under conditions of stress. In the last ten years of political oppression and social dissolution in Rumania—to start with a recent example—the revival of the old ballads, old songs and folk-dances has taken on the proportion of a mass phenomenon. Of course, it can easily be said that this forms an item in the cultural policy of the communist régime, but the remarkable success of such a policy has been made possible by a reversion to an earlier type of social emotionality. The revival of the old ballads is a way by which the individual belonging to this community satisfies his frustrated need for security and self-assertion by identifying himself with the imaginary heroes of the past who fought for the poor against the tyranny of the strong.[1]

A characteristic example of emotional regression is offered by the Athenian community during the 'age of anxiety', i.e. the period of decline of the city-state. Two collective phenomena were symptomatic in this respect, a heightened religious emotionality and a heightened need for social integration. The former was manifested in the revival of a series of mystic beliefs and practices, principally the Eleusian and Orphic cults, which promoted a closer contact between man and God. As the term revival suggests, this constituted, to a great extent, a regression to religious beliefs and attitudes characteristic of the archaic period of Greece, and which were suppressed by the Homeric Olympian religion. Now, with the decline of the city-state, whose religious foundation consisted in Homeric mythology, the people reverted in their religious emotionality to an earlier stage in the development of their civilization. This withdrawal from the unpleasant present into the past increased their feeling of security.[2] It was the same search for security that caused a heightening of the feeling of social 'belonging' among the Greeks of the period. Considering the impressive number of unofficial associations, half religious, half secular, which sprang up in the fourth century B.C. one could say that the heightened need for solidarity was one of the most characteristic psycho-social traits of the period. This phenomenon, remarked upon by many historians, needs no detailed treatment here. A heightened spirit of 'groupism' can be interpreted as a symptom of regression when it is displayed by members of a democratic, individualistic and cosmopolitan society; it is a reversion to a pre-individualistic social order of a community type.

[1] In the national competition of 1955—Bucharest—there were 600 entries of folk-dance teams and choirs.

[2] According to some views the archaic mystic beliefs and practices persisted among the common people throughout the Homeric and classical periods. Their revival towards the close of the fifth century was mainly due to sociological causes. The rise of the lower classes as a result of democracy lies at the basis of this revival. For details see Chapter IV.

Ample evidence of the close connection existing between religious revivalist movements and regressive group feelings is offered by the religious sects in Western Europe during the late Middle Ages. This has been clearly demonstrated in a recent study by N. Cohn.[1] Cohn's central thesis is that these revolutionary movements rose and developed during periods of stress provoked by social disruptions, over-population, famine and calamities of all sorts; they were 'collective efforts to cope with situations of strain, or conflict'. Most of what is said in this study about the behaviour of the individuals belonging to these movements is, in one way or another, symptomatic of regressive behaviour in general and regressive emotionality in particular. Among such symptoms there were the proneness of these individuals to mythical thinking, their over-dependence on providential leaders and particularly their expectation of the imminent coming of a new Messiah. All these forms of delusional behaviour are unmistakable signs of the serious impairment of their sense of reality which is normally provoked and associated by mental regression to early infantile stages.

In the psychological description of these salvationist movements Cohn is inclined to use terms of psychopathology. He speaks, for instance, about a 'syndrome of paranoia' in group behaviour which is obviously another sign of regression. Perhaps it would be more adequate to describe this specific aspect of group behaviour as a 'Manichean' attitude in life often displayed by groups under conditions of stress. It consists of a strong in-group feeling which can develop into self-adulation of the group, and in messianic aspirations. This is paralleled by strong out-group feelings manifested as aggression towards other groups, and in an advanced stage, as group autism. In this latter case the group is perceived by its members as the 'centre' of the world, the embodiment of supreme virtue with the mission to exterminate any resistance to its great designs.

We can go back here to the double role played by certain collective emotional states in the historical development of a community. The feelings of insecurity, resentment, or messianic calling set up in a group of people by specific historical circumstances, can become spring sources of new historical developments. This idea deserves close consideration for a twofold

[1] *The Pursuit of the Millennium*. London. 1957.

reason: it reveals the dynamic character of emotional climate in the historical process, and also it gives a certain insight into the psychology of social revolutions.

The above details about the religious revolutionary movements suggest that certain emotional attitudes created in a group of people by (historical) situations of stress have a double, or rather an ambivalent character. Firstly, they arouse an attitude of withdrawal from the present situation. The feeling involved in such an attitude is a mixture of fear, resentment, and apathy. The retreatist, the regressive, and some of the displaced emotional states described above are examples of this. But, on the other hand, the same situation of stress normally creates an opposite feeling, one of aggression, which stimulates attack upon, rather than withdrawal from, the situation. In other words, it motivates a revolutionary action in the group. Now, psychologically, it is sound to assume that both attitudes are present in a group under conditions of strain, though only one of them leads to overt behaviour. In other words, most groups under conditions of stress are emotionally motivated towards both a retreatist and towards a revolutionary type of action. What course of action is taken depends on the historical situation, i.e. on a set of socio-cultural factors.

It is merely stating the obvious to say that the first course of action is more likely to be taken in a situation of despair in which the oppressing forces are strong to the degree of excluding any rational expectation of relief or victory in the oppressed group. This is the case of the anchoristic movements and to a certain extent that of the religious millennarian movements. In such cases the individuals, separately, or as a group, withdraw from the present situation into themselves, into a world of fantasy. Sometimes this withdrawal into themselves reaches that degree that even their resentment and aggression become inwardly orientated, i.e. thay are turned into penitent and self-punitive attitudes. The case of the flagellant sects is a case in point.

But as soon as the situation contains an element of security the action of the group takes a different course. Indeed any element of security perceived by a group under conditions of stress constitutes a stimulus for a revolutionary attitude, i.e. for an attack upon an external object believed to be the cause of the stress in the situation. The growth of the revolutionary mood in some groups of industrial workers during the nineteenth century illustrates this point. There was, in the initial stages, a situation of stress resulting from unemployment, low wages, uprootings, etc., which aroused in the workers either complete apathy, or a mixture of this with an unfocused resentment so characteristic of the mid-nineteenth-century nihilism. It is this mood that was so severely condemned by the fathers of communism. Marx's lifetime ambition and work were to convert this passive anarchism of the workers into a positive, real revolutionary anarchism. He obviously succeeded, and the key of his success can be expressed in one word, 'organization.' In this 'togetherness' consists the element of security which was introduced into the situation and it was precisely this element which accounts for the change in the workers' attitude from a retreatist to a revolutionary one.[1] Tocqueville—who is a gold-mine for historical psychology—was aware of this aspect of the motivation of revolutionary action. In his view, one of the main determining factors of the French Revolution consisted in the position held by the French peasantry in the pre-revolutionary society. This position offers a classic example of a situation of stress with a flaw in it, i.e. with an element of security. The peasants, on the whole, oppressed by a complicated system of social obligation, were, at the same time, possessors of land, a fact which allowed them a certain degree of independence and security. This incongruity in their status was reflected in their emotional attitudes. Both a retreatist, and an aggressive revolutionary attitude were clearly discernible. After describing the peasants of the pre-revolutionary period as 'submissive and even placid', Tocqueville continues, 'but open to them a door of escape from the evil they seem to bear so lightly, and they will rush towards it with such a violence as to pass

[1] This point has been experimentally illustrated by Dembo and Barker, followed by Wright. They used for their experiments pairs of children in frustrating situations. The pairs were divided into 'weak' and 'strong' friends. One of the main results was that the pairs consisting of 'strong' friends became comparatively more aggressive towards the specific element in the external situation—the experimenter in this case—perceived as the cause of frustration. This has been attributed to the elements of security provided by the presence of a friend in the situation. On the other hand, the reaction of the 'weak' friend-pairs contained a strong element of 'puzzlement' and unfocused aggression. See Wright, M. E. 'Constructiveness of Play as Affected by Group Organization and Frustration. Char. & Pers. 1942, XI.

In the same order of ideas it is worth mentioning that apathy and resignation are often found in the behaviour of groups under conditions of stress. Unemployment and concentration camps are typical in this respect.

over your body'.[1] Towards the end of the eighteenth century, the latter attitude prevailed in the behaviour of the peasants' group. This was mainly due to the fact that several 'doors' were opened which let hope and security come into the peasants' world. Firstly, there was the original element of security derived from the possession of land which raised the peasants' aspirations above the level of a social group completely dependent upon the aristocracy. Then there followed other elements of security such as economic prosperity—the two decades preceding the Revolution were particularly prosperous—the growing weakness of the aristocracy, the spread of revolutionary ideology. All this contributed to the crystallization of a revolutionary mood in the peasants.

In conclusion the above idea can be formulated thus: a group of people oppressed and frustrated on all levels of life are to a lesser degree prompted to revolutionary action, than a group of people whose level of aspiration had been raised in a specific direction only. The gain in security resulting from a specific rise in the level of aspiration serves as a catapult for the revolutionary mood always present in a group under conditions of stress. Again, Tocqueville is ready to support such an hypothesis when he writes: 'It is not always by going from bad to worse that a country falls into Revolution. It happens most frequently that the people which had supported the most crushing laws without complaint . . . throw this off with violence as soon as the burden begins to be diminished.'

HISTORICAL CIRCUMSTANCES AND EMOTIONAL AMBIVALENCE

This is not the place to explain the sources and the inner mechanism of ambivalence in human behaviour. However, any attempt towards the understanding of this complex problem should start from a simple primordial fact: the antithesis of reason—sometimes intellect and consciousness are mentioned in the same context—and emotionality. Reason is a balancing structure; its main function is to establish a certain degree of gradualness, continuity and consistency in human behaviour. To achieve this it has to struggle against—to repress, as the psychoanalyst would

---

[1] *On the State of Society in France before the Revolution.* Trans. H. Reeve, London. 1873. p. 165.

have it—emotionality which, on the whole, works in an opposite direction. It has often been said that the 'logic' of emotional life is that of black and white, of the 'all-or-none' principle. There is no neutral ground between extreme tendencies. Love borders on hatred, courage on fear, arrogance on servility, piety on impulsiveness and violence. This implies that individuals whose minds are dominated by emotional factors are liable to inner contradictions in their behaviour; they swing in their emotional behaviour from one extreme to another, viz. from the extreme of love to that of hatred, from aggression and arrogance to servility, from piety to violence.

This brief consideration gives a first insight into the connection between ambivalence in human feelings and various historical circumstances. For, it had been commonly observed that certain historical circumstances, certain cultural climates have, on the whole, disrupting effects on the rational structure of the mind, and, at the same time, stimulating effects on emotionality. In such cases, one can notice frequent symptoms of ambivalent feelings in the behaviour of a group. To illustrate this let us take a concrete case as presented by one of the most famous historians. In his history of Rome under Tiberius, Tacitus describes in some detail the sycophantic habits of the people, of the Senators in particular, that is to say, their exaggerated need 'to protect their position by subservience'; they were, in Tiberius' own words, 'men fit to be slaves.'[1] After saying this, Tacitus somehow unexpectedly continues: 'Then gradually (their) self-abasement turned into persecution.' By this remark he seems to grasp the very essence of the case, i.e. the ambivalent attitudes created in a group of people by fear and insecurity. The only superfluous word in his formulation is 'gradually'. This is because attitudes of servility and flattery existed in the people described by him side by side with suspicion and aggression; so did love and hatred. The people's attitudes towards the strong were ambivalent: admiration and love were mixed with denigration and hatred. The same people showed servile submission towards the powerful, and aggressive domination leading to persecution of the weak. Hence the swing in their behaviour between lack of self-respect and a morbid need for self-assertion and power.

Naturally, Tacitus saw in this the distinctive feature of a

[1] *On Imperial Rome.* p. 147.

specific historical period. Moreover, he was aware that this kind of emotional behaviour was the result of an extremely autocratic régime. The atmosphere in Rome under Tiberius was permeated with fear: fear of intrigues, of informers, of Imperial caprice. In such an atmosphere, servility and dependence upon the Emporer's will grew hand in hand with mutual suspicion and denunciation; it was an atmosphere in which any kind of offence was easily turned into 'high treason', in which children denounced their fathers, in which poisoning and accusations of poisoning were regular occurrences. The proto-type of the period, Sejanus, the Commander of the Guards, is described by Tacitus in terms of this basic ambivalence: 'a blend of arrogance and servility.'[1]

The significance of Tacitus' insight therefore goes beyond a specific historical situation. Such feelings and attitudes are characteristic of most human groups living in an atmosphere of terror. But, before generalizing, it would be better to analyse other cases.

Few, if any, technical historians saw more deeply into the ambivalent character of social sensibility than Huizinga in his famous book: *The Waning of the Middle Ages*. This is due both to his psychological insight, and to the nature of his subject. A 'violent tenor of life' was, according to Huizinga, the dominant note of the late Middle Ages in France, and in Burgundy in particular. This dominance of emotional factors constituted a source of ambivalence in people's behaviour. Huizinga phrases this point suggestively: 'So violent and motley was life that it bore the mixed smell of blood and roses.' The fear of hell and the naïve joy of life were so near each other in people's minds that they often intermingled. They displayed in their behaviour a quick alternation of irritability and serenity, of violent revenge and gallant mercy, of cruelty and piety, love and hatred, cupidity and generosity. Their inner tension was high: they laughed and wept easily. The people's attitude to women and love was also marked by the same ambivalence; they veered between crude sensual and highly polished, almost idealistic love.

---

[1] Tacitus' objectivity has always been a debatable point. It might well be that he retrojected his view about the Rome of his time on the Rome of Tiberius, intending by this to criticize the public corruption of his contemporaries. Even if this is true, the present argument still remains valid.

Symptoms of the same state of mind were reflected at the cultural level. The painting, the costumes and the pageantry of the period reveal an unmistakable preference for vivid contrasting colours. This is the manner in which Huizinga describes the manifestation of this mental condition in the religious field: 'When we see side by side the most striking contrasts of passionate piety and mocking indifference, it is not so easy to explain them by opposing, as if they made up distinct groups, the worldly to the devout, the intellectual to the ignorant, the reformers to the conservatives.' Further on, he continues: 'To explain the astonishing contrasts of religious life towards the end of the Middle Ages, we must start with the recognition of a general lack of balance in the religious temper, rendering both the individual and the masses liable to violent contradiction and sudden changes.'

Anyone attempting to explain this psycho-historical situation has to grapple first with the following questions: are some historical periods more dominated by emotional factors than others? If so, why? Why this excess of ambivalence in the period mentioned above?

The answer to the first question is a positive one. The emotional motives in people's behaviour play a greater part in patriarchal, agricultural than in modern industrial societies; the same motives are stronger in an authoritarian than in a democratic organization; they are also stronger in a society under conditions of stress than in one under conditions of leisure. The 'waning of the Middle Ages' can, therefore, be considered as a period in which emotionality played an important role in human behaviour.[1]

Much more important in this case are the questions starting with 'why'. Why was the pattern of life in this period so much influenced by emotionality? Unfortunately much more information than is available at the present is needed, before such a question can be answered satisfactorily. Huizinga's study is hardly a beginning in this direction. However, as things are at present, the best one can do is to make some general suggestions to help future explorations in this field. With regard to the dominance of emotionality in life, as well as with the ambivalent character

---

[1] As to the precise limits of this period there can be no generally accepted answer. As will be shown later, L. Febvre finds important symptoms of ambivalence in the emotional behaviour of the sixteenth-century French.

of human behaviour, two points have to be considered; in the first place, the system of emotional security, and the system of control of primary impulses.

To start with, the degree of security could not be high in a period in which the protection against plagues, epidemics and calamities of any sort was almost non-existent. Politically, the society described by Huizinga was an autocratic system in which the value of the individual's personality was not taken for granted. It was a society in which 'the soldier' and 'the monk' constituted two predominant personality types. This shows already the presence of a basic ambivalence in the pattern of life in that the two personality types correspond to two opposing attitudes, an aggressive, and a retreatist one. From the cultural point of view, it is important to note that it was the 'waning of the Middle Ages', that is to say, the beginning of the disintegration of the medieval world. Heretical sects mushroomed in Western Europe; they were but symptoms of deeper disrupting processes. Humanistic knowledge had begun to increase rapidly, thus spoiling the traditional image of the universe. Perhaps unconsciously the 'doubt', the 'Lucianic spirit', so characteristic of the Renaissance, started to creep in, in the minds of the people. It is true that religion was still holding its ground, offering security for everyone. But facing an ever growing enemy, its spirit had to be bolstered up. Thus, the fear of hell, as well as the yearning for salvation, were pushed to an extreme. With both the seed of doubt and the terror of damnation in his heart, the individual was in a permanent struggle with himself: his personality was 'highly-strung', as Huizinga notices. This has a direct bearing on the ambivalent character of human emotionality and, at the same time, clarifies the idea of ambivalence which is essentially this: a low degree of security resulting from disrupting processes in the individual's environment, social or physical, increases the emotional character of his behaviour and, at the same time, intensifies the basic ambivalence of his feelings.

There is little doubt that the world in which the man of the late Middle Ages lived was highly 'emotionalized'. It was dominated by supreme powers which man could not understand, with which he could not deliberate, let alone master. The adjustment to such a world involved a basic ambivalence, for, to put it figuratively, the world became easily the symbol either of God, or of the

Devil, as man was possessed by love, serenity, and acceptance, or by hatred and destruction.

The origin of this basic ambivalence will be discussed more fully below, but before this, it is interesting to see what system of control medieval man had over his primitive drives. Though drawing to a close, the period covered by Huizinga's study still belonged in some important respects to the Middle Ages. The main sign of this was, as Huizinga himself says, that 'individual and social life in all their manifestations were imbued with the conception of faith'. In the spirit of medieval Christianity, this meant that human life was entirely oriented towards spiritual values. In this central belief in the transcendental meaning of human existence lay the root of the perfectionist attitude in life characteristic of medieval man. This expressed itself in the tendency, individual and collective, to pattern human behaviour according to highly idealized models of life: the saint was the model of a perfect Christian, the knight was the model of a perfect gentleman. In other words, the tendency to squeeze life within rigorous canons of behaviour was an important psychological trait of the period.

The adjustment to such a pattern of life implied, naturally, a specific system of organization and control of the individual's mind. It determined in the first place, the formation, at the conscious level of the mind, of an acute need for conformity, or a strong feeling of what was right, or wrong, good, or bad, acceptable or unacceptable. But the same condition of life made necessary the formation, at the unconscious level of the mind, of a strong repressing mechanism. This meant a ruthless control of all unacceptable impulses. The deeper the individual repressed these impulses in his unconscious, the purer he felt at the conscious level.

In this strong repressing mechanism lay one of the main sources of ambivalence in the behaviour of late medieval man. For any rigid repression accentuates the contradiction between the upper and the lower levels of the individual's mind, between what is acceptable and not acceptable in the light of his system of values. Owing to the requirements of his culture and particularly to the pressure put upon him by the transcendental models of life, the man of the late Middle Ages developed this contradiction to an extreme. The low level, the unconscious repressed level, was the exclusive seat of his unacceptable tendencies and desires, that is to say, of hatred, aggression, cruelty and sensuality. The upper level, that of conscious aspirations, became the exclusive seat of pure, tender love, or piety, charity, pity and of all the Christian virtues. It is this high tension between the two levels that explains the oscillation of his behaviour between two extremes, viz. the extreme of love, and that of cruelty, the extreme of pity and revenge, of spirituality and sensuality. This basic polarity of his mental structure did not allow for compromising and balanced attitudes.

AMBIVALENCE AND CULTURAL POLARITY

At this stage, one can look more closely at the influence of cultural factors on the ambivalent feelings and attitudes of a group of individuals. There are two levels at which such factors operate. At a primary level, a certain cultural climate as a whole can determine a specific type of mental organization which predisposes towards ambivalent feelings and attitudes. Thus, it is obvious that the system of control of primary impulses and the system of emotional security which, in the view of this study, were closely related to the ambivalent behaviour of late medieval man, were, to a great extent, determined by a specific social and cultural climate. This amounts to saying that the cultural climate of the late Middle Ages determined a highly tense mental organization, a mental structure based on a strong contradiction between its upper and lower levels, which was in itself a source of ambivalence. But the very manifestation of this general mental condition brought forth a secondary, more specific, influence of cultural factors upon the individual's ambivalent behaviour. Remaining within the present example, this can be formulated as follows: the people of late medieval times projected their inner contradiction by means of cultural symbols. The result was that, in the course of generations, their social and cultural environment became organized round these symbols. At this stage, their ambivalence became doubly conditioned. A first source of ambivalence lay in the depth of the individual's mind as a result of strong repressing processes. But the cultural climate also included factors such as verbal symbols, beliefs, prejudices, and institutions which entertained and even strengthened the individual's basic ambivalence. These later factors can be called secondary motives of ambivalent behaviour.

The cultural climate of the late Middle Ages was organized in terms of basic contradictions and polarities. The moral world, for instance, assumed a duality at a quasi objective level, in the sense that both virtues and vices were projected on to the external world. Moreover, they were objectified. The medieval picture of the moral world was always tinted with the spirit of Manicheism; the moral world was in fact a battlefield between the armies of the angels and those of the demons. Now, there is hardly need to point out that for late medieval man this was not a simple figure of speech; it cannot be classified in terms of modern psychology as delusional behaviour. For the people of the Middle Ages did more than 'believe': they believed in the reality of their beliefs. The homogeneous character of their cultural climate was the factor mainly responsible for this. Most people—if not everybody—saw, heard, and even met angels and demons. Ronsard—to give an example from a later period—while on the way to his mistress, saw with his own eyes '*dans l'air la Chasse Infernale*' so vividly and so alive that he felt compelled:

> De tirer son epée et de couper menu
> L'air tout au tour de lui avec le fer nu.

'Reification' is the right word for such phenomena. Virtues and vices had their own voices; they had mind and body too. In his journey the hero of *The Pilgrim's Progress* met 'the Evangelist', 'Pliable', 'Despair', 'Wiseman', 'Badman' and many others. And this was not simple allegorical language. These words were as representational as any other. For medieval man the levels of reality were not as sharply divided as they are for us.

As the pattern of life was organized between two opposite poles, the individual's behaviour tended to oscillate between the extreme of sensuality and cupidity and that of piety and purity, between the extreme of temptation and that of guilt and repentance. This was a way of life determined by emotionality as opposed to that determined by reason which is more and more characteristic of the modern era.

A final and most important point is the negative relation of ambivalence to rational thinking. Bearing in mind the balancing function of reason, one can say that the ambivalent behaviour displayed by the people of the late Middle Ages was indicative of the undeveloped state at that time of a rational frame of mind, or even its total absence. But it has to be stressed again that a rational frame of mind is dependent in its rise and development upon specific social and cultural factors. More precisely, the development of a rational frame of mind in a group of individuals is an historical process. In this respect L. Febvre, who was the first to look at the phenomenon of ambivalence from a historical perspective, made a few pertinent observations.[1] He rightly connects the ambivalent behaviour of the people living towards the close of the Middle Ages with the lack of rational organization of their environment. These people lived in an environment of contrasts, a fact which, according to Febvre, contributed to their disposition to swing between extreme passions. In other words, the extremes of nature left their impact upon human behaviour. Firstly, there were the extremes of climate between exceedingly cold winters, and hot summers, and the extremes of light between day and night. Then there were the extremes of socio-physical environment resulting from a primitive natural economy, i.e. periods of superfluous abundance were followed by periods of starvation, or, abundance in one place and starvation in another, with no proper means of transport.

All these extremes have since been smoothed over by a rational organization of the environment, physical and social. The extremes of winter have been tempered by the discovery of new kinds of fuel and by a well organized system of heating; those of summer by artificial cooling. On the other hand, the invention of electricity has considerably reduced the difference between night and day. A rational economy has also helped men to avoid the extremes of poverty and of unnecessary abundance and waste. Thus, science, as a system of rational thinking and action, has contributed to the building up of a more homogeneous and constant environment. This stabilized medium of living has, in its turn, acted upon human behaviour: it reduced man's tendency to swing between extremes, i.e. it reduces his ambivalence.

PSYCHO-SOCIAL MODELS OF EXPLANATION IN HISTORY

The historical development of collective emotionality is still virgin soil both for the historian and the psychologist. This is due partly to the lack of interest in this direction, and partly to the

[1] *Combats pour L'Histoire*. Paris. 1953.

lack of a body of adequate hypotheses on which to organize the relevant facts. For the former, the historians are to be blamed, for the latter, the psychologists. The result is that progress in this field of human knowledge has not gone beyond suggestive comments on isolated facts. In the field of religion one knows, for instance, that the ancient Greeks, in the course of their historical development, invested their gods with various attributes; one knows also that the Byzantines knew Jesus of Nazareth as Christ Pantocratos (the Lord of the Universe), that the High Middle Ages knew a Christ in Majesty, and that, not later than the fourteenth century, everybody knew him as the Christ in the Passion. Further, one knows that religious representations are closely connected with emotionality, individual and collective. Nevertheless, the questions remain wide open: why this change in religious representations; why this change in collective emotionality? Historians like L. Febvre rightly deplore this lack; he feels that the history of human emotionality can fill an important gap in the field of historical knowledge. For this purpose he wants a history of the feelings of fear, of love, of hatred, of joy and pity. It seems, however, necessary to stress again the fact that there are two approaches to the history of human emotionality. Firstly, one can regard an emotional climate as an effect of various social and cultural conditions specific to the historical development of a community. On the other hand, one can regard it as a dynamic factor, i.e. a source of historical events within a specific community. Since the former approach has been our central concern so far, it remains to say a few words about the second. This may throw light on the importance which the study of human emotionality has for historical knowledge.

It has often been said that the reduction of a social, or historical fact to a psychological one, or the mere description of the former in terms of the latter, means a definite loss in the precise and rigorous character of scientific knowledge. This is probably true, and the reason for it lies in the very nature of psychological phenomena. Psychological phenomena have a lower degree of determinability, consequently, a higher degree of freedom than social phenomena, and historical events in general. If we were to refer an economic phenomenon, such as a case of monetary inflation, to a certain emotional state of 'panic' in a social group, we would certainly gain some knowledge of that specific case of inflation. But it can easily be seen that the gain is not an essential one. For what in fact happens is a translation of an objectively observable phenomenon into a subjective, moreover highly irrational, one. 'Irrational' is a very important word in this context, for it indicates the degree of indeterminability of a phenomenon such as that of panic. While in some circumstances panic may lead to inflation, in some others, it may not; moreover it may determine an opposite process, i.e. deflation. Thus, in spite of the fact that a certain gain in knowledge has been achieved, the process of knowledge as a whole falls to a lower degree of determinability. This can be illustrated with another example: If the historian were to describe an important event like the nomination of Adolf Hitler as the leader of Anton Drexler's tiny political group, in 1920, and all Hitler's subsequent career, in terms of the feelings of insecurity and aggression widespread among all members of the German community of the time, an important aspect of the event would certainly be explained. But this is done at the same risk as before, that is to say, the risk of falling into an area of low determinability. For the feeling of insecurity may lead to authoritarian leadership of the right, or of the left; it may lead to social anarchy, and even to religious revivalism.

There is, however, another side to this problem. When a historian describes, or explains in psychological terms he may lose a certain degree of precision, but in quite a different way, he makes an important advance in his knowledge of historical events. His grasp in the determining field of these events goes deeper. The reason for this is that most mental phenomena, particularly those belonging to collective emotionality, play the part of 'general factors' in the determining field of historical events; they determine more than one event. They determine the structure of events. Thus, the disadvantage arising from the indeterminability of mental events is compensated for by the advantage derived from their structural character. This can be illustrated by the case of the historian who considers the feeling of collective insecurity as one of the determining causes of Hitler's access to power. Provided that he is aware of the irrational character of such feeling, he has now in his hands a factor of a kind which can give him the clue to a series of other events of the period, such as the specific character of economy, of political institutions, of international relations, of ideological trends. In other words, this very phenomenon opens his eyes to the structure, the '*innere Zusam-menhang*' (Ranke) of events in a given historical period.

It is this structural character that gives to the phenomena belonging to collective emotionality an important place in historical knowledge. Febvre is quick not only to notice but also to use it. In his study of the French sixteenth century, he often points to certain collective emotional attitudes which he interprets as a background to various historical events of the period, or as structurizing factors in the field of historical events. For instance, the emotional attitudes characteristic of the people in the political field, were, according to Febvre, gradually extended to the religious and social fields. Thus, the Calvinist God was fashioned according to the image of the absolutist monarch of the time. '*Car le Roy donne sa grace; il ne tient pas compte d'un mérite. Tel le Dieu de Jean Calvin.*'

One can easily reverse the process indicated by Febvre and say that the medieval French kings were modelled upon the people's image of God. But this makes no difference to the argument. The important point is that one and the same emotional factor works through the whole field of social and cultural life. As such it can be considered as an active background to a multitude of events out of which was built the history of the period.

IV

THE EMERGENCE OF
PERSONALITY IN THE
GREEK WORLD

The soul which moves within two distant points is neither
stable nor cheerful.   DEMOCRITUS.

THE GREEKS AND THE HISTORY OF THE MIND

WE go back to the ancient Greeks whenever we try to
understand the foundations of our ways of life both
as individuals and as communities. There we find the
basic patterns of our social organization, the roots of our deepest
feelings, the model of our rational thinking, and even the prefi-
guration of our scientific outlook of nature.[1] Christianity itself,
our specific religious mode of being, can hardly be understood in
its origins without its Hellenistic background. We have built up
and still live in a 'Hellenocentric civilization'.[2]

'Back to the Greeks' has a particular appeal and significance
for historical psychology. As far as we know, Greece was the
place where that irreversible process, which we call history, began
its course. To understand this one need only bear in mind the un-
folding of social and cultural forms which took place between the
age of Homer and the Roman conquest. The historical development of Greece between the eighth and the second centuries B.C. is
comparable in magnitude and richness with that of Western

[1] Schrödinger, E.: *Nature and the Greeks*. 1954.
[2] Jaeger, W.: *Paideia. The Ideal of Greek Culture*. Engl. Trans. by G. Highet. 1944.
Vol. I, p. xv.

Europe over twice as long a period. This should not be taken as a value judgement, but rather as an indication of the significance of historical change in the Greek world, and particularly in the life of some Ionian communities. In Athens, the Greeks created the first model of an open society, that is, a society with a flexible and changeable structure.

Normally, four main periods or eras in Greek history are distinguished; the Homeric era up to the end of the eighth century, the archaic era including the seventh and the sixth centuries, the classical era covering the fifth and the fourth centuries, and the Hellenistic era. All these, and particularly the latter three are socially and culturally well defined structures and as such they constitute marked stages in the life of the Greek communities. This highly articulate historical character of Greek civilization presents a definite advantage for the historical psychologist whose main task is to investigate the relationship between historical development and human behaviour. For the fulfilment of this task he will proceed firstly to an analytical descriptive study of the main features of human behaviour characteristic of each era. Then, as the next stage, he will consider his findings from a comparative-evolutionary standpoint, with a view to establishing the main behavioural changes—such as changes in attitudes, feelings, beliefs—which took place during the historical development of Greek civilization. This will enable him to reconstruct the thread of historical process at the psychological level by following the gradual change in the patterns of human behaviour in general, and in the mental organization of the individual in particular.

The question of whether the Greeks themselves were conscious of the historical character of their society, though important in itself, cannot be examined here. However, no one can possibly answer such a question without considering the view taken by the Sophists of the nature of society, or without examining from this specific point of view the writings of Thucydides or Polybius, to mention only two outstanding examples. The objective description and analysis of social, political, and even psychological events, with constant reference to 'what it was', and to 'what it is', to 'then' and 'now', the occasional stress put on the growth and the cumulative effect of some psycho-social processes—the appetite for power, for instance—the eagerness to bring into relief the specific character of historical events should allow no one to doubt the awareness of such historians of the historical process.[1] But even a negative answer to the question raised above will not alter the aim of the historical psychologist: he can proceed to the reconstruction of the psychological thread of history by assuming that historical changes are normally reflected in the behaviour of the people. Whether this is a conscious or unconscious process is of secondary importance.

It is not only through its prominent historical character that Greek civilization appeals to the specific interests of the historical psychologist. Even more important in this respect is the sense, or rather the pattern, of its historical development. Greek civilization has remained a model of humanistic civilization: all the main social and cultural processes taking place between the archaic and the end of the Hellenistic era—and specially during the consolidation of the Attic civilization of the fifth century—can be seen as stages, or aspects in the discovery and development of man's basic qualities, physical, moral and spiritual. Thus, the pattern of historical development is eminently anthropocentric; it consists both in the emergence of man as the central figure in the picture of the universe, and in the gradual increase of the value of the individual's personality in the world of man. This is a complex psycho-historical process which requires a closer examination.

It was a new, moreover unique development which can be fully appreciated only if it is seen within a wider complex of ancient history. Few have expressed this more colourfully and convincingly than Jaeger when he wrote: 'As against the Oriental exaltation of one God-king far above all natural proportions . . . and the Oriental suppression of the great mass of the people, the beginning of Greek history appears to be the beginning of a new conception of the value of the individual.' It is clear that one has to deal here with a process of transition between two distinct types of civilization. In terms borrowed from the anthropological School of Lévy-Bruhl, one can say that the pre-Hellenic civilizations of Egypt, Babylon, and Persia were more or less of pre-individualistic type; at this stage of ancient history, man knew himself only as a 'participant' in the life of his community; the personality of the individual, the organization of his mind as a whole, was submerged into the structure of the group. The

[1] Exceptionally good examples of this are Books I and III (5), of Thucydides' *The Peloponesian Wars*.

Greeks were the first to build up a type of civilization which enabled man to become aware of himself as an individual. In Greece, the history of the ancient world passed from a pre-individualistic to an individualistic stage.

This distinctive mark of Greek civilization has been expressed in many different forms. Jacob Burckhardt, for instance, speaks about three main historical periods favouring the emergence of human personality: the sixth century in Greece, the period of the Prophets in Israel, and the European Renaissance. The first is undoubtedly the most important one. Within this specific historical context, created by the dissolution of the old traditional order and the rise of the classical era, there took place 'the discovery of individuality', as a follower of Dilthey puts it.[1] This was a many-sided process culminating in man's awareness of himself as a rational being. In a somehow similar manner, this idea is expressed by Jaeger when he considers 'the rationalist consciousness of selfhood' as the distinctive mark, and at the same time, the chief achievement of the Greek culture. For Bruno Snell, a psychologically minded classical scholar, the ancient Greeks were the discoverers of 'the individualized mind'.[2] A series of more recent studies have made it their specific task to throw some light on the rise of the feeling and the concept of the *personal* in the religious,[3] moral,[4] and political[5] spheres of Greek life.

Though it is by now apparent, it should nevertheless be stressed that man's awareness of himself as an individual did not come spontaneously with the advent of Greek civilization. Nor was it a spontaneous-discovery made by the Greeks at a certain specific stage in their history. On the contrary, it was a slow psycho-historical process which started off in Ionia towards the end of the archaic era, and continued to grow to the very end of the Hellenistic period. Consequently, one can detect within Greek history itself a process of transition from a pre-individualistic to an individualistic civilisation.

Through broad in its approach and scope, the present study does not attempt to present a comprehensive history of the mental structure of the ancient Greeks. Its main interest is focused on the

[1] Misch, G.: *A History of Autobiography in Antiquity.* 1950.
[2] Snell, B.: *The Discovery of the Mind.* Eng. Transl. by T. G. Rosen. 1953.
[3] Festugière, A. J.: *Personal Religion among the Greeks.* 1954.
[4] Dodds, E. R.: *The Greeks and the Irrational.* 1953.
[5] Havelock, E. A.: *The Liberal Temper in Greek Politics.* 1957.

period of transition in Greek society and culture from the pre-individualistic to the individualistic stage. The field of vision has been deliberately restricted in the belief that this historical context is of crucial importance to the mental development of the Greeks. Owing to this transition, the Greeks have established their distinctiveness and uniqueness from a psychological point of view; by this they have become creators in the history of the mind. This study is chiefly concerned with the development of a specific form of self-awareness in the members of the Greek communities, which determined the emergence of the individual's personality as the basic unit and supreme value in life. In more general terms, this study attempts to analyse the process of personality formation in a specific historical context. Since, however, this context is Greek civilization, the present investigation has an epistemological value of its own. The matter is about what might be called the ' *locus classicus* ' of personality formation.

For the understanding of the process of personality formation in Greek civilization two basic aspects (they can be called basic types) of man's awareness of himself should be distinguished. The first can be described as the discovery by the individual of his own inner life. It starts from an introspective interest and a general inclination towards self-scrutiny and ends with an attitude of valuation. In the course of this process the individual becomes aware of the united and unique character of his inner life. Moreover—and this is the most important stage in this process—he becomes aware that the source of his actions lies in himself, in his needs, wishes, feelings, and ideas. In other words, to the feelings of unity and uniqueness he adds the feeling of self-determination of his inner life.

This particular mode of self-awareness had a long history in the Greek world. Faint signs of it can be traced as far back as the end of the seventh century. After this timid start, however, its progress was steady and even spectacular. Between Hesiod and Menander, or even between Solon and Antiphon the Sophist, there took place an impressive growth in the individual's power of self-scrutiny, and with it a considerable rise in the value he placed on his inner life. Bearing in mind that as a result of this psycho-historical development the members of Greek society became aware of themselves as independent units in life, this aspect of self-awareness is referred to in this study as the process of individuation

But the growth of man's self-awareness in the Greek world was not exclusively centred round the individual's sense of the uniqueness of his inner life. The individual grew aware of himself as the bearer of social values, as a 'character', or as a particular embodiment of the ethos of his society. The basis of this form of self-awareness is another psycho-cultural process described in this book as the process of rationalization. This process also had a long history in the Greek world. From the end of the seventh century onwards the Athenian perceived himself less and less as a passive tool, and more and more as a rational agent, i.e. as the possessor, and sometimes the creator of objective values and rules on which the order of his society, and of his world as a whole, was based. As the awareness of a 'common mind' grew in each individual, the relationship between the members of the community changed from one based on mechanical conformity and unconscious identification to one based on reflective consent.

Individuation and rationalization are basic processes in the formation of human personality in general. While the former is the expression of the individual's inner integration, the latter is the expression of the individual's social integration; while the former leads to the individual's feelings of separatedness and uniqueness, the latter leads to his feeling of belonging; the former lies at the basis of the ego formation, the latter at the basis of the super-ego formation. But personality formation in Greece, particularly in the classical era, seems to have been characterized by the perfect balance between these two processes: both the individualizing and the rationalizing of the individual's mind were equally developed. As a consequence of this, one could say that the Greeks had created a classic model of personality, i.e. a model of man's realization of himself as an individual, and at the same time, as a member of his group. To prove this it is necessary to make a detailed analysis of the historical development of human personality in Greek civilization and in its two main aspects, individuation and rationalization.

INDIVIDUATION

This is a diffuse mental process, the end product of which consists in the individual's awareness of himself as a spontaneous agent in his environment. It requires a series of preparatory stages by which an individual establishes a flexible balance between his inner drives and the conditions of his environment. It requires in the first place a certain amount of introjection, that is to say, the acceptance by the individual of certain basic conditions of life characteristic of his environment, physical and social, as well as of the inner changes resulting from this. It requires, at the same time, a certain amount of projection, the main effect of which consists in the moulding of the environment according to the individual's drives, feelings, and established patterns of behaviour. When accomplished, the process of individuation is signalled in the consciousness of the individual by the feeling of the unity of his inner life and by the conviction of, or the belief, in the inner motivation of his behaviour.

For the sake of clarity, this section is confined to the phenomenal aspect of the process of individuation in Greece, i.e. to a descriptive account of the main symptoms of the development of self-awareness in Greek individuals. This will be followed, in the next section, by an attempt to consider this process from a socio-cultural point of view.

There are grounds for believing that the Greeks of the Homeric era were not aware of themselves as having a mind of their own. From the analysis of the people's behaviour, of their beliefs and opinions, as portrayed in Homer's works, it emerges that, at this historical stage, the Greeks held the view that their mental life was organized around a series of independent centres: the *Psyche,* the *Thymos,* and the *Noos.* This can be described as a mosaic conception of the mind. The same sources allow us to infer that the individuals of this era had no notion of the existence of the mind as a source of their feelings and actions. In more technical terms, the people described by Homer did not feel that the 'motives' of their behaviour lay in themselves; on the contrary, they believed that their behaviour was determined from outside, by the gods. A typical example is Achilles in his predicament at the beginning of the Iliad when 'Athena stepped behind him, caught him by his golden hair' and helped him to make his decision. From the analysis of a series of such cases Snell concludes that: 'Homer lacks the knowledge of the spontaneity of the human mind; he does not realize that decisions of the will, and many other impulses and emotions have their origins in man himself.' Then in the same breath he goes on: 'Homer's man does not yet regard himself as the source of his decision,' this source lies outside himself in a divine apparatus.

The question of whether such conclusions can be justified arises. Snell, for instance, derives his evidence from the psychological analysis of the language used by the people of the Iliad. Since the present writer is not a classical scholar, the question of linguistic interpretation must be left out of this analysis. But there are other grounds on which the view mentioned above can be supported. Both genetic psychology and anthropology refer to stages in the development of the human mind as following a similar pattern. The mind of a child has a diffused, incoherent character; mentally, a child is not differentiated from his environment, at least, not to the degree of regarding himself as a source of his own behaviour. The same can be said about the mental structure of the individual of primitive society.[1] Furthermore, some historians have reached similar conclusions with regard to certain stages in the development of Western societies. For Jacob Burckhardt, for instance, medieval man 'was conscious of himself only as a member of a race, people, party, family, or corporation—only through some general category'.[2] The medieval peasant, for example, was aware of himself only as a class; his usual form of reference to himself was 'I peasant N.N.' Even if one cannot go all the way with Burckhardt in this assumption, it is only reasonable to assume that what he says is applicable to the mental development of the medieval peasant. Since the feelings, desires, or aspirations which such an individual might have had were consciously or unconsciously related to his being a peasant, i.e. to a class, his awareness of himself had a diffuse character.

We can now say, therefore, that the mind of a child, of primitive and, according to Burckhardt, of medieval man is at a pre-individualistic stage. If the sociological term 'pre-individualist' is translated into a psychological one, i.e. 'pre-individuation' the meaning is that the individual has not emerged yet as an integrated mental structure. One cannot speak, at this stage, about the existence of an individualized mind. The individual has not yet the feeling that his inner life forms an enduring structure with its own

---

[1] Heinz Werner has done much to clarify this stage in the development of the mind both from the ontogenetic and the philogenetic point of view. See in particular: *Comparative Psychology and Mental Development*. Chicago. 1940.

[2] *The Civilization of the Renaissance in Italy*. 1945. p. 81.

axis; he expresses his ties with his environment, not simply as parts of himself, but rather as a diffuse form of himself. Thus, the child reveals in many ways his inability to distinguish between the inner and outer world, between thoughts and things. Moreover, he gives the impression that his personality—if this term can be applied here—is an extension of the personality of his mother. Primitive and medieval man reveal a similar mental organization when they identify themselves with their status, class, or with their community at large.

In contemporary Western society, the personality of the individual, his ego, is determined by his separatedness; it is socially and psychologically a distinctive entity. His ties with his environment can be imagined as divergent lines springing up from the solid core of his mental life. On the other hand, primitive man exists by his ties, by his social ties in particular. As life in a primitive culture is completely ritualized, the greatest virtue is to be similar to others. Primitive man cannot see the connection between himself and his actions; his thoughts and feelings are revealed to him from outside. In opposition to the personality of Western man, that of primitive men consists of a series of convergent lines representing his ties with others with a complete void in the centre. In terms used by the Lévy-Bruhl School, his personality is '*un fait de participation, de réciprocitees, d'actes convergeants de groupes*'.[1]

It is precisely at this pre-individuation stage that the Greeks of Homer's age found themselves. The animistic, anthropomorphic, and magic element, in their behaviour constitute an undeniable proof of this. To start with, in the mind of the individual of this period there is little, if any, difference between the animate and inanimate world. Rivers, rocks, winds, are appearances of animate beings, demons, or gods. The world is run by universal forces which express themselves as things, animals, and humans. In such a world of close communion between man and things, on the one hand, and man and animals on the other, the sentence 'Hector is a lion' is not merely a metaphoric or allegoric expression. It really means that the universal vital force, the 'forward impulse' works through Hector as well as through the lion. This is a world of participation accessible only to the magic way of

---

[1] Meyerson: '*Les Apports de Maurice Leenhardt à la Psychologie Historique.*' *Journal de Psychol. Normale et Pathologique.* Vol. 55, 1955. p. 377.

thinking, a world in which the individual's impulses, feelings, and ideas come from outside. The factors composing the mind are immersed into the whole environment; they have not yet formed a nucleus in the individual. The mind is as yet not individualized.

Now, the important point is that this type of mental structure can be seen as an historical evolutionary stage: it is in fact a mental structure characteristic of Greeks of the Homeric, and part of the archaic eras. From the beginning of the sixth century onwards, one can follow the growth of an individualized mind, that is, of a type of mental organization which enables the individual to perceive himself as an entity differentiated from his environment. The historical circumstances in which this change in the mental development of the Greeks took place are of crucial importance. A period of radical transition started off with the decline of the old traditional order which set off a series of conflicts and tensions within Greek society, i.e. conflicts between the rising and declining social groups, between new and old values and patterns of behaviour, which in a somehow unexpected manner constituted a favourable climate for the process of individuation. As the analysis of these historical circumstances will form the specific concern of the next section, it would be appropriate to precede this with a description of the main stages in the growth of an individualized mind within Greek civilization.

The first clear symptoms of an emerging individualized mind can be found in the lyric poets of the second half of the seventh and the beginning of the sixth century. As compared with Hesiod and particularly with the elegists, Tyrtaeus and Kallinos, this poetry reveals a new source of inspiration and a new attitude to life, both centred in the poet himself as an individual. While Tyrtaeus—who considered himself a Homerid—is entirely imbued with the supreme collective values, with ideals of citizenship and patriotism, both Archilochus and Sappho, and later Anacreon, make a mental volte-face. They focus their interest on their person, relegating the life of their community to the background of their mind.[1] Thus their poetry, normally referred to as

[1] According to some views Hesiod displays a certain introspective attitude and a certain self-confidence which may be taken as symptoms of an individualized mind. To a certain extent he sets his own vision of god up against the traditional epic songs. Misch believes that he 'achieved the confidence and the courage for personal conviction through the devotion of his whole being, not merely through reflection.' Op. cit. p. 74.

'personal lyric', reveals an important stage in the process of individuation within Greek civilization which can briefly be described as self-representation of the individual in a poetical form. These are the main aspects of this new mental development.

One notices first of all a certain detachment of the poet from his social and cultural background. This is shown by his readiness, if not eagerness, to express feelings and opinions which are either indifferent to, or in conflict with the conventional values. Take for instance Archilochus' own account of his flight in the battle of Paros: 'Some Saian is priding himself on my shield, which I abandoned reluctantly beside a bush; but I escaped death. Let the old shield go—I shall buy another just as good.' It is almost incredible that the soldier poet should have used such language in a society whose main values were courage and gallantry. The mystery is, however, partly dispelled when the same Archilochus tells us that 'if one cared for the gossip of the people one would never have much pleasure in life'.

But there is more than a feeling of independence of public opinion in Archilochus's poetry. Under the steam of his own passions he moves outside conventionality confident that even there he represents something positive for his compatriots. Whether scolding the officials of his city, or abusing men older than himself, he expresses the confident expectation that the public will applaud. And in most of what he says he gives vent to his most personal feelings and particularly to his weakness for fault-finding. (Pindar referred to him as 'the fault-finder Archilochus'). Obviously, this self-confidence springs from Archilochus's awareness that his private feelings, his personal approach to life, represent a value not only for himself but for others too.

The positive value placed on the world of personal experiences and on private feelings constitutes a basic symptom of the emergence of an individualized mind. This is revealed in so many ways by the Aeolian lyric. As it has been pointed out, the drinking songs of Alcaeus presuppose a drinking party of friends, and the love songs of Sappho presuppose a group of young girls, musicians, who were her friends. Such poetry confirms, therefore, not only the existence of 'personal' ties but also a praise and a cultivation of them.

In Sappho, the inner world of emotions is exalted so much that it dominates the life of the individual. In the emphasis she puts on her own feelings, on her 'personal taste', she says, 'the fairest thing is one I love,' one can see a clear sign of the emergence of a personal self as an important factor in the individual's world. For it is from this self that things get their importance and value rather than from themselves or from gods. This points to a significant aspect of the process of individuation, that is, to the individual's awareness of the inner motivation of his conduct. This is certainly the case with the lyric poets mentioned so far who sometimes seem to be able to look at the whole world from a central point in their inner life, i.e. from their 'I'. Even the deity is addressed by Sappho as *thou*; a prayer on her lips becomes a 'personal' contact with god. This is a long way from the impersonal collective world of Tyrtaeus.

A brief analysis of the psycho-genetic conditions of this process of individuation among the Greeks may help here. As common experience shows, the rise of self-consciousness in the individual is particularly stimulated by two closely inter-related mental conditions, frustration, and inner conflict. Thus, it was primarily the experience of unhappy love and unfulfilled expectation that aroused in Archilochus the need to spot, and give a certain relief to the hurting area. Take for example the following lines: 'Desire, looser of limbs, has overwhelmed me, my friend,' or, a characteristic example of a primary experience of the self as 'absence': 'Wretched I lie, unsouled by desire . . .' One should note, in particular, the poet's intraceptive attitude: he feels that a crime has been committed, obviously not because an external norm was broken, but because something in himself was neglected and crushed out. Thus, the genesis of the self seems to be related to a negatively toned emotional experience, to an inner tension and anxiety. Snell makes this point clearly when he says that the self, or the personal soul, as manifested by the lyrists, is a 'source of reactions which set in when the feelings are blocked. Love is not a passion which wells up from within, but a gift of Aphrodite and Eros. *Only emotional discord released by unhappy love is truly personal*'.[1]

It is clear, therefore, that the individual's self-awareness is stimulated by a situation of conflict created by a clash among various impulses within the individual himself, or by a clash between the individual and his environment. This process reaches a

[1] Op. cit. p. 65. Italics mine.

definite stage when the blocked impulses and frustrating experiences are organized in a more or less stable structure. The function of this new structure in the individual's mind is, firstly, to establish the difference between what resists, and what does not resist the inner impulses, and secondly, to bring into relief the difference between what is inside and what is outside the individual. Some lyrical situations express this vividly: when the poet is made unhappy because of unfulfilled love, he finds himself alone in a universe indifferent, if not hostile to his turmoil. The feeling of separateness and uniqueness is on such occasions heightened to an extreme.

It is necessary to point out at this stage the specific difficulties of this study: the limitation of a purely psycho-genetic approach, and the constant need for two levels of thought. This emerges clearly from a short comparison between the mental climate depicted in the works of the lyrists mentioned above, and that depicted in the work of the seventh-century Ionian elegists, Mimnermos of Kolophon, Semonides of Amorgos and Kallinos.

The Ionian elegists also show a certain introspective attitude and concern with the individual's life. This can be deduced particularly from the 'hedonistic' element of their poetry. But one hastens to say that, though a cry for pleasure represents an important tone in the emotional harmonic of this poetry, it can by no means be considered as the fundamental one. What seems the most striking in all the elegists is their 'impersonal' vision of the human life. 'Like are we to the leaves . . .' is a common adage. Man's life is entirely dominated by the blind power of Fate. No less 'impersonal' is the elegists' vision of the human heart, for neither the depths of sorrow, nor the heights of joy can light up in the individual the awareness of the unique character of his inner life. There is no inner-directed, no inner-centred character in the individual's feelings: pleasure, joy, and glory come with the vigour of youth and manhood, pain and sorrow with old age. There is no throbbing of a personal soul in Semonides' lines: 'My son, the end of all things is in the hand of Zeus the heavy thunderer. There is no wit in man. Creatures of a day we live like cattle . . .'; neither is there in Mimnermos' approach—if this can be called an approach—to Aphrodite: 'What life is there, what pleasure without golden Aphrodite.' Compare this with Sappho's friendly personal request to the goddess of love: 'If ever in the past you listened to my prayers, now also you must listen to me.'

Why is there this difference between the lyrists and Ionian elegists who, admittedly, belonged to different communities, but who, on the other hand, were more or less contemporaries? To answer this question two sets of psycho-cultural factors have to be taken into account, firstly some specific traits in the socio-cultural status of the lyrists Archilochus and Sappho, secondly, the more general trends of their society and culture. For a social psychologist of today it is not surprising to find out that the beginning of 'personal poetry', and on the whole, the first articulate manifestation of a personal vision of life in Greek civilization are connected with an adventurer, an outcast almost, and with a woman. Archilochus had a stigma attached to him. He was a member of a knightly estate, but of illegitimate birth. This may explain the restless life led by this soldier poet, as well as his hyper-sensibility to frustrating situations. But, the same socio-psychological conditions can be taken as the main spring of his strong feeling of separateness, of his own individuality, which lies at the basis of his poetical vision. The non-accepted, the outsider, ridicules conventional values and makes a plea—the first plea in the Greek world—for a self-chosen life. The same feeling of separateness, of a woman living in an essentially male society, is to a great extent responsible for Sappho's heightened awareness of herself as an individual, and consequently for the self-orientated character of her poetry.

But however suggestive in itself, this biographical background is in fact incidental, and as such has a limited value for the understanding of a complex psycho-historical process. There is the additional drawback of having no comparative data on the elegists. Other more general and objective factors have also to be considered in order to understand the difference between the lyrists and the Ionian elegists from this point of view. Unfortunately, our historical knowledge is, on this point, only conjecture. One knows for instance, that the seventh century in Ionia was the heyday of aristocracy, and that the socio-cultural climate of the period still belonged in many respects to the Homeric world. This is clearly borne out by the impersonal element so dominant in the elegists' vision of the human life. Like Homer, who sees human life as dominated by the powers of *Tyche* and *Moira,* the elegists constantly reminded man, even when he was enjoying life, of 'the black fate standing by . . .' (Kallinos). Now, this is only partly true of the lyrists, and in this lies an important difference between them and the elegists, relevant to the process of individuation. This difference consists in the relative degree of distance from the Homeric socio-cultural climate. In some important respects, the elegists can no longer be considered as Homerids. In order to understand this one has to make a bold step by assuming that some socio-cultural processes which became so obvious in the sixth century, were under way. It may be that, at least in some parts of Greece, the patriarchal authoritarian order as a whole began to show signs of weakness and decline; it may be, on the other hand, that the change was confined to a specific sphere of life, such as religion. At any rate, at this early stage one can notice a certain growth of the individual's reliance on himself which can be taken as a sign of the declining authoritarian features of Greek society and culture. This can be illustrated by the difference between Homer and Archilochus in their attitude to Fate. It is not that the latter does not believe in, or does not rely on Fate. He advises men to trust the gods and endure misfortunes patiently. But in his own moments of misfortune, the gods and Fate are not the ones to whom he appeals and on whom he relies. When something goes wrong in his life, in his friendships or in his fortunes, he finds another source of advice and strength: this source is in himself. It is in such moments of trouble that the poet talks to himself like this:

Heart, my heart, convulsed with helpless troubles, rise up, defend yourself against the foe, meet them with truculent breast. With firm stance receive the enemy's onslaught, and neither rejoice openly, if the victory is yours, nor crouch at home and wail if you lose. But when life brings joy, rejoice, and when it brings suffering, do not grieve over-much. Understand the rhythm of life which controls man.

This is the first genuine monologue in the Greek world, and a perfect model of an ego-oriented human situation.[1]

The self of a lyric poet is a kind of inflated self: one can say

---

[1] Admittedly, in Homer's *Odyssey* the hero often takes counsel with his 'heart' but this statement should be understood within the specific context of Archilochus's poetry and personality.

that it is the essence of any lyric situation to epitomize the emergence of the personal self in the individual. That is why the psychological analysis of cultural products of this kind normally yields important evidence for the study of the process of individuation in a given civilization. But, obviously, this constitutes hardly more than one single aspect in this complex psycho-historical development; the mental climate created by the Greek lyrists discloses the rise of self-awareness and of an individualized mind at its beginning only. From the end of the seventh century onwards, this process grows continually until it reaches its climax in the fifth and fourth centuries of Attic civilization. This idea can be illustrated by a brief analysis of two other cultural symptoms of this particular development of the Greeks.

It has been shown in a previous chapter that the discovery of the self is bound up with a discovery of the external world; that the structurizing of man's inner world is in a dialectical relation with the organization of the outer world, and that the feeling of the selfhood grows hand in hand with the feeling of otherness. Some basic trends in the sixth century pre-Socratic philosophy are highly relevant from this point of view. The particular concern of the representatives of these schools with the physical aspect of the universe, with the basic and differential qualities of matter, can be interpreted as an effort of the human mind to define itself in juxtaposition to the reality lying outside it. It is not without significance that it was one of the pre-Socratics, Heraclitus, who made the first attempt to establish clear logical distinctions between the soul and the body. Admittedly, at this early stage, the pre-Socratics' concern with the distinctive character of the mind cannot be taken to indicate more than a vague initial form of man's awareness of himself. There are, however, other aspects in the pre-Socratic thought which suggest at least the possibility of interpreting this cultural development as a definite state in the rise of an individualized mind.

The pre-Socratics are the founders of a new tradition of thought based on critical discussion. Now, the very use of such a method of thinking is an important symptom of an individualized mind. This becomes apparent if one compares the critical method used by the Ionian physicists with the dogmatic religious one used by the Pythagoreans in particular. While the latter presuppose a revealed form of truth and its communication in a more or less static form, the former see the truth as a stage arrived at by discussion and criticism between two individual thinkers, normally between teacher and pupil. As an ingenious interpreter of pre-Socratic thought remarks, 'Thales must have been the first who said: "This is how I see things . . . how I believe things are, try to improve upon my teaching."'[1] Thus, Thales was criticized and advanced by Anaximander, Anaximander by his pupil Anaximenes, and finally Heraclitus took the same attitude towards his predecessors. Admittedly, the relation between teacher and pupil can, in this case, be described as an abstract and rational relation. But it has its personal element as well: the pupil criticizes not only the logical flaws in the argument, but also the general assumptions of his teacher which are obviously dependent upon a personal attitude. The critical method of thinking of the pre-Socratics was notably prolific of new philosophical schools and doctrines. The significance of this is that a logical argument can to a certain extent be individualized.

But this is not all. A critical method presupposes a high degree of personal freedom: he who uses it has achieved a certain independence from stereotyped modes of thinking as well as a certain degree of confidence in the powers of his own mind. There is no lack of evidence for this in the pre-Socratics. Their self-confidence is apparent from their creative originality and powerful personalities. Heraclitus gives signs of an almost aggressive self-confidence when he asserts, 'Of all sayings I have heard, no one advances so far as to recognize that widsom is apart from all other things.' And there is ample evidence for his self-awareness. 'I have searched myself,' he says when trying to point to the source of his thoughts.

Nevertheless, it would be premature to look to the pre-Socratics for symptoms of a fully emerged individualized mind. Their special concern with 'the common mind', or, in Heraclitus' words, 'the world in common,' is a proof that they were inclined to conceive human individuality primarily as a vehicle for the rational mind. However, as we have seen, the pre-Socratics made an important step towards the emergence of the individualized mind, which reached its apogee in the classical era. This is borne out by certain basic features of Greek tragedy, particularly of the tragedies of Aeschylus and Euripides.

[1] Karl Popper *Back to the pre-Socratics*. Presidential Address, Aristotelean Society, Oct., 1958.

Aeschylus is often considered as having the two faces of Janus; one turned towards the heroic legendary past, the other to the present and future democratic era. In one sense, however, one can regard his drama as full proof of the emergence within Greek civilization of the individual as a free agent. His plays—*Oresteia,* in particular—illustrate some of the main features of individual self-consciousness, such as deliberation and free decisions. Orestes in his struggle frees himself from the impersonal forces of the universe as well as from the influence of the mystic ties of blood, into a world of his own. His decision to punish his mother's crime seems to be taken at the level of rational consciousness; it is in this sense made by himself. This indicates personal responsibility, which is undoubtedly a symptom of self-consciousness. His trial also takes place on a rational plane, as the Areopagus regards him as an individual deciding for himself, not as a mere tool in the hands of super-human forces.

The verdict given by the Areopagus gives cause for further speculation as to the nature and degree of the individual's self-consciousness at this stage in Greek civilization. The votes are equally divided between 'guilty' and 'not guilty'. Athene, the goddess of reason, casts the final vote as the result of which Orestes is acquitted. The meaning of this is certainly not that the gods decide upon man's fate, but rather that a rational law prevails over the traditional morality against which Orestes is guilty. The equal number of votes on either side suggests also that it remains with Orestes himself to pronounce the final meaning of his conduct. Socially he is clear, free of blame, but he cannot easily solve the conflict within himself aroused by his ambivalent feelings towards his mother, love and hatred at the same time. As he cannot blame any person or thing for his crime, his only way out is to blame himself[1]. This is self-consciousness at a highly developed level.

Though almost a contemporary of Aeschylus, Euripides belongs entirely to a new stage in the psycho-historical development of the Greeks. In the battle between the conservative and

---

[1] The guilt is purged away by Apollo: 'The pollution of matricide can be purged away,' cries Orestes with relief. The context in which this takes place allows for the interpretation that there took place a change in Orestes' self-insight: 'Katharsis' operated a rationalization, or socialization of his inner feelings of guilt. Apollo cleansed Orestes from his irrational guilt (Erinyes) by increasing his awareness that his action was an implementation of justice.

progressive-liberal spirit which was the main focus of interest in the symposia of late fifth-century Athens, the defenders of liberalism normally rallied round the name of Euripides. In their eyes he stood for expansion of individual freedom. It is therefore little wonder to discover in Euripides' drama not only symptoms of a high degree of the individual's self-awareness, but also a high value placed upon the inner personal life of the individual. Here are a few illustrative examples.

To start with, Euripides' drama reflects what one might call a 'demythologizing' attitude which was an important feature of the mental climate of late fifth-century Athens. Though, as a poet Euripides could be neither as critical nor as explicit in his attitude to mythology as some of his contemporaries were, nevertheless he took a detached view of mythical tradition by re-interpreting it in the light of new conditions of life particular to his age. Euripides was—as one of his commentators says—'the first poet who deliberately worked on the principle that poetry should depict a reality as *he* saw it; and since the mythical traditions were at hand he used them as a vehicle for expressing the new reality as *he* saw it.'[1] There is no need to point out to what a great extent this attitude implied the emergence of the individualized mind: mythology itself started to be individualized.

It would not be an exaggeration to assume that the individual's awareness of himself, the insight he has into, and the value he places on his own desires and feelings constitute an essential element in the psychological fabric of Euripides' drama: Indeed this self-awareness throws important light on the origins, and on the nature of the dramatic situation. Most revealing in this respect is the desperate battle fought by some of Euripides' heroes, the long speeches made by them, in order to prove their specific case and justify their own desires and aspirations. Thus, Phedra, in *Hippolytus,* is at pains to demonstrate that a married woman is not wrong to give her love to another man. Her appeal is made in the cause of subjectivity, or of the value she places on her personal passions as against the super-personal values of religion and social custom. The denial of her claims is for Euripides a source of tragedy.

A different aspect of the same value of subjectivity is seen in

---

[1] Jaeger, W. Op. cit. p. 339. Italics Mine. Much of what is said here is based on Jaeger's interpretation of Euripides' drama.

Medea. The claims of convention to which her personality is subjected, the traditionally established roles of a woman and wife, are weakened, if not completely swept aside, by her overwhelming desire. Thus she becomes to an extreme degree both the creature and the victim of her inner life. Helen, in *Orestes,* reveals the same forces within her when she analyses her own adultery—the source of so many tragedies—as an act committed under the pressure of sexual desire. The value of subjectivity creeps in also in the *Women of Troy.* Here, Euripides tends to 'demythologize' the great exploits of the past, with the obvious purpose of letting his contemporaries see beneath the glittering façade of national pride and glory the dark undertone of human suffering and innumerable personal tragedies among the defeated.

To say that Euripides' heroes endeavour to see life from their own point of view as individuals is not enough. In Euripedes' drama individual consciousness becomes a revolutionary force aiming at the complete transvaluation of the cosmos in terms of its own. Even divinity itself seems to derive its modes of existing from this. When Hecuba prays to the ether: 'Thou earth's support, enthroned on the earth, whoever thou mayst be, hard to discover; Zeus, be thou nature's law, or the mind of man, I pray to thee . . .' one cannot help feeling that it is only the 'I', i.e. the suppliant's ego, that is firmly grounded in reality; the rest is veiled in the mists of doubt. It is this heightened self-awareness in the individual that constitutes the main dramatic element in human life, as Euripides sees it. No wonder that the same Hecuba realizes that: 'No mortal is free: he is the slave of money or fate; or else the mob which rules the state, or the bonds of law keep him from living as he wishes.' It remains only to be said that this intense awareness of the encroachment upon his life of the impersonal forces of 'money', 'fate', 'the mob', 'the state', and 'the law' is preceded in the mind of the individual by its contrary, his acute awareness of his personal life, and his desire to live 'as he wishes'. Here one can say again that it is the crushed, the denied self that makes its existence so obvious and necessary to the individual concerned. The self, like God is a limit concept; the experience of God's absence is often more relevant to His existence than the experience of His presence.

Euripides' drama offers full proof of the emergence of an individualized mind among the Greeks. The two main aspects of this are: firstly that the individuals portrayed by Euripides have a strong awareness of the resistance which society at large offers to their inner life. To this they react by a heightened self-awareness, the result of which is a strong opposition between the 'I' and 'non-I'. This aspect in the growth of an individualized mind can be described by analogy with what some sociologists call the feeling of negative freedom so characteristic of the beginning of modern democracy when the individual affirmed his 'I' mainly by fighting against the levelling influences of social institutions, of the State and the Church in particular. It is no wonder that so many of Euripides' heroes are women, therefore more liable to be crushed in their aspirations by society. Secondly that one can infer from Euripides' drama the importance which the individual attaches to his personal life. Thus the individualized mind appears not only in its negative character, as resistance and opposition, but also as a positive value, moreover, as a conscious rational purpose in human life. In this way Euripides is a true representative of his age; he expresses in dramatic form the most typical aspects of life in fifth-century Athens. This cannot be better described than in the words of one of his contemporaries, Pericles: 'We do not grudge our neighbour his private pleasures, nor do we make him repent them by our bitter looks.' In fifth-century Athens, the process of individuation manifests itself in all spheres of life: the Athenian community of this period belongs to an individualized social and cultural order.

THE SOCIO-CULTURAL BACKGROUND OF INDIVIDUATION

The mental evolution described so far was not an isolated phenomenon. The growth of the individualized mind among the Greeks was in fact part of a complex process of social and cultural changes which took place over a long period, and particularly between the sixth and fourth centuries. During this period the whole pattern of Greek life became more and more individualized. It is convenient to discuss this development in Greek history from the following points of view: (a) the economic and class structure; (b) the political organization of the community and (c) the pattern of relationships between the individual and his community.

(a) Signs of the growing predominance of a commercial over

the traditional argricultural economy could be seen as early as the seventh century. Some historians trace back to this period the beginning of an ancient capitalism (*chrematistike*).[1] This new development in the economic field had a quick and powerful impact on the class structure of the Greek communities. It led in the first place to the formation in the cities of a wealthy middleclass, and by this, to the creation of a strong opposition to the oligarchic aristocracy. But the same system of commercial and monetary economy stimulated the formation of the lower middle classes and lower classes comprising a great variety of occupational groups, from the shopkeepers and small artisans, at the top, to the great mass of labourers and hired men, at the bottom. As the new classes rose and developed in opposition to the upper classes, throughout the sixth century, the Greek communities were torn by internal strife. This was a period of great social unrest marked by the struggle of the people, of the many and the poor against the powerful and the rich. This was the period of the tyrants, the champions of the lower classes, which led through a series of broad reforms to the establishment in many cities of a democratic régime, and through this to the complete reformation of the class structure of these communities.[2]

The main effects which this phenomenon had upon the historical development of the Greek communities can briefly be described as the growth of a more flexible economic and social order, and on the whole, of a more individualized pattern of life. The reign of money created gradually a new mentality so aptly expressed in Alcaeus' words 'money makes the man'. One can easily imagine what happened to a society whose class structure was determined by the dominance of an aristocratic oligarchy when wealth and luxury began to connote both social mark and political value. The rigid social order based on the right of birth gave way to a more flexible order based on the right of wealth.

Some mention should be made of the development of a type of social and moral behaviour based on self-interest, since this is normally stimulated by a commercial and monetary economy. But this would take us too far afield into the realm of speculation.

[1] Glotz, G. *The Greek City and its Institutions*. London 1950, p. 101.

[2] Sparta should be mentioned as an outstanding exception. There, the struggle of the people against an oligarchic aristocracy which took place at the beginning of the sixth century ended with the defeat of the former, and with a stronger autocratic régime.

It is, however, reasonable to assume that the high degree of freedom in the economic field produced and increased a feeling of self-confidence in a great number of individuals and at the same time a considerable weakening of the external authority of tradition. In other words, a more flexible economic order allowed for more scope for the development of an inner-directed type of behaviour. All these were powerful individualizing processes in the pattern of life of the Greek communities.

(b) The rise of the city state which had been accomplished by the close of the sixth century, was the main event in the period of transition from the archaic to the classical era. A closer examination of this event will follow below when the relationship of the individual to his community is discussed. For the moment it is enough to mention that this socio-political development contained within itself a series of important individualizing processes. As Glotz aptly puts it: 'The city had grown strong by freeing the individual from patriarchal forms of servitude.' In Athens, however, and in some other smaller cities, the rise of the city state coincided with a series of other socio-political developments which brought about the collapse of the archaic order of society, culminating in the birth of the democratic era. Since a democratic is almost synonymous with an individualized society, only a few main aspects and stages of the emergence of this new social and political order within the Athenian community will be mentioned.

The publication of laws was one of the main achievements of the popular uprising of the end of the seventh, and beginning of the sixth centuries. This was a necessary protective measure against the arbitrary interpretation of the law based on oral tradition. The step was first taken in the colonies (Locri and Catana), then in Corinth and Thebes, and finally, in Athens, by Draco and Solon, in 621 and 594, respectively.

This event marked a decisive step towards the emergence of the individual as an independent unit in the organization of his group. To understand this, it is necessary to bear in mind that one of Draco's main intentions was to minimize collective responsibility for criminal conduct. And indeed, as a result of his legislation, the fierceness of blood feuds was considerably mitigated and eventually replaced by the State regulation of trials; the State could only charge the individual with acts for which he himself—not any other member of his family—was responsible. Moreover, by distinguishing between intentional and accidental killing, and between wanton attack and self-defence, Draco made the first attempt to render the law pliable to the specific personal conditions of the individual. In order to attain its main aim, i.e. 'peace and safety for the kinsmen of the accused', the legislation had first to individualize responsibility.

As Solon's legislation paved the way for the rise of democracy, there is no need to stress its individualizing effects. Two points, however, need to be re-emphasized. Firstly, as a result of Solon's political reforms, the distinction of fortune replaced that of birth. In the eyes of the State, there existed only free citizens organized in four classes according to the productive capacity of their property. As mentioned above, any transition from a social structure based on the right of birth to one based on the right of wealth leads normally to a higher degree of individual freedom and consequently to a more individualized pattern of life. This was certainly the case with Athens. Secondly, Solon's economic reforms suppressed all remaining collective property, and liberated the soil by regulating the laws of dowry, the right of succession, and freedom of bequest. Thus, Solon increased considerably the degree of individual freedom by placing restrictions upon paternal authority.

An important step forward towards the individualizing of the social and political order in Athens was made by Cleisthenes' constitutional reforms which replaced the traditional system of 'phratries' by the more rational system of 'demes'. As a result of this there emerged a new form of social organization based on co-operation among individuals who were to a great extent freed of the traditional bonds of their tribes. The emerging society was an association of groups and of individuals motivated in their actions by conscious rational goals. This amounts to saying that the pre-individualized period of the Athenian community was at this time rapidly drawing to a close. In his social behaviour, the individual became less and less dependent on external factors, such as his blood ties or his group status, and more and more on personal factors associated with his interests, his capacity and his power of reasoning. This state of affairs is admirably expressed by Pericles when he lays down the ruling principle of equality in Athenian democracy: 'Advancement in public life,' he says, 'falls to reputation for capacity, class considerations not being allowed to interfere with merit; nor again does poverty bar the way; if a man is able to serve he is not hindered by the obscurity of his position.' It is obvious that under such circumstances the socio-political order of the groups is completely individualized, i.e. it becomes a matter of agreement and consent among individuals.

(c) Much of what has been said above throws light on the changes which occurred in the system of relationships between the individual and his community. Generally speaking, there took place between the archaic and classical eras of Greek civilization what some sociologists may call the transition of a social group from a community to a society stage. Though the objection may be easily raised that the use of such terms is not completely justified, this kind of approach has at least the merit of pointing very clearly to the nature of the change which took place in the sphere of social relations. In a 'community' the individual's integration with his group is rooted in the unconscious bonds of tradition. Normally, community represents a form of social order at a pre-individualized stage. The 'self' being not fully developed, the individual accepts uncritically the communal norms and values conveyed to him by the authority of tradition. The development towards society comes with an increase in self-awareness in the sphere of social behaviour. This implies an increased ability of the individual to establish a more conscious, more direct and more personal contact with the institutions, values and norms on which his society is based.

Glotz summarizes admirably the evolution of Greece in this sense when he writes: 'The history of Greek institutions thus falls into three periods: in the first, the city is composed of families which jealously guard their ancient right and subordinate their members to the common good; in the second, the city subordinates the families to itself by calling to its aid emancipated individuals; in the third, individualism ran riot destroying the city and necessitating the formation of larger states'[1]. In the first period, corresponding more or less to the Homeric and archaic eras, the individual related himself to his society as a member of a family, the family being the proper social unit. At this stage, even responsibility *vis-à-vis* the law was collective. The publication of the laws was a decisive step forward from this

[1] Op. cit. p. 5.

stage. In this way, the individual came into direct contact with the basic norms of the organizations of his group. As mentioned, one of the main aims of Draco's laws was to put the individual in direct contact with the State on matters of responsibility and punishment. This direct contact between the individual and the politico-social structure of his group was the main characteristic of the second period, that of the city state. At this stage, the individual in his capacity of a citizen was both a participant and a maker of his society. Though 'citizenship' is essentially an attribute of the individual its functions are both individualizing and socializing. In the city state the two terms of the relationship individual-society had the same weight: the citizen is equally self-centred and community-centred.

This almost ideally balanced relationship between the individual and his society came to an end with the disintegration of the city state starting in the fourth century. Glotz refers to this period as that of 'individualism run riot'. This is probably an exaggerated view arising from too close an analogy between this period in Greek history and our early twentieth-century civilization. It is nevertheless true that during this period the relationship between the individual and society underwent important changes. With the decline of the city state, and the building up of larger states during the Hellenistic period, the direct and existential contact between the individual and society withered away. As a citizen of the world, the individual could only vaguely experience his own participation in the formation of his society, or the participation of society in the formation of his personality. As the social horizon was too remote for him to see, he could not relate his desires, aspirations and values but to himself: he became more and more self-centred in his behaviour. This is the period in which the individualizing processes in Greek civilization reached a peak. Society, morality, art, philosophy, religion became, to a great extent, the expression of the individual's private life.

At this stage the main theme with which this section began can be restated: with the decline of the archaic era, the whole pattern of life in Greece had been submitted to a growing individualizing process. This was both a cause, and an effect of the feelings of self-awareness and self-determination in the individual. Though the process was continuous, two historical periods, the sixth and the fourth centuries, have a particular importance. Both periods showed an exceptional increase in the individual's awareness of himself, and on the whole, in the emergence of his personality as the basic unit of life. The reason for this must be obvious by now. These two periods are marked by rapid and radical socio-cultural changes, both having a strong transitional, therefore 'anomic' character. With a certain adjustment of vocabulary, Dilthey's remarks on the psychological effects of the European Renaissance can to a great extent be applied both to the sixth and the fourth centuries of Greek history. 'Every time a culture dies out,' Dilthey writes, 'and a new one is to arise, the world of ideas that proceeded from the old culture fades and dissolves. The individuals' experience is, as it were, liberated for a time from the fetters of conceptional thought, and becomes a power in itself over men's minds.' During such periods of transition, when the old-established patterns of behaviour are dying out while the new ones are not yet crystallized, the individual falls back on his own resources in his adjustment to life. His inner life, released from the mould of the socially established forms of behaviour gains freedom as well as value. The individual takes from within himself both the content and the forms of his existence. This explains the spurt of self-awareness which such periods normally stimulate.

The two periods under consideration need a closer definition. The sixth century is the period of disintegration of the old patriarchal social order. It was the crumbling of these patterns of life that enabled the individual to become, for the first time in Greek history, conscious of himself as an individual, and not only as a member of the family, a tribe or a community. The main symptoms of this self-consciousness as they appeared in the lyric and the dramatic poetry, as well as in philosophy, were described in the previous section. It was this growth in self-consciousness that directed the future psycho-historical development of the Greeks. The social and cultural order, and the whole pattern of life characteristic of the classical era were strongly dominated by a conscious reflexive element, i.e. by conscious deliberation and agreement among free citizens.

Now, needless to say, this kind of psycho-historical development affected man's mental organization as a whole: a new personality structure emerged. As compared with the community-centred mental organization characteristic of archaic civilization,

[1] W. Dilthey: *Die Anthropologie XVIII Jahn. Ges. Schriften, IV.* p. 437.

that of the classical era was more self-centred. Bearing in mind what has been said so far on this point, it would be more adequate to describe it as a citizen-centred mental organization. While the behaviour of the individual in the archaic era was mainly outer-directed, that of the individual belonging to the classical era was equally inner- and outer-directed.

The fourth century was the period of the decline of the civilization of the city state, on the one hand, and of the birth of Hellenistic civilization, on the other. The main characteristic of the latter was cultural pluralism. In this atmosphere of social 'disfunctioning' and ambiguity of values, the individual had to face his inner life in all its nakedness. This dramatic act of self-discovery had two aspects, or rather two stages. In the first stage, that of negative freedom, the individual felt strongly inclined to regard all the institutional forms of life as simple 'conventions', as a set of rules which prevented his own development. Antiphon the Sophist—the Angry Young Man of his time—is sensitive even to the subtle interference of society with the function of his senses: 'It has been by custom and law determined for the eye what it is supposed to see, and not to see; for the ear, what it is supposed to hear and not to hear . . . and for the heart, what it is supposed to want and not to want.' This negative attitude towards the objective reality of society and this withdrawal into one's self created the conditions for an ego-oriented mental structure and for a highly individualized world which became important psycho-social aspects of Hellenistic civilization. But, one hastens to add, this was only one aspect. This negative attitude of withdrawal into oneself soon became a positive creative attitude. Starting from his awareness of himself, and perhaps from his loneliness, the individual made a plunge towards integrating himself both with the cosmopolitan social order of his age, and with the larger rational order of nature, as the latter was expressed in Stoic philosophy. The psychological significance of this will be dealt with elswhere.

FROM 'SHAME' TO 'GUILT'

Shame-culture and guilt-culture are terms used by some anthropologists to discriminate between two types of moral behaviour. In a wider sense they connote two forms of social behaviour. As there is little agreement, and even less clarity among anthropologists with regard to these terms, it is advisable to indicate briefly their main connotations as follows.

In a shame-culture, the moral behaviour of the individual, and his social integration in general is outwardly oriented. Moral authority is external, and can broadly be defined as social pressure. The individual respects the basic values of his community because they represent traditional rules of behaviour observed by everyone. The external authority which lies at the basis of his moral behaviour is invested in parents, elders, in the representatives of social and spiritual order. The most powerful psychological regulators of moral behaviour are fear and embarrassment at being disapproved, scolded, laughed at by others. In other words status-consciousness constitutes a basic criterion of moral conduct.

In a guilt-culture, on the other hand, social conformity is inwardly directed, being based on the inner authority of conscience. The mechanism of moral behaviour presupposes a split and inner conflict within the individual's mind. The individual's failure to behave morally is signalled by the feeling of guilt. This is in essence the experience of an inner conflict which means that part of the individual's mind is hurt and disapproves of his behaviour. Self-disapproval is experienced positively as atonement, and negatively as remorse. One speaks in this sense about an *internalized,* or autonomous, morality, for the individual's social conformity is determined by inner conviction.

Certain aspects of Greek history suggest the possibility of seeing the development of the Greek communities from a shame- to a guilt-culture.[1] It has to be said, however, that the last stage of this development was fully realized only by Attic civilization. A short analysis of Greek history from this particular angle, is not only useful, but also necessary at this stage, for it throws new light on the formation of the Greek personality structure, and particularly on the process of individuation. The aim of such an analysis is to show the main stages by which the Greek had internalized the norms and values of his society, the obvious result of this being the emergence of an individualized society and culture. These are the main aspects of this psycho-historical process.

---

[1] Dodds has suggested such an interpretation (op. cit.). Jaeger also is suggestive in this respect.

To start with, the evolution from a patriarchal aristocratic, to a democratic social order which took place during the sixth century was, on the whole, a transition from a shame- to a guilt-culture. This becomes apparent if one bears in mind that, owing to its rigid class structure, an aristocratic society contains strong elements of shame-culture. In such a society the individual's personality is externally determined by his status. Consequently, the individual's status-anxiety—to use a stock phrase—constitutes the main source of his morality: his qualities, merits and virtues are rigorously measured in terms of social approval or disapproval, of social distinction and hierarchy. Needless to say, the Greek patriarchal aristocratic society makes no exception to this. 'Honour thy gods','honour thy father and thy mother', 'respect the stranger', were in such society supreme commandments handed down by tradition. 'Law' and justice meant customary behaviour, or as Guthrie aptly puts it: 'Justice then, for the Greeks, consisted first of all in doing what custom alone had established as being suitable for a particular station in life, whether that of serf, king, or even god'.[1] Thus the individual's development was permanently moulded and squeezed within the narrow framework of social approval and disapproval. 'Epainos' and 'Psogos', i.e. praise and blame, were the source of honour and personal merit. 'Fame' was the supreme virtue.

On the other hand, a democratic society contains strong elements of guilt-structure. This is on account of its individualistic character. In such a society, the individual is frequently presented with the opportunity of deliberating and choosing among various courses of action, and various values. This obviously implies the development of an internal mechanism to regulate conduct which is the mark of a guilt-culture.

The above remarks show only the bare outline of a complex psycho-historical process. For a more detailed picture of the transition of Greek civilization from a shame- to a guilt-culture, one has to follow up step by step the progress made by the individual in this civilization towards the internalizing of his behaviour. The internalizing of (a) moral, (b) social, and (c) religious behaviour are the main aspects of this development.

(a) An internalized moral behaviour expresses itself in the individual's awareness that the motives of such behaviour lie in

[1] W. K. E. Guthrie: *The Greeks and their Gods*. London. p. 124.

himself and not in an external agency. This awareness can grow to the point of causing the individual to feel that he is a free agent. Internalized moral behaviour is also normally expressed by the feeling of personal responsibility. The individual does not, therefore, project the responsibility and blame outwardly, on things, persons, demons, or gods. Hence the consequence of moral infringement comes from within, as the feelings of guilt, remorse, or expiation.

Now, in Greece, the internalizing of moral behaviour was an historical process. For Homer the motivation of moral behaviour lay in a divine apparatus. When Achilles, seized with anger, assails Agamemnon with the sword, Athena puts on the brake of moral control by asking him to put an end to his 'menos', i.e. to his impulse. Both in the Homeric and archaic eras the individual's worth and virtues, his morality in general, were normally regulated by the external social agency of praise and blame. However, from this early period up to the close of the classical era, one can notice a gradual evolution from an externally to an internally determined morality. Needless to say, this change, like any long historical process, follows a zig-zag path, and there are serious gaps in the evidence for it. Nevertheless its main direction is sufficiently clear.

The first example of this is the change in the concept of moral purity–impurity, or in the concepts of guilt and sin. For reasons which will become apparent at a later stage, one can consider these concepts together. In the archaic era, the general attitude is that the state of moral impurity, or guilt and sin is impersonal in its nature; it is determined by external circumstances. One feels guilty, for instance, because of the sins of one's own father, because of a 'curse', or because of having come in touch with polluted things. Responsibility is also impersonal; as one has to pay for someone else's sins, others may pay for one's own sins. Certain evidence for this can be found in Theognis' complaint: 'Father Zeus, I wished it were the gods' pleasure that whoever did act abominably and of intent, disdainfully with no regard for the gods, should thereafter pay penalty himself, and that ill-doing of the father become no misfortune to the children after him.' Solon also described the hereditary victims as 'anaitioi', i.e. non-responsible. Under such circumstances, the experience of guilt and sin would not amount to more than a feeling of helplessness and doom aroused by an implacable fate. Though direct evidence is hard to produce, it seems that this is a magic stage in which moral categories such as 'virtue', 'guilt', or 'sin' are cosmic agencies affecting human life according to a system of their own.

In comparing this attitude to morality with that of later periods, one cannot help noticing the evolution towards a kind of internalized morality by which the individual takes on himself both the authorship and responsibility of moral behaviour. As early as the end of the archaic age, one notices the existence of a doctrine according to which the sinner would no longer be punished in his descendants but would pay his debt personally in another life. Culturally, this may have a certain connection with the Pythagorean and Orphic conception of the soul, but the important point is that the feeling of personal responsibility makes its appearance, however uncertainly. A certain evidence for this can be extracted from Draco's laws. According to these laws, the state of pollution arises only from 'intentional' killing and wanton attack, and not from accidental murder or self-defence.

Both the idea of pollution (miasma) and that of purification (katharsis) underwent the same change. In the archaic age, the general belief was that pollution was infectious and hereditary. Consequently the state of guilt and sin resulting from it was determined by external circumstances. A few details about moral attitudes in the classical era can easily prove how far away the Greeks had moved in this respect. There is little doubt that towards the classical age—if not earlier—purity is commonly believed to be a personal condition, that is to say, dependant upon the individual's feelings and actions. Dodds speaks in this context about the 'transference of the notion of purity from the magical to the moral sphere', a process which was completed by the end of the fifth century. The notion of purification had also, by that time, undergone the same transformation. While in the archaic age, purification was a mechanical ritual, a quasi-physical cleansing, in the late classical age, it involved the idea of inner conflct which set in motion the feelings of guilt and atonement.

But the experience of guilt and atonement presupposes a highly articulate inner life in the individual. It presupposes in the first place an inner structure of which the function is to regulate the moral behaviour of the individual. This structure consists not only of a system of values and norms which guides the process of inner deliberation, but also of a system of controls, that is, a system of repressing and repressed drives, as well as an organized emotional system. In other words, the experience of guilt and atonement presupposes the formation of an inner structure which can be called internalized morality, or simply conscience. Since the term conscience has a comprehensive and often elusive meaning, the emergence in the Greek of such a structure requires more detailed consideration.

Conscience implies first of all conscious distant ends and pur-posive control of behaviour. In this respect it is worth noting that as early as the archaic age, the individual in the Greek com-munity is advised to 'see the end'. What the nature of this end is, does not matter here. The important point is that the individual is systematically advised to resist the pressure of circumstances and expediency and to orient his behaviour after an inner norm. This can be taken as an initial proof of the existence of a system of inner control which allows the individual a certain degree of autonomy in his behaviour.

A full inquiry into the origins of this system of control raises too many questions. However, one can easily show that as early as the sixth century there existed attempts to formulate moral con-duct in terms of an inner structure in the individual's mind. Consider, for instance, the following precepts: 'Avoid the pleasure which creates displeasure' (Solon); 'Look after your health and be moderate in food, drink and sports' (Pythagoras); 'Maintain the mean between thirst and drunkenness' (Theognis). Of a total of 128 sayings of the Seven Sages, eleven counsel caution in the use of tongue, six warn against pleasure or gain, five advise deference to parents, two emphasize the importance of obedience to law, and a great number advise sobriety and measure in the choice of the heart. It should be stressed that this forms the skeleton of the Greek's conscience, at least up to the end of the classical era.

Admittedly, some of the above statements contain some am-biguity and refer not only to moral behaviour. Nevertheless, they are strongly suggestive of the origin of the function of self-con-trol in the Greek mind. They suggest in the first place that this origin lies in the individual's need for inner order, more precisely, in a strong feeling of balance and harmony. Remember how colourfully Archilochus advises his heart to 'understand the rhythm of life which controls man'.

But with the Greeks this feeling does not remain an organic subconscious force; it becomes a spiritual force by being projected at the conscious level. 'Know thyself' is one of the maxims of the Seven Sages—perhaps the most typical one—inscribed in the entrance of the temple of Delphi. Thus, from the end of the archaic age measure and moderation constitute for the Greek a moral value, i.e. a conscious rational goal in life. It is important to note that all this is formulated in individualistic terms. It can be put as follows: keeping control and order over your life is good for you as an individual, for it satisfies an inner demand. Moreover, we are left in no doubt that the individual is endowed with a specific function for this purpose. This is 'sophrosyne' which is the Greek term for self-control. 'Sophrosyne' is an elementary form of wisdom resting on a specific ability of the individual to order his life according to rules accepted by himself. Whether this ability is called reason, or intellect, does not matter. The important point is that it indicates a reflexive attitude, an inner directed conduct, and a kind of morality based on internal authority.

The development towards an internalized morality reaches a peak in the classical era. Its most powerful expressions can be found in the motive of guilt—sometimes described as pangs of conscience—predominant in the fifth-century drama, and in the Socratic concept of the 'inner voice'.

Much that is relevant to this point has been said earlier in discussing the individualizing processes in Euripides' drama. However, it should be noted that fifth-century drama makes a departure from the archaic idea of guilt and responsibilty as purely external objective conditions in which the individual may find himself unknowingly or unwittingly. Though not discarding altogether the archaic idea, the classical drama tends to express guilt and responsibility as inner conditions, as internalized states. Jaeger points to a certain evolution in this sense which took place between Aeschylus and Euripides. In his view, Aeschylus and Sophocles strove to mitigate the power of external conditions 'by making the guilt-laden man play a more active part in his destiny'. This striving reached a peak in Euripides whose heroes indulged in long introspective analysis in order to put across a subjective facet of their action. The meaning of this is clear: they feel that their guilt or innocence depend to a great extent on their intentions, on their reasons for doing or not doing certain things, on their feelings about their actions. In other words, their morality depends on an inner process of deliberating, valuating and choosing.

It seems that the Socratic concept of the 'inner voice' epitomizes the emergence of an internalized morality in the Greek world, and that the similarity between, if not identity of the function of the 'inner voice' and that of moral conscience are almost obvious. To start with, Socrates advises the individual to resist the uncritical acceptance of the conventions and usages of his community; he urges the individual to think before conforming. This would imply that the criterion of moral behaviour cannot be derived from the external authority of social convention: this criterion reveals itself in the act of searching the self or of self-consultation, in a word, self-knowledge.

Stated in such terms, Socratic morality can be considered the prototype of internalized morality. However, this statement needs careful qualification. First of all, the following important question has to be examined. What does Socrates really mean by self-knowledge? Does he mean that self-scrutiny enables the individual to establish a contact with himself as an individual, and to base his moral choice on this, or does he mean that it is merely an act by which the individual clarifies the moral notions and values existing in his community, and that his intention is, in this case, to 'know' what he is supposed to accept? A detailed discussion of such questions lies beyond the scope of the present study. It is nevertheless worth mentioning that, according to Plato's interpretation of Socrates, the inward experience and the 'inner voice' revealed in Socrates' method do not refer to the individual as such, but to his 'ethos', that the 'inner voice' is in the last analysis not an individualized voice but the voice of man in general. But there is another Socrates, interpreted by Antisthenes, the father of the cynics, who speaks about an inner drive in the individual as a source of morality in itself. To side with one version or another is not an easy matter; the ambivalence underlying Socrates' thought may be the main reason for this. Fortunately, this choice, whatever it may be, does not affect the essence of the present argument. For what is important is the fact that, according to Socrates, the elements of moral behaviour whatever their origin may prove to be, can be found, or established by a process of inner knowledge. This is in itself a symptom of a guilt culture.

(b) It has become obvious from what has been said under (a) that internalized moral behaviour implies internal social behaviour, i.e. the internalizing by the individual of the norms, values, and in general the patterns of behaviour characteristic of this community. In fact these two processes are closely linked.

There are reasons for believing that in the Athenian community the internalizing of social behaviour started to take place round about the end of the archaic era. Most relevant in this respect is the change in attitude towards the law which occurred between the archaic and classical eras. In the archaic era, the common belief was that the laws had a totally external (heteronomous) character. They were God-given. According to Tyrtaeus, for instance, the Spartan constitution was given by Apollo through Lykurgos. Though it is difficult to trace in strict chronological order the changes which took place in such an attitude, one can, nevertheless, speak confidently about a gradual internalizing of the law. Thus, Solon's laws, despite all the mystery created round their origins, took their authority primarily from the citizen's assent to them, and only partly from divine power. Solon himself was aware of the relatively human, as opposed to the divine character of his laws; when asked whether he gave the best laws to the Athenians his answer was—'No, but those which best suited them.' In the fifth century, Herodotus, contrary to Tyrtaeus' opinion, was inclined to think that Lykurgos brought the Spartan constitution from Crete, consequently, it was man-made.

Evidence of the same trend can be derived from the semantic analysis of the two concepts referring to public law, 'Thesmoi' and 'Nomoi'. 'Thesmoi' signified in the oldest days the fundamental rules of public law. They consisted of ritual prescriptions as well as legislative enactments regulating property, marriage, succession, crimes, and public relationship. As the term suggests these rules were essentially religious, based on the sacred authority of the gods, transmitted through oral tradition and interpreted by the priests. Most relevant in this respect is the fact that the 'Thesmoi' were invested with supernatural power; they fell automatically on whoever had transgressed them. In this way a criminal was in a state of 'Atimia' (outlawry) even if he was not discovered and tried. It is obvious, therefore, that, in ancient days, public order and legality functioned in a quasi-magic atmosphere. Like Piaget's children, the Greeks of the Homeric and archaic age believed in the heteronomous character of the laws. And, like Piaget's children again, they evolved towards a conception of the laws which stressed their autonomous character. This is revealed in the meaning of the word 'nomos'. 'Nomoi' were man-made laws, known to all, and belonging to all; they were of a more recent date and bore the name of their author. Their incorporation into the body of legislation came only after the people had voted for them. One can say, therefore, that their authority rested on public consent.

A most revealing stage in the internalizing of social behaviour is the emergence of what Grote describes as 'Constitutional morality' which is, in his view, the greatest achievement of Cleisthenes' reforms. It consisted in the infusion into the individual's mind of readiness for 'voluntary action in the interest of the community', on the one hand, and 'self-imposed restraint', on the other.[1] 'Self-imposed restraint' obviously implies that the individual has the basic norms and values of his community in himself, as constitutive principles of his mind. This is just another way of saying that society has been internalized.

There is no lack of evidence for such a mental development among the Greeks. As we have seen, there was voluntary consent to Solon's laws. The best proof of this is offered by the famous financial arrangement known as the 'great disburdening' by which the well-off classes came freely to the rescue of the poor. It is this aspect of Solon's reforms that Democritus, a century later, had at the back of his mind when he said that the roots of society lie in the individual's feelings of compassion and altruism. In terms more pertinent to the present study, Democritus had reasons for believing that in the Athens of Solon, and of his own time, the public conduct of the individual was determined from within. This presupposed the presence in the individual of strong habits of self-determination, and self-blame, i.e. of an inner structure directing his social behaviour. Additional evidence for this can be derived from the main trend of political and ethical thought of the fifth century. The Sophists, for instance, based their ideas on the

[1] G. Grote: *History of Greece*, Vol. III, pp. 131–2.

assumption that society and morality are end results of a conscious process carried out by the individual on the basis of his inner sociality, or, more precisely, of his 'internalized society'. As has been already remarked, the Sophists did not distinguish between man's personal ethics and his political sense, between man's 'morality' and his 'civility'.[1] As a characteristic detail, it is worth while mentioning that, during this time, there took place an important change in attitude towards punishment. As opposed to a retributive conception characteristic of earlier eras, the Sophists stressed the deterrent and corrective nature of punishment. This transition from a retributive to a corrective stage seems to be symptomatic of the general evolution from a shame- to a guilt-culture. According to a retributive conception, 'law', 'punishment', 'revenge' are outside, moreover, have little to do with the individual's consciousness. The 'eye-for-an-eye' principle is mechanically applied, often without discrimination between the actual offender and his family, or his community. On the other hand, the corrective-deterrent view is based on the active part played by the offender's conscience in the process of punishment. Punishment is intended primarily to instruct, i.e. to create, or to stimulate in the individual an inner-directed moral mechanism. Thus the external function of society in preventing crime is partly handed over to the inner processes of guilt and atonement.

(c) There are many other aspects of the process outlined above which are worth mentioning. Cannot the rise of tragedy itself, with its centred motive of guilt and expiation, be taken as symptomatic from this point of view? One wonders indeed whether the birth of tragedy in any civilization is not a symptom of guilt-culture, or of the beginning of guilt-culture.

But, as this question will be taken up in the next chapter, it would now be appropriate to look at a more general psycho-cultural phenomenon closely associated with the transition of the Athenian community from a shame- to a guilt-culture. This is the change in the people's attitudes towards the gods and religion in general which started to take place around the end of the archaic age, and continuing throughout the classical into the Hellenistic age. The direction of this change is indicated by what Festugière describes as 'personal religion'. He means by this the develop-

[1] The quoted terms belong to E. A. Havelock. Op. cit. p. 172.

ment in the members of the Greek community of the desire and ability to be in close personal contact with the gods, moreover, to worship and dedicate their lives to the god of their choice. Obviously, 'personal religion' was opposed to State religion, in which the individual was involved communally in acts of public worship. Briefly, 'personal religion' was individualized religion. On the other hand, the gods of the civic religion were communal and external: contact with them was, at least, partly determined by social pressure.

Now, it is true that Festugière may easily give the impression that he prefers an anhistorical approach to this problem. His eagerness to prove the existence of a personal religion among the Greeks sometimes makes him overlook the differences which exist from this point of view between various stages in Greek civilization. When he starts illustrating his thesis, he speaks in the same breath about the 'intimate personal bond' between Achilles and Athene, about the sixth and seventh centuries' 'private dedications' to Athene, about personal ties of friendship between Sappho and Aphrodite, about the god of inner devotion of Hesiod, and finally, about the gods of the great tragedians and those of the Eleusian Mysteries. But, at the same time, Festugière seems to realize that all this can be seen as various stages in the formation of an attitude. For, as soon as he comes to a closer grip with his subject, he significantly writes: 'Because certain features of the Hellenistic age—notably the decline of the city state and the prevailing influence of Plato—favoured the growth of personal religion, my examples will be chosen principally from the Hellenistic and Greco-Roman period.' Obviously, one is concerned here with an historical process; the development of personal religion among the Greeks started in a vague form, in the archaic age, and reached a climax during the period marked sociologically by the decline of the city state, and culturally, by the 're-vival' of a series of mystic cults in the field of religion.

Why did the development of personal religion follow this historical course? The answer to this question sheds light on various aspects of the transition of the Athenian community from a shame- to a guilt-culture.

It is appropriate to note here that the development of personal religion went hand in hand with the general process of democratization. However, more specific determining factors of such a development can be found only by a closer examination of the psycho-historical situation of Athens round about the close of the fifth century.

A growing disbelief in the Olympian gods, as represented by the Homeric mythology, was characteristic of this period. It was, obviously, associated with the formation of a more enlightened rational attitude to life characteristic of the classical age. But there were other more specific causes. Firstly, the Olympian dynasty of Homer had always a strong aristocratic flavour, secondly, the Homeric mythology was closely woven into the social and cultural fabric of the city state. Now, at the close of the fifth century, after a relatively long period of democracy, the Homeric religion could no longer keep a strong hold upon the mind of the people. In purely sociological terms, this means that the decline in belief in the Olympians reached its nadir in an advanced period of democracy. This corresponded to the rise of new classes, and of the common people in particular, whose specific religious needs were not satisfied by the Homeric mythology. In fact, the beliefs and attitudes of the Olympian religion faded, and gradually died out. Their place was taken by all sorts of mystery cults, i.e. by a body of religious beliefs which allowed for a more intimate contact between man and God.[1] One can conclude from this that the change in religious beliefs and attitudes was an expression of the change in the class structure of Athenian society.

But the change in the social structure of Athenian society was only one aspect of this period. That is why the sociological explanation has to be completed with a psychological one. The close of the fifth century marked the beginning of a new era for the Greek world, and for Athens in particular. It was round about this time that the 'age of anxiety' began. A long period of wars and civic strife had certainly much to do with the coming of this age. But, as things looked in Athens at the turn of the fifth century, the cause of anxiety seemed to be much deeper; the whole social and moral framework—the city state itself—was crumbling.

[1] Two main hypotheses have been put forward for the explanation of this phenomenon. According to one view, the mystery cults constituted a body of primitive beliefs suppressed by the more recent Olympian religion. In this case, their 'revival' implies a psycho-social process of regression provoked by the disintegration of the city state. According to other views, these mystic beliefs constituted the religion of the common people which was intensified by democracy.

The two main characteristic traits of this period were the failure of the corporate spirit, and the growth of cosmopolitan individualism. They reached a climax in the fourth century with the conquest of Alexander of Macedon. The whole period was one of radical reorganization, and consequently, one of anxiety. The sense of the instability of human affairs was particularly acute. In Festugière's view, 'no more tormented period of world history is to be found than the first century of the Hellenistic age.' The collapse of the corporate spirit, and generally speaking, the weakening of all social bonds, might have aroused in a few individuals the feeling of relief and freedom—in the Cynics for example—but they certainly aroused in many others disorientation, anxiety, and by compensation, a heightened need to belong.[1]

In this psycho-historical situation lie the roots of a great change in religious attitudes among the Greeks; the rise, or the unusually rapid growth of personal religion is closely associated with it. Firstly, the civic cults of the Olympians, typical of the city-state, became less and less appropriate in the growing cosmopolitan world. Secondly, the individual deprived of the security given to him by his communal ties, and facing alone the new open and fluid Hellenistic world, felt the need of a more friendly and personal communication with God. As Festugière remarks, the age of anxiety stimulated in the people two opposite sets of beliefs. On the one hand, there was a growing belief in an indifferent, if not hostile Fate. On the other hand, there was the belief in the redeeming power of certain gods, hence the need for an intimate and personal approach to them as shown by the practices of initiation, purification and personal devotion.

Therefore, as the religion of the civic cults was, on the whole, a symptom of a shame-culture, so personal religion was a symptom of a guilt-culture. Moreover, personal religion was, in this case, a sign of an advanced stage in the development of a guilt-culture. At this stage, civic religious practices, and communal gods were replaced by private devotion and personal gods. God,

---

[1] This need found its expression in Plato whose totalitarian views are normally considered as a reaction from the spirit of individualism resulting from the decline of the city state. Even more revealing in this respect was the growing spirit of 'groupism', that is to say, a pronounced inclination among the Greeks of the Hellenistic period to form voluntary and unofficial associations. The motivation of such an inclination lay in unsatisfied social need. See on this point: Tod, M. N.: *Clubs and Societies in the Greek World.* In, *Sidelights of Greek History.* 1932.

or the gods became symbols of supernatural power on which the individual pinned his hopes for personal salvation. In other words, salvation or doom depended on the personal initiative of the individual, rather than on a civic rite. As the intermediary role of the community receded, the individual himself had to negotiate with divinity the fate of his soul. Thus, contact with God became gradually imbued with personal feelings of love and hope, or fear and guilt.

A last point should be mentioned before concluding this section; it is the evolution of the system of values in Greece.

The archaic traditional society was ethically well integrated; the moral code of 'Arete' was generally accepted. After the decline of this society, one can distinguish two lines of development in the ethical field, one towards ethical monism, the other towards ethical pluralism.

Spartan society is a typical example of ethical monism. Bravery and patriotism are supreme virtues. The moral code of the individual is rigidly determined from outside by social pressure. Inner deliberation is discouraged, for in Sparta, 'men are courageous from ignorance, but they hesitate upon reflection,' to paraphrase Thucydides. All this points to the fact that, in Sparta, the development of the Greek mind remained at a patriarchal stage. In Sparta, Greek civilization showed to the very end clear signs of a shame-culture and little, if any, growth of the process of individuation. No wonder that the Spartans represented a special problem for the Delphic oracle: 'they were simple soldier men,' writes Charles Seltman, 'who needed direction so that they were ready to surrender personal initiative, and to seek on every trivial matter a wise advice from the god through the Pythia'.[1]

In Attica, the evolution went towards an ethical pluralism. As early as the sixth century, Solon recognized that there were various virtues, and that men could pursue their goals along diverse paths. This in itself is an important sign of the decline of the patriarchal society, and of the rise of democracy. Snell puts this clearly: 'By enumerating one by one the various professions and skills, Solon shows that the new society of citizens is diametrically opposed to the ancient aristocratic order. The uniform ideal of the ruling class is no longer acknowledged'. Since the psychological implications of an individualized social order have been dis-

[1] *The Twelve Olympians.* London. p. 120.

cussed elswhere, for the moment it is enough to point to the significance which ethical pluralism has for the mental development of the individual. Firstly, the emergence of pluralism in ethics can be both a cause and an effect of individual differentiation in the sphere of moral behaviour. Secondly, ethical pluralism places the individual in a position to choose between various values and means. In other words, it implies inner processes and structures which enable the individual to decide in terms of his own experiences and purposes upon the course of his actions. As a result of this he includes himself and his personality in his moral decision. This is precisely the basic psychological condition of internalized morality, and of a guilt-culture in general.

Following from all this, it can be stated that between the archaic and classical ages, the Greeks had evolved from shame- to guilt-culture. This suggests that 'shame' and 'guilt', as psycho-cultural concepts, can be regarded from an evolutionary point of view, in other words, that the psycho-cultural development of certain communities leads from a shame stage to a guilt stage. It would be tempting at this point to say that there is something natural and reasonable in this kind of evolution, if one did not come up against the difficulty of finding direct evidence for such a statement. One can, however, use for this purpose a certain amount of indirect evidence. For instance, J. Piaget describes two stages in the development of a child which can easily be assimilated to what has been described here as shame-culture and guilt-culture. Piaget speaks about heteronomous morality characteristic of children up to the age of six, and autonomous morality developing after that age. In the former stage, the moral behaviour of a child is externally determined; he looks upon the norms of his group as upon objective laws. In the second stage, he internalizes the social and moral code of his group. Thus, his moral behaviour becomes determined from within, by inner compulsion. This process of internalizing the social and moral code can equally be applied to the historical development of a community. As a result of this, the individual members of the community pass from a stage in which their social integration and moral behaviour are externally determined, to a stage in which this aspect of their behaviour is determined from inside. This is a transition from a shame-culture to a guilt-culture.

The internalizing of the social code, though a normal form of psycho-cultural evolution, is not realized to the same degree in every community. Moreover, some communities stop their historical evolution at the level of heteronomous morality. There are also cases of regression, i.e. the reversion of a community of people from an autonomous to a heteronomous morality. The ancient Greeks, however, not only developed through both stages, but were the first community known to history which built up a society whose order was based on the inner authority of the individual's reason. The process of rationalization which is the subject of the next section will throw light on this aspect of Greek civilization.

RATIONALIZATION

Though individuation and rationalisation are inter-dependent processes, they are opposed to each other in their results. Individuation presupposes the emergence of a specific mental structure whose function is to clarify and increase the individual's awareness of himself. This is an individualizing structure in the sense that it enables the individual to translate his relationship with the external world in terms of his own needs and experiences. Such structure can be named the 'self', or in a restricted sense the ego. Rationalization works, on the other hand, in an opposite direction. It does not lead to the adjustment of the environment to the unique character of the individual's mind, but rather to the adjustment of the individual's mind to the general and objective conditions of this environment. As a result of this there emerges a new mental structure by which the individual recognizes the basic principles governing his mind, the mind of the others, and his environment as a whole. In other words, the individual becomes aware of himself as a member of an organized whole. This structure can be called intellect, reason, and in a restricted sense, super-ego.

Rationalization was an historical process in Greece. Since it would be difficult to follow this process in a strict chronological order, the scope of the present section has to be limited to a brief account of some of its main aspects and stages.

The Greeks are considered as the creators of rational thought. This is relatively easy to demonstrate at a cultural level. It would be enough to show the transition by stages from a magic and mythical explanation of the world, so characteristic of the Homeric and the archaic period, to a growing realistic interest in things and events, displayed for instance by the pre-Socratic thinkers, or by historians like Herodotus and Thucydides. And though this can by no means be considered as a unilinear process, one can go further, to the stage of conscious systematic effort towards the discovery of the formal universal principles governing the relations between things and events as displayed, for instance, by the Eleatics, by Socrates, by Aristotle, or by a whole trend of mathematical thought. But cultural evolution is in this sense a symptom of mental evolution. Thus the real concern of the historical psychologists is with psychological processes such as changes in interests and attitudes, new inner balances, and new forms of relations between man and his universe, which led to a gradual change of the Greek mind from a magic to a rational stage. Here are a few significant aspects of these processes.

The change from a magic to a rational attitude requires first of all a certain re-orientation of human curiosity. This is manifested as interest in things as such, in their intrinsic nature and in their inter-relations. The beginning of this new development in the Greek mind was made by the pre-Socratics during the end of the archaic era. There is nothing magic or mythical in, for instance, Empedocles' bent of mind when he compares an eye with a lantern. His curiosity is kept at the level of reality; both terms, the eye and the lantern, belong to the same order, and their comparison with each other serves the purpose of increasing human knowledge about their intrinsic nature. Had Empedocles been interested, not in the eye, as an empirical phenomenon, but in its ultimate origin, in the force which created the eye, he would have certainly compared it with something supernatural. But this is precisely what does not happen. For the Greek mind as expressed through the pre-Socratics shows an obvious inclination towards a kind of understanding and explanation of physical environment which is given by things themselves and by their inter-relation, with no appeal to the supernatural.

The word appeal should not be misunderstood. One can hardly say that the Greeks had at this early stage, or at any later stage, completely eliminated the supernatural from their understanding of the world. This has never happened in any civilization. The Greeks started, however, to grasp, or to draw the dividing line between the natural and the divine. This they did by a systematic effort to heighten the amount of consciousness in their contact with the world. In the first place, they checked the interference of the divine by trying to confine both the contents and the form of knowledge to what is found in the focus of introspective consciouness, that is to say, to sense data and canons of mental activity. Signs of such development can be found as early as the sixth century. For Xenophanes, for instance, the dividing line between the natural and the divine is so clearly drawn that he refused to ascribe human properties to gods. This is a striking change since the Homeric period. He refuses also to ascribe divine qualities to men, i.e. the power of divination. Heraclitus gives a similar impression when he writes: 'the wisest man beside god, appears like an ape, in wisdom, beauty and all else'. Here the divine appears either as an ideal concept referring clearly to a reality of a different order from the order of natural events, or as a limit concept, the supreme end of a series from which a certain classification can be made: god—man—ape. Both senses show a clear discrimination between the divine and the natural. The development of this critical attitude is illustrated by a series of efforts towards the secularization of myths.[1] Prompted by such an attitude, Hecataeus, for instance, found it difficult to believe that Aegyptus could have fifty sons; twenty would have been more probable considering some natural conditions of life. Thus a myth was unmasked as 'unnatural', consequently it was untrue, for it did not correspond to certain norms governing human knowledge—that is to say it did not correspond to reason. As an expression of the same mental trend one has to mention again Euripides' own difficulty in taking myths at their face value: under his pen, the Orestes myth becomes infused with a strong element of farce. And Euripides was not alone. To his generation there belonged people such as Anaxagoras, with his

[1] According to Abel Rey, Thales, with his first principle, 'Water', lies at the very beginning of such an enterprise. Though derived from mythology—Egyptian, Babylonian and Aegean—this principle becomes in Thales a naturalistic concept. 'Okeanos' is no longer personified, but conceived as a thing, an external reality, 'Water.' 'With Thales,' writes Rey, 'we are in the presence of a purely physical first state, of the type from which all others come.' This implied a reorientation of consciousness which is admirably described by Rey: 'The attention is clearly turned towards the things which are independent of us, for it is definitively decided that there are things, and an order of things which are independent of us: the universe around us, in which we are.' Op. cit. p. 31.

concept of expanding reason, Diogenes of Apollonia who attributed the beginning of the world to the principle of active reason, and Thucydides who maintained that the road to truth leads away from myths.

The examples mentioned above—to quote only a few—testify clearly to the emergence in the minds of the Greeks of an enduring disposition towards rational thought. In order to understand this mental development it is necessary to describe its nature. The development of rational thinking is closely associated with what, in present-day dynamic psychology, is called reality testing function, a term which often can be rendered as rational consciousness. The formation in the mind of the individual of such a function presupposes in the first place a shift in the orientation of his consciousness, and of his mind as a whole, from inner-emotional to external factors. As a result of this, things and events are no longer, or are to a lesser degree, perceived as symbols or functions of obscure magic or mythical forces lying beyond them: things and events become reality itself. Signs of such mental development in Greece can be found as early as the sixth century. The pre-Socratics with their interest in the physical world can be mentioned as an example.

But, as suggested above, the development of the reality-testing function presupposes a certain liberation of consciousness from the pressure of emotional life, an operation normally carried out by repression. In this respect it is important to note that the Greeks had succeeded to a greater extent than the members of other communities in minimizing the influence of certain primitive emotional factors upon their adjustment to environment. A certain evidence for this can be obtained from what has been said about the development of self-control in the minds of the Greeks. At any rate, by the beginning of the classical era, this mental trait is clearly expressed at the cultural level. 'Men attain good cheer,' Democritus writes, "through moderation in pleasure and a life well measured. Want and excess cause metastasis and produce great disturbances in the soul. The soul which moves between distant points is neither stable nor cheerful.' Since this attitude towards emotional life is closely bound with the rise of the sense of reality, it deserves a more detailed consideration.

The presence of strong emotional factors causes knowledge, or broadly speaking, the conscious perception of the world to be inwardly oriented, i.e. determined to a high degree by the individual's impulses, fears, love, hopes. One speaks in this case about a strong mechanism of projection, the result of which is a pronounced inclination in the individual to perceive in the external world his own needs and feelings. This is a sign of a weak reality-testing function. The child's perception of the world, or that of certain people suffering from delusions, are extreme examples of this. When the reality-testing function is strong, the perception of the world is determined both by inner and outer factors. This cannot be achieved until and unless the effect of emotional factors is minimized by a sustained conscious control or by their temporary relegation into the unconscious. If one describes this mental condition in terms normally applied to physical phenomena, one would say that the control and withdrawal of inner emotional factors enable the external world to break through the barriers of projection, and impose its own terms on its relation to the mind. One can call this new relation with the external world relation at the reality level. This means that the individual's mind has formed an enduring disposition and an ability to perceive things, objects and persons as reality in themselves, and not as merely disguised appearances of spiritual forces. For these forces are obviously projections of the individual's emotionality, and as such they are accessible to magical thought and to mythical forms of representation. In other words, they disclose an inclination towards a mythic and irrational thought which is diametrically opposed to the reality-testing function and rationally constituted consciousness.[1]

---

[1] One should avoid the error of confining the role of the reality-testing function to that of eliminating by repression the inner emotional drives from the individual's perception of the world. What is more characteristic of this function is that it creates a compromise and balance between the inner and the external factors. It prevents the individual from falling into the extreme of transforming the external world into the function of his inner drives which is in fact a characteristic of magic or delusional thought. And yet, this is not done at the expense of going to the other extreme, namely to the extreme of crushing the dynamic force of the inner factors. The reality-testing function means in fact a dynamic harmony and equilibrium between the external and internal world. The mind is transformed by the external world to the same extent in which the external world is transformed by the mind. In this dynamic relation between inner and outer factors lies one of the main sources of the Greek sense of inner balance which is perhaps a prime condition of rational thinking. For in this inner sense of balance, lies the deep motivation of the individual's inclination to perceive what is common, regular, normal in things and in events. This deep sense of order and harmony expresses itself at the conscious level in a code of rules which regulates the relationship between the individual and his environment. The most complete and clear form of this code was given by the Greeks of the classical period in the principles of formal logic.

There is one point regarding the genesis of rational conscious-ness which deserves special mention here. As previously stated, a basic condition of such mental development in Greece consisted in an outward orientation of the individual's mind. As a result of this the world of perception became differentiated into inde-pendent units—things and objects—having their intrinsic qualities and being in formal objective, or, rational relation with each other. But a brief examination of the historical context in which this took place, shows clearly that the outward orientation of the Greek mind had two directions: one, as just mentioned, towards the physical, the other towards the social world. The second direction was at least as important as the first in the for-mation of rational consciousness. To avoid a possible misunder-standing, it should be said that this orientation of the individual's consciousness towards his social world does not simply mean in-creased interest and involvement in the life of his community. It means in the first place an increased curiosity and power of obser-vation in this specific direction. As a result of this, his perception of the social world developed on similar lines with that of the physical world: the individual formed the habit of perceiving his fellow-men objectively, i.e. as having their intrinsic qualities, and above all, as having their own mind. If the analogy can be stretched so far, one can say that the social world too became differentiated into independent units, i.e. individuals. This is just another way of saying that the Greek social structure was on the point of passing from its pre-individualized to its individualized stage. While at the first stage the individual's perception of his fellow-men was dominated by the category of 'sameness' and 'community' at the second stage, it was dominated by the cate-gory of 'otherness' and 'differentiation'.

This development in the psycho-social sphere of life is of par-amount importance for the development of rational consciousness. The reason for this is very simple—the individual's percep-tion of his fellow-men as 'others', as units differentiated from himself and from each other, increases his conscious effort to-wards communication, that is to say, his need to work out at the conscious level the basic norms and rules of communal life. His social adjustment as a whole depends on this. In Greek history at least one significant fact supports this hypothesis: it was precisely during this period of transition from a pre-individualized to an individualized stage that Heraclitus made the attempt to formulate the concept of the 'common mind' which is a tool, as well as a criterion of rational knowledge. The premises and train of thought leading to this formulation are not known; hypothetically they can, however, be reconstituted as follows: Heraclitus started from his observation of the differences existing between individuals with respect to their perception and their opinions about things and events, in other words, he started from his awareness of a highly differentiated psycho-social structure. This aroused in him the legitimate question: how, under such circumstances, is understanding or knowledge possible? The answer was, by relying on what is common in the experiences and perceptions of several individuals, of all individuals if possible. The result of this proceeding is the emergence of what Heraclitus calls 'the world in common' (Xunon, or Koinon) which is nothing else but the hypostatizing of the mind in common made up of the overlapping parts of several consciousnesses.

It goes without saying that what is common is our perceptions, or the overlapping parts of our consciousnesses consists of a set of rules, norms, or principles which lie at the basis of rational thinking. Consequently, the concept of the common mind, as defined above, is a primitive formulation of the concept of rational consciousness, or rational mind in general. But this is not the whole point. What is important is the socio-genetic aspect of this concept, namely, this concept was coined in a socio-psychological climate characterized by a rapid process of individual differentiation, in a society which half a century later became a prototype of democracy. The temptation is great, and not without justification, to jump from this factual consideration into the core of the problem: it seems that the emergence of a rational consciousness, i.e. of a type of conscious mental activity based on formal general laws is greatly stimulated by socio-psychological differentiation. No wonder that the Greeks are the founders of rational thought. Paraphrasing an important idea found in the Sophists, one can say that logical rational thinking is a form of 'sociability', or a technique of living (which can be taught) in a highly individualized society. In terms more pertinent to this study, individuation entails rationalization.

Now, one can pass on to a more systematic historical account of this problem. For a better understanding of the historical origin of rational thought in Greece it would be useful to look more closely at one specific aspect of the Greek mind, its social aspect. The problem is in this case to describe in historical terms the emergence of reason in the field of Greek social life, namely, the formation of rational attitudes towards authority, or rational social relations, and in general a rational social order.

Some important socio-psychological phenomena characteristic of the period of transition from the patriarchal to the democratic social order shed light on this aspect of the process of rationalization. First of all one notices during this period a change in the character of social authority; there is a gradual transition from a social order based on the traditional quasi-religious authority of a personal ruler, or group of rulers, to a social order based on the formal impersonal and abstract authority of the law. The rational character of the law as against the irrational character of traditional authority is self-evident. The authority of the law rests on the nature of its purpose, while of tradition is implicit and external to the individual's consciousness. Thus, the individual's obedience to tradition is based mainly on unconscious emotional motives while his obedience to law is based on conscious goals which he shares with other members of his community. While change in tradition takes place slowly and outside the individual's consciousness, the change in the law presupposes not only conscious and deliberate effort in its makers, but conscious efforts of readjustment in each member of the group.

The transition of the Greek community from a social order based on traditional authority to one based on the formal authority of the law starts in the sixth century, and reaches a definite form in Athens during the democratic period. By his written code of laws, Solon made a conscious attempt to lay the foundation of a social order based on the citizen's personal respect for and obedience to the law. Admittedly neither the concept of law, nor the citizen's obedience to the law are, at this early stage, purely rational in character. Solon, for instance, links justice with religion; he believes that the gods punish infringement of the law. Despite this, however, the seed of rationality was sown. In the mind of the Athenian citizen law emerges gradually as an authority in itself regardless of whether it was backed by another kind of authority, religious or otherwise. This shows itself primarily as a deep interest and confidence in the law and in its representatives which is a fundamental characteristic of the Athenian public life during the democratic era. The impressive number of courts of law and justiciary settlements of all sorts is only one aspect of this phenomenon. Much more important in this respect is the unique readiness of the Athenian citizen to go to the courts even on matters which today would look trivial. The institution of Euthynos founded in the period immediately preceding democracy, is a characteristic example of this. Each tribe appointed an 'examiner' to sit during the regular market hours at the statue of the eponymous hero and collect the charges against the magistrates which any citizen had the right to make. The 'examiner' then brought the charges to the local judges. This shows, apart from a prevalent practice in Athenian public life, also the individual's habit of dealing rationally with his social (communal) conflicts, or, of disengaging these conflicts from their personal emotional context and applying to them the impersonal formula of the law.

This is not all. The famous Greek partiality to, and ability for law making, indicate the same enthusiasm. If one is to believe Aristotle, Athens had no less than eight constitutions from Solon's to his own time. Consequently, the Athenian community had within this period reformulated eight times its basic principles of organization, not to mention a multitude of more specific laws. This certainly shows social dynamism, if not instability. But in this specific case it shows the ability, or even the ease with which a group of individuals formulated their common interests in a set of general principles and laws, i.e. ability to rationalize social life.

The growth of a rational frame of mind in the members of the Greek community is a deep and many-sided process. One historical event, Cleisthenes' reform, has exceptional significance in this respect. To start with, Cleisthenes deals the final blow to the declining patriarchal order based on the system of phratries by replacing it with the administrative system of demes. Naturally, this means that social life became significantly more rational in character. For the individual's integration with the old tribal order was determined mainly by unconscious traditional bonds, by family and blood ties. A deme was, on the other hand, an abstract administrative unit appealing to the individual only as a rational necessity. Thus, in the new system of demes, the Athenian citizen gradually formed the habit of considering his relations with other members of this community as grounded in, and leading to rational purposes. In this lies a fundamental psycho-social condition of democratic society. One could describe it as the ability of the individual to regard his society as a flexible scheme resulting from conscious deliberate agreements between him and other members of his group.

There is still more to be said about the impact of Cleisthenes' reforms upon the rationalization of the Greek mind. Obviously, the creation of a rational social order as described above, implies the individual's capacity to see common ends in their relation with each other and to achieve them by methods and means generally agreed upon. In other words, this requires the formation of certain habits of behaviour in the social sphere. It is exactly the period of Cleisthenes' reforms that can shed light on the formation of these habits in the mind of the Athenian citizens. To explain this one has to go back to what Grote considers as the greatest achievement of Cleisthenes' reforms, namely the creation of 'constitutional morality'. Here is Grote's description of this phenomenon: 'It was necessary to create in the multitude, and through them to force upon the leading ambitious men, that rare and difficult sentiment which we may term a constitutional morality, a paramount reverence for the forms of the constitution, enforcing obedience to the authorities acting under and within those forms, yet combined with the habit of open speech, of action subject only to definite legal control, and unrestrained censure of those very authorities as to all their public acts—*combined too with a perfect confidence in the bosom of every citizen, amidst the bitterness of party contest, that the forms of the constitution will be not less sacred in the eyes of his opponents than in his own.*'[1]

It can be seen now that the phenomenon termed by Grote 'constitutional morality' can easily be described as internalized law, introjected social order, social consciousness, or even the super-ego. Difference in terms matters very little in this case as all of these terms refer to the same psycho-social phenomenon, or rather describe various aspects or stages of the same process. The important point is that at a certain stage in the historical development of his civilisation, the Athenian citizen experienced his social conformity as being determined from within; the external authority of the law had, at this stage, become the inner

[1] Op. cit. Vol. III., pp. 131, 132. Itals. mine.

authority of consciousness or reason. It is at this mental stage that the individual of Greek civilization in general, and of the Athenian community in particular, developed a specific structure within his mind which enabled him to establish, or to create the organizing norms of his environment. Once this organizing structure was formed, the whole realm of life was gradually rationalized, i.e. became 'cosmos'.

The rationalizing of religion was closely connected with what has sometimes been described as the moralizing of the Greek gods, the time interval between the writing of the Iliad and that of the Odyssey, that is to say between the first half of the eighth and the first half of the seventh centuries—or according to Finley, between mid-eighth and mid-seventh century—has a certain importance in this respect.[1] The gods of the Iliad are arbitrary, if not capricious in their actions. It is only in the Odyssey that Zeus becomes sensitive to moral criticism, that is to say he becomes motivated in his actions by certain pre-established rules embodied in the concept of justice. From this point on one can follow in Solon, Hesiod, Theognis, Aeschylus, how the gods' actions become more and more rationally oriented. Finally the major Olympians become the symbols and supporters of a rationally organized physical, social and moral universe. They become the embodiment of cosmic order.

There are many other important aspects of this phenomenon which cannot even be mentioned here. The Greeks went so far in their drive towards rationalizing the divine forces, that they tried to wrap up in a rational form even their most obscure religious experiences. The Pythia would talk only reason.[2]

We come now to another important aspect of the process of rationalization, the rationalization of the physical universe. This has, however, been touched upon at an earlier stage when dealing with the transition of the Greek mind from a magic to a rational stage. Moreover, this is by far the best known aspect of the process

[1] M. I. Finley: *The World of Odysseus*. London, 1956

[2] The Delphic divinations passed through three stages before they reached the ears of the inquirer. A priest interpreter memorized the Pythia's words. Then this first version passed on to a second interpreter, the *prophètes*. Lastly a third priest, an *exegetes Pythochrestos* approached the inquirer. The *exegetes Pythochrestos* distinguished himself for his 'natural good manners and adroitness', as well as for his knowledge of matters regarding international policies. See Ch. Seltman: *The Twelve Olympians*. pp. 115–16.

of rationalization. Direct evidence for it can be found in the evolution of Greek philosophical thought from the Ionian school to Plato, as well as in the evolution of Greek science. All this constitutes a gigantic and unique attempt to infuse the physical universe with the laws of reason, the clearest image of which is given by Plato when he conceives the creator of the world as a geometer.

In the rationalization of social relations lies perhaps the most characteristic, and at the same time, important symptom of the rationalization of the Greek mind. In a patriarchal social order characteristic of the archaic age, the relationships between the individuals are mediated if not entirely determined by unconscious irrational motives, such as class prejudices, emotional or family tribal ties, and social status rooted in traditional values which are indiscriminately accepted by all members of the community. It would perhaps be wrong to say that this kind of relation takes place between individuals, for they are obviously shaped by supra-individual or rather supra-personal factors such as class, tribe, or family. Now, there are grounds for believing that with the advance of Greek society into the democratic era, inter-individual relations became more and more personal in their nature. Firstly, they are more and more based on the intrinsic values and qualities of the individuals involved, that is to say, on the individuals' intelligence, temperament, virtues, or vices. Secondly, they are influenced very decisively by the situation in which two individuals establish relations with each other. In this lies their rational nature for they presuppose the conscious and critical attitude of two or more individuals towards each other. Nothing can better illustrate this state of affairs than the type of inter-individual relations described by Menander in his comedies —in so far as one can rely upon Gilbert Murray's version of these plays. In this late period of Athenian democracy, the patriarchal pattern of inter-individual relations, i.e. the traditional categories of master and slave, father and son, or daughter, of husband and wife had little more than a symbolic meaning. As the old emotional and unconscious connotation of these social realities was dying out, inter-human relations became more and more dependent on the intrinsic qualities of the individuals involved. In 'The Arbitration', for instance, Abrotonon, the slave flute player, is by her virtues, qualities and deeds a free woman. All the relations between her and other characters are determined by this consideration rather than by her official status. If this is the spirit conveyed by Menander, then in few known societies were human relations more rational, that is, rooted in individuals' critical assessments of each other, than in the fourth-century Athenian community. Of course, one had to bear in mind that this fragment of life belongs to literary fiction. But even as such it shows certain basic trends and aspirations of the Greek mind in a given historical period.

These impressions can be considerably strengthened if one examines the nature of inter-group relations as practised by the Greeks of the democratic era. The evidence on this point seems to make the task of the historical psychologist relatively easy. One has only to read Thucydides with a psychological eye to realize how often relations between groups, and particularly between city-states are kept and often solved at a rational level, even in a surrounding atmosphere which is heavily charged with passion. Alliances, coalitions, friendships, hostilities, and even wars seem to be matters of rational arrangements between communities. Take an example at random; the relationship between the Plataeans and the Spartans during the Peloponesian war, as depicted in the debate after the defeat of Plataea, between the Spartan and Theban representatives on the one hand, and the Plataeans on the other. At a certain moment the Plataean speaker says: 'Nevertheless in this war we never acted against you in an *unreasonable manner,* nor were we likely to have done so.' The manner in which the speaker supports this broad statement, however brilliant, does not concern us here. The important point is that he believes that a reasonable attitude and conduct towards the Spartan, in other words decisions and actions derived from cold logical considerations, are points in favour of his argument. Moreover he gives us to understand that the other side entertained the same belief. For was it not the Spartans who promised that if the Plataeans 'would voluntarily give up the city . . . the guilty would be punished, *but no one without a fair trial*'?[1] Now, one can easily say that all this is nothing more than a manner of speaking, and that in fact the city of Plataea was finally 'razed to the ground from its very foundations'. But a manner of speaking is in this case not as insignificant as it may seem. For not all diplomats, even in more recent times, make the same kind of effort to frame rationally the case for their

[1] *Idem*, pp. 191–2. Italics mine.

countries. Is this not due to the fact that they do not believe, or believe to a lesser degree than the Greeks, that relations between human communities are based on reason? Coming back to Thucydides one can easily prove not only that the Greek diplomats often made such an effort, but also that they were frequently successful in their enterprise. The relations between Mytilene and Athens following the defeat of the former fully illustrate this. One can see in the evolution of these relations the gradual triumph of reason over passion.

The objections may be raised that these are inter-group relations as seen by Thucydides, and that the speeches referred to are at least partly arranged by him.[1] But what was said earlier about Menander's vision of inter-individual relations applies here too. What Thucydides says indicates at least a tendency of the Greek mind in a given historical period. And avowed tendencies and goals are no less important and real than actions; in the long run life is moulded by them.

Starting with Herodotus, an increasing tendency can be noticed among the Greek historians to perceive historical events in the function of the basic logical principles of the human mind as well as to see the historical evolution as following a certain (rational) pattern. Herodotus himself was, as A. W. Gomme rightly points out, not a simple chronicler.[2] A simple empirical succession of events was not his main concern. He stresses certain events and places them in a certain order so as to illustrate the meaning of the course of events. In other words, he organizes his material logically. Moreover, Herodotus sees the evolution of events directed towards certain universal norms and values. Gomme formulates some of these norms as follows: 1. Zeus punishes the perjurer; 2. Zeus helps the suppliant; 3. Prosperity is a slippery thing; 4. Power is corruption, it leads to 'hubris'. Admittedly, it is not easy to describe these norms and values as rational. On the contrary, it seems more appropriate to call them beliefs. But Gomme is quick to tell us that in Herodotus' case they are not primitive beliefs, and that at least some of them are based on empirical observation. For example, Herodotus himself had seen rich

---

[1] Historians like Tacitus, for instance, do not feel the need for such arrangements. In the speeches rendered by him, in the Annals, the backbone of the argument is formed by emotional traditional values, i.e. our fathers . . .

[2] *The Greek Attitude to Poetry and History.* 1954.

people whose richness went to their head, made them over-confident, and thus pushed them to ruin. One can say that these norms on the basis of which Herodotus organizes the course of historical events are rooted in rational process, or, generalization out of a limited number of particular cases. Thus it seems justifiable to describe them as reasonable beliefs.

If Herodotus leaves us in doubt as to the rational character of human history, any such doubt melts away when one comes to Thucydides. For with his partiality and respect for particular events and their empirical succession, Thucydides' aim is to reveal the permanent in events, or the rational thread in human history. He writes about 'events which happened in the past and which, *human nature being what it is,* will at some time or other and in much the same ways, be repeated in the future'. He also claims that his work was 'done to last for ever'.[1]

Human history acquired a rational character at this stage in Greek civilization because of the development in individuals of two mental traits—critical attitude, and objectivity. Both these traits are displayed by Thucydides, and in various degrees, by all subsequent historians. It is impossible to give here the full meaning of these terms. Broadly speaking they presuppose a certain mental alertness and flexibility by which one grasps the individuality of things and events, and at the same time, their general and universal character. They also presuppose a capacity for regarding things, events, persons and groups of people dispassionately, that is to say, in their formal relations with each other rather than in their relation with the observer.

The alertness of Greek intelligence is often referred to as a natural inborn quality. But this does not help the historical psychologist. For his very aim is to show how this alertness in Greek intelligence developed in the course of history and how the spirit of objectivity emerged in the course of Greek civilization.

The Greeks have left us the first model of objective writing of history. As has often been remarked, most Greek historians have observed a certain amount of impartiality even in their description of the enemy: the enemy is not necessarily bad. Gomme assigns this quality not only to the historians, but also to some of the poets concerned with the historical past. Homer and

[1] Italics mine.

even Aeschylus describes the 'Barbaroi' as full of good qualities. Such is Hector and the Trojans in general, such is Xerxes and particularly Darius, who is tolerant and just. Needless to say, Thucydides describes the Spartans in the same manner. Moreover, the same attitude of detachment and cold balance of facts is noticed when Thucydides describes the part played by himself in the battle of Amphipolis.

Thibaudet suggests that the origins of this outstanding spirit of objectivity lies in the fact that all great Greek historians were uprooted.[1] Herodotus, Thucydides, Xenophon, and Polybius lived for long periods in other countries. Gomme objects that though they were outside Athens, they lived in the Hellenic world and as such they cannot be considered outcasts and uprooted. He suggests instead that their objectivity springs from a mental rather than a sociological quality which is eminently Greek, their sense of balance and symmetry. The Greek historians naturally attributed to each event, to each personality or community, that role which was necessary for the (logical) meaning of the whole story.

Both hypotheses contain a grain of truth, but one cannot build too much on either. The spirit of objectivity is a complex mental trait and the Greeks did not confine its use to the understanding of human history; they displayed the same, or a similar attitude in science as well as in philosophy and ethics. It is, therefore, futile to link its origin with one particular socio-psychological condition of the Greek historians, their uprootedness. In fact the spirit of objectivity is one aspect, an important one, of the process of rationalization. Thus, to grasp its origin, one has to consider the formation of the Greek mind from this point of view. One has to take into account the specific balance established between individuals in Greek civilization and their environment, the formation of the reality-testing function, and most of all a series of conditionings and mental habits which determined the individual's readiness to grasp what is formal, abstract and general in things and events, rather than what is immediately dependent on his impulses and feelings. One can see in this case why one should avoid linking too closely the spirit of objectivity with the sense of form or harmony, however characteristic of the Greeks this sense may have been. The sense of form is primarily an

[1] Thibaudet, A.: *La Campagne avec Thucydide*. Paris. 1922.

aesthetic and emotional trait of the mind. In using it the individual organizes his data and facts according to one of his basic feelings or moods which happens to express, at that moment, his personality as a whole. (This leads to good patriotic and religious writing of history.) On the other hand, the aim of an historian like Thucydides is to see what is universal in events and people; he is not affected by his moods. Even in the enemy of his country he perceives what is general, i.e. his human nature. From that he derives his actions and the historical events resulting from them.

This throws light on the rationalization of human behaviour. Symptoms of this can be found as early as the sixth century. A critical attitude towards myths and religious beliefs as manifested by Heraclitus, Hecataeus, Xenophanes and others, the gradual separation of emotionality from knowledge, an attitude of control and repression towards emotional factors in behaviour are stages and aspects in the rationalization of human behaviour. Towards the mid-fifth century this process reached a peak. One of its best expressions is to be found in the Sophists' and Socrates' dismissal of the part played by emotions in the motivation of human behaviour. Emotional states such as pleasure, pain, anger, and fear, lead according to Socrates, to false judgements and thus a morally bad action. Moral conduct is based on knowledge. Hence, Socrates' effort to prevent any emotional, subjective, or unconscious factor, any custom and traditional belief from interfering with moral decisions. Moral conduct is motivated by abstract goals and norms acceptable only to the intellect and reason. Moreover, moral virtue and rational knowledge are inseparable. This obviously implies that the individual fails in his moral intention and action unless by a process of abstract knowledge he becomes aware of what is universally valid for mankind.

Two points ought to be clarified here. Firstly, the process of rationalization of the Greek mind cannot be seen as an historical continuum. Between the sixth and fourth centuries there had been temporary reactions and regressions towards mysticism. There is no need to deal with them in detail. But despite all this it is hard to deny the existence within this interval of time of a powerful, though sometimes dicontinuous tendency towards more and more rationality in the behaviour of members of the Athenian community. Secondly, and this is a more serious objection, one often says that rational thought and attitude were characteristic of a few. Regarding this point, Dodds quotes Burckhardt's saying about the nineteenth-century religion: 'Rationalism for the few and magic for the many'.[1] However, one can hardly see how this can be applied to fifth-century Athens. It is more likely that the position of Greek rationalism was this: There were few who could formulate the ideal of rational life, but there were many who aspired, and even practised in various degrees the prescriptions of such an ideal. There is hardly need to say that culturally Athens was more homogeneous than nineteenth-century societies.

THE MODEL OF HUMAN PERSONALITY

Individuation and rationalization are two formative processes of human personality. As personality, the individual shapes concomitantly his experiences in two directions; inwardly and outwardly, around an inner and an outer pole. In the first case, he becomes aware of what is 'himself', in his experiences. Thus he establishes his specific difference from his environment. In the second case, he becomes aware of what is common between himself and his environment. The mind has within itself two sets of structures or functions, individualizing and rationalizing structures. Trying to identify these structures and to name them, such as the 'self', the ego, or, on the other hand, reason, intellect, the superego, does not help very much. For there is little agreement in today's psychology as to the definition of these terms. On the other hand, this is not important for the present purpose. What is important is that, owing to these mental structures, an individual is able to adjust his experiences both to himself and to the general conditions and norms of his physical and social environment. One speaks in this case about an 'inner' and 'outer' integration which are basic aspects of human personality. The former leads to an organized awareness of the 'self', the latter, of the 'non-self'. But in spite of its polarity, personality is an integrated whole. This implies a balancing and compensating relation between the individualizing and rationalizing structures. Inner integration works hand in hand with outer integration. This gives a certain indication of the paradoxical nature of human personality. For personality is normally defined as an individual integrated *qua* individual, with his society or civilization. This paradox explains

[1] *Idem*, p. 192.

the common belief that creators, in a spiritual rather than a technical sense, possess a model personality. They have a relatively richer inner life, and at the same time, a greater facility than other people for shaping their unique experiences according to the norms and values of their civilization.

We should look more closely at the historical character of the concept of human personality. In its current use the term personality connotes the enduring shape taken by an individual's mental life as a result of his living in a given culture. This implies firstly that, with the exception of extreme pathological cases of disintegration, every individual has a personality, and secondly, that every society and culture, whatever their structural qualities, provide the individual members with adequate conditions for the formation of their personality. In this sense the concept of personality has a universal validity. An individual possesses a personality as he possesses two eyes or a nose. It is true that some recent anthropological studies have thrown certain light on the sociological relativity of the concept of personality. They have produced considerable evidence to support the idea that the personality of every individual contains a strong socio-cultural co-efficient resulting from its conformity to a behaviour pattern characteristic of a given culture. Terms such as ' basic personality ', or 'modal personality' express this socio-cultural co-efficient. But, one hastens to add, this development in the field of anthropology has by no means invalidated the general idea according to which each individual has a personality whatever his society may be. It merely specifies that the personality of a member of Balinese society is in some important respects different from that of a member of ancient Egyptian society, Nazi society, or contemporary French society.

As this study makes a new, more radical attempt to bring into relief the socio-cultural character of human behaviour, the use made here of the term personality differs in some respects from the commonly accepted one outlined above. To start with, the definition of human personality is framed in terms of two basic psychological processes, individuation and rationalization. It has, however, to be stressed that this is not a simple arbitrary methodological device. On the contrary, it seems logically compelling to assume that the emergence of an individual's personality requires two basic conditions. The first one consists of the individual's active—as opposed to reflexive—awareness of himself, which enables him to refer most of his experiences to a stable inner structure, the self, or the ego; in other words, to individualize the meaning of his experiences. The second condition consists in the individual's ability to integrate himself with the structure of his culture, more precisely, to become actively aware of himself as a member of a social whole. This enables him to give a more general meaning to, or to rationalize his experiences.

It is hoped that what has been said about the historical development of the Greek personality structure has proved sufficiently that individuation and rationalization are not only psychological, but also socio-cultural processes. This constitutes in fact the first stepping stone in the historical approach to the problem of human personality. For it implies that the process of personality formation as such is socio-culturally conditioned, more precisely, it takes place only in those psycho-cultural climates in which individuation and rationalization operate freely and equally. A few examples will illustrate the negative side of this principle. In a primitive community, in an authoritarian group, or generally speaking, in a totalitarian cultural climate, the process of individuation is either defective or non-existent. Since, in such cases, the individual cannot grow aware of himself as an individual, he cannot develop his personality. In other words, as long as an individual fails to individualize his behaviour, i.e. his perception of the world, his feelings, attitudes and ideas, because he is compelled by objective social circumstances to identify himself with the behavioural patterns of his group, he has no personality. Saying that he has a collective, or corporate personality, amounts to the same thing. The results are similar when rationalization is defective, or, when the individual cannot integrate himself *qua* individual with the order of his society, when he fails to appropriate his socio-cultural cosmos by internalizing it. It sounds almost a truism to say that to have a personality implies a certain degree of autonomy in the field of social and moral behaviour.

The first conclusion from this is that the term personality can be applied only to a specific mental structure in the individual, that which results from a free interplay and final fusion between individualizing and rationalizing processes. The second conclusion is that both individualizing and rationalizing processes depend on the social and cultural order to which the individual belongs.

This means that some social and cultural structures lead to the organization of the individual's mind in the form of personality, while others do not. Furthermore, one and the same society passes through different stages from this particular point of view: at one stage in its historical evolution, it prevents the emergence of the individual's personality, while at another stage it promotes it. It is within this specific conceptional framework that one should understand the central idea of this study, which is that the historical conditions of Greek civilization have led gradually to the organization of the individual's mind in the form of personality.

The next step is to try and demonstrate that the basic mental structure produced by the Greek civilization can be considered as the prototype of human personality. The reason for this is that this civilization had created, at least during its classical era, almost ideal conditions for a harmonious and balancing relation between the individualizing and rationalizing structures of the individual's mind. Certain details of the specific milieu in which the Greek developed his personality illustrate this fact.

To start with, in Greece, the process of individuation was neither extreme nor forceful. The individual grew aware of himself smoothly in a way which precluded any trauma. This was due mainly to, (a) the Greek climate, (b) Greek religion, and (c) the Greek social setting.

(a) Men's adjustment to a temperate Mediterranean climate is effortless. The contact with the environment, even by a simple act of perception, is on the whole charged with pleasant feelings. This primary condition of life has an important impact upon the development of the individual's mind: it reflects itself in the first place in the individual's system of self-control and inner security. Since there is little antagonism and tension between the individual's needs and the conditions of his environment, the mechanism of repression is soft and flexible. Gratification of basic needs is achieved with no particular effort. On the other hand, frustration is partial and normally compensated for. In such a climate, the individual grows conscious of himself in a positive manner, he grows towards, not away from, or against his environment: he is normally gratified and accepted.

Though having a clear awareness of his own ego, the Greek is at all times open to the non-self, to his community, to what is generally human. The barriers between his ego and the world are flexible. In this may lie the roots of his curiosity and creativity, of his vivid intelligence, and above all, of his unsurpassed ability for communication. The Greek is seldom, if ever, withdrawn into himself. This is of paramount importance for the understanding of so-called Greek individualism, a concept all too often construed according to our modern idea of this phenomenon.

The idea of a more detailed analysis of the specific connection between the Mediterranean and the Greek mental structure is a tempting one. Valuable conclusions could be drawn from a comparative study of the process of individuation in a Mediterranean climate, on the one hand, and a northern climate, on the other. The unfriendly frustrating conditions characteristic of the latter are partly responsible for the formation of strong repressing functions in the mind of the individual, as well as for the emergence of an inflated ego so characteristic of the Puritan or Prussian personality structure. However, there are strong reasons for resisting this temptation. Firstly, far too much has been said about the intimate relation between the Mediterranean climate and the Greek mind, or Greek civilization in general. Consequently it is not easy to avoid the traps laid down by fascinating theories on this matter. Secondly, in a study of historical psychology, geographical setting has little, if any relevance for the obvious reason that it is anhistorical, i.e. unchangeable in nature. As such, it cannot account for the development of the Greek personality structure in the sense meant here. Greek religion and social setting are much more relevant.

(b) The influence of Greek religion upon the process of individuation is on the whole similar to that of the Greek climate. Generally speaking, the Greek gods, like the gods of many other communities, were invested with great power over the destiny of man; they were the guardians of order and justice. Consequently human behaviour was strongly conditioned by the gods' will. One of the main features of Greek religion, however, consisted in its prominent historical character: the Greek's relation with his gods changed gradually from one based on fear, to one based on friendliness. As a result of this the cleavage between the sacred and the secular grew smaller and smaller. Thus, unlike the primitive gods (Demeter), the Olympians were more human, or at least, they were part of man's natural environment. Though more powerful, they were often chivalrous in their dealings with man:

they advised rather than commanded. Moreover, they were 'rhea zoontes' (easy living), i.e. anything but models of disciplinarian life. The main psychological consequence of this was that the moral habits of the Greek were formed in an affectionate atmosphere of permissiveness. In this lay yet another condition of a smooth and harmonious development of the individual's consciousness of himself. Though clearly aware of his own desires, aspirations or duties, the Greek did not need to develop a rigid self-control, or an 'athletic' inner structure, whatever this may be called, ego, superego, or conscience, in order to fulfil or repress them. This can be more readily understood if one bears in mind the difference from this particular point of view between the Greek and the Christian religion.

The polytheistic character of Greek religion had a particular importance for the formation of the individual's personality and especially for the emergence of his self-awareness. Nothing can illustrate this better than comparison with ancient Jewish monotheism. In the Jewish religious climate, the relation between God and man was one between an almighty father and a helpless child, between creator and creatures. This gave rise to strong opposition between good and evil in the practical and moral spheres of life, and a rigid monism in their system of values. One god, and only one represented the 'law'; he was the *way*, the *truth*, and the *life*. This unbridgeable gap between the divine and the worldly, and particularly the transcendental monism in their system of values, had considerable influence on the development of the individual's personality. They were, in the first place, sources of strong repression. In order to be able to comply with the 'law', to follow the *way*, the individual needed a rigid control and repression of parts of himself. This obviously resulted in inner tensions and conflicts, and finally in an asymmetrical development of his personality. The individual formed either a rigid and strong super ego, or a powerful, super-flexible ego.

On the other hand, Greek polytheism led to pluralistic moral standards. The Greek gods regarded man in various ways, each having his own 'law', i.e. his own system of permissiveness. What was forbidden for Zeus, was less so for Aphrodite, or Dionysos. From this specific point of view, the Greek climate of personality formation can be understood by analogy with some polyandric family patterns. The plurality and flexibility in the world of values determined soft and flexible repressing mechanisms, as well as plurivalent mental development. This should not be taken to mean that the Greek was not repressed; the emphasis should lie on the qualitative rather than quantitative aspect of his repressing mechanisms. A drive was repressed not because it was bad in itself, but because it might create unbalance and disharmony in the individual. In other words, repression was applied to 'excess' rather than to the drive as such, and the criterion of repression consisted in a need for inner balance and wholesome development rather than a rigid system of values. The concept of the organic, though often misused, expresses in the clearest way possible the characteristic of the Greek personality structure.

(c) The most important factor influencing the process of individuation is the social setting. This is mainly illustrated by the most mentally advanced Greeks, the Athenians. In the nature of the small-scale democratic society characteristic of the city state, lies one of the main causes of the moderate and harmonious character of the process of individuation. 'We live at ease . . .' says Pericles. Though being to a considerable extent a 'product of the mind', the city state did not take the individual far away from his private interests, material or spiritual. The individual discharged his public burdens in an atmosphere of ease and naturalness. Moreover, these burdens were decided upon by public deliberation and consent. All this created in the individual a soft and flexible mechanism of repression. The Athenian did not need to deny himself much in order to be a good citizen; there was little need for him to bolster up his ego feelings as a defence against his society.

Many other aspects of Greek life influenced the process of individuation in the same direction. The family atmosphere, the system of education, particularly in Athens, might be revealing. However, what has been said so far throws sufficient light on the main aspects of the climate of individuation in ancient Greece in general, and in Attica in particular. Since the individual in this community developed in an atmosphere of friendliness and security, it would be psychologically sound to believe that his awareness of himself seldom involved feelings of isolation and loneliness. Consequently, he did not feel the need to go to the extreme of rationalization, that is to say, to escape from the dread of isolation by building up a rigid social order. This leads to the second aspect of the formation of the Greek personality structure, rationalization.

Individuation and rationalization being compensatory processes, one can assume that, in Greek civilization the process of rationalization was not carried to an extreme. The rationalization of inner life provides the first example. What has been said above about the nature of repression in the members of Greek society—the Spartans making an exception—throws particular light on this. According to what is known about their everyday life, the Greeks of the classical age were flexible and tolerant towards their basic impulses and drives, as shown for instance, by their attitude towards sex. There is little doubt that they were spontaneous and natural about it, though perhaps not as spontaneous and free as they are sometimes described.[1] The same can be said about their attitudes towards their emotions and feelings. They cultivated their emotional life side by side with their intellect. Their art is the main proof of this. Though they are the fathers of rational thinking they never gave up mythical thinking. On the contrary, they used it and developed it on a parallel with rational thinking. In this respect Dodds is right when he stresses the continuous irrational element in the Greek civilization. The magic practices of the Epidaurus Temple flourished side by side with the Greek empirical and scientific medicine.

The same sense of moderation applies to the rational organization of their social life. There was nothing more foreign to the Athenians of the classical era than over-rationalization in the social field. The best proof of this lies in the fact that they were creators of a flexible society, i.e. a society with a well defined order, and at the same time 'thrown open to the world' (Pericles). Thus they created a model of open democratic society which combined harmoniously freedom with order.

To say that the way in which the Greeks rationalized nature was not excessive is rash, if not completely untrue: it is flatly contradicted by the hyperlogical universe of the Eleatics, to mention just one example. But any historical judgement conceals within it an analogy between the present and the past. As compared with the modern Europeans, the Greeks appear moderate in their rationalization of nature. To start with, the order governing the Greek universe, though clear, was more flexible than the

[1] C. T. Sletman: *Women in Antiquity.* London.

mechanical order so characteristic of the modern scientific conception of nature. It was more 'concrete', to use a term borrowed from the German romantics, that is to say, more directly derived from the nature of things. The Greek idea of order in nature is expressed by the words 'cosmos' and 'Eukosmia' which is the very opposite of the idea of mechanical order. This suggests that the Greek's need for order is primarily an aesthetic and moral one, i.e. a need for form and justice. As such it is not incompatible with the free play of his imagination. On the other hand, modern man's need for order is essentially practical, i.e. a need to act upon and change nature.

The only modern concept of order in nature which comes near to the Greek 'Eukosmia' is the romantic concept of 'panlogism', and particularly Goethe's sense of form and harmony. But one should bear in mind that it was the spirit of this period that overstimulated human practical needs for rationalization. Hegel paved the way for Marx and the communist movements of today which have extended the mechanical model of order from physical nature to human life as a whole. This is just another example which illustrates the asymmetrical mental growth of modern man. Because of his strong need for rationalization he has lost touch with the individuality of things, and above all with his own individuality.

The objection may be raised here that the present study oversimplifies the problem by stressing too much the balanced and harmonious character of the Greek personality structure. Was not this structure, at least at a certain stage in Greek history, liable to fall into the extremes of individuation and rationalization? What about the Hellenistic period with its individualistic trends, on one side, and its highly rational ideal of life epitomized by the Stoic philosophy, on the other?

In order to answer such questions, certain facts must be recognized. It is undoubtedly true that examples of extreme individualistic as well as of extreme rational behaviour are more frequently found during the Hellenistic than during the classical era. However, facts in themselves, whatever their number, do not yield knowledge; their meaning must be construed, and not their meaning *for us*, but for the Greeks. The important thing is to establish the significance of such behaviour—egocentric, or overrational—within the mental climate of the Hellenistic period.

This is precisely what the historians of this period often fail to do. In the absence of an adequate psycho-historical study, they follow the path of common sense interpretation which, sometimes, amounts to little else but retrojective interpretation. The result is that feelings, attitudes, aspirations, and ideas held by the Greeks of the Hellenistic era are interpreted not only within the conceptual framework of a contemporary historian, but often also within the frame of mind of a contemporary community. Thus, the Greeks were 'liberal', or 'totalitarian' like us, individualistic or rationalistic like us, and naturally, disoriented and ambivalent in their minds like some of us in the twentieth century. Two examples suffice to illustrate this. They are by no means untypical.

Towards the end of his comprehensive and penetrating study, Glotz describes in dramatic terms the growth of the spirit of individualism within the Hellenistic world. He produces an impressive number of facts to illustrate the gradual disintegration of institutionalized life. To start with, marriage was no longer considered a strict duty for the individual, as it was in the old days, but rather a convention, moreover, an artificial institution. The decline of conjugal fidelity is the main proof of this. Illicit unions no longer shocked the people: to the poet Amphis a concubine was preferable to a wife; Praxiteles took for mistress his model Phryne; Menander lived with Glycere, Diphilus with Gnathaena . . . In such a world dominated by a demi-monde spirit, the individual withdrew himself from his society into the realm of his own interests. The birth-rate fell step by step with an increasing desire for comfort and luxury; men avoided as much as possible the duties of fatherhood; daughters were not wanted at all; abortion and exposure were frequent and seldom punished. When he attempts to account for the cause of all this, Glotz quotes Polybius: 'People who had no children,' says Polybius, about his contemporaries, 'in place of leaving the property to their collaterals, as was formerly the custom, spent it on banquets and drinking parties.' This is, in Glotz's view, an alarming stage in the evolution of the Greek spirit of individualism which, in the Hellenistic period, 'ran riot' and 'degenerated into egoism'.

Admittedly, the examples mentioned above prove sufficiently the existence of individualistic, and even egoistic attitudes in the behaviour of the Greeks of the Hellenistic period. But the main question which the historical psychologist has to ask is this: Were the individuals of this period as isolated and as self-centred as the term 'individualism' coupled with 'egoism' suggests? Any attempt to answer such a question has to take into account the main features of the psycho-cultural climate of this period. Particular attention should be paid to the integrating forces operating within this climate. Two points, both concerning the system of beliefs, are highly significant. Firstly, during this period, there rose and developed the Stoic philosophy and movement which fostered in the individual his rational awareness of himself as a member of the human community at large, as well as his belief in his 'organic' integration with the rational order of Nature. Secondly, the same psycho-cultural climate provided a fertile ground for the revival, and the rise of a series of mystic religious beliefs—Christianity itself was greatly enhanced by it—which satisfied the individual's need for integration with a higher spiritual order in the universe. This is enough to make one grasp the true meaning of all those 'individualist' and 'egoist' forms of behaviour described by Glotz. Individualism and egoism say nothing in themselves; one has always to establish the meaning of such terms in a given psycho-historical context. Thus, the Greek of the Hellenistic period might have been often concerned with his private interests and pleasures, he might have often withdrawn from certain spheres of social life, but he never went as far in his isolation as to lose sight of the framework of the human community at large, or of the great design of the world of man. His individualism and egoism were never completely divorced from his vision of, and integration with, a larger unit than himself. Consequently, he seldom, if ever, experienced feelings of loneliness and desperation which only life in a purposeless and opaque universe can arouse. This cannot be said about the 'individualism' and 'egoism' of contemporary man.

The second example illustrates another tendentious approach to the problem of Greek personality structure. The exaggeration in this case is made in the direction of rationalization. After a detailed and enlightening account of various forms of self-representation as revealed in the extant Greek autobiographical writings, Misch reaches the conclusion that the Greeks, though achieving a highly individualistic civilization, 'were not yet fully aware of the importance and the formative power of the experiences of personal life'.[1] What they perceived in the individual was mainly his 'ethos', his 'reason', his 'character'; they remained blind to the innermost life of the individual in his uniqueness, i.e. to any kind of experience which cannot be expressed by reason. The unique character of the individual's inner life as a positive value was discovered later on by Christianity.

This is a surprising conclusion, and can be disproved easily by Greek lyric poetry, and particularly by Euripides' heroes who, as shown earlier, were obsessed with their innermost life; in their desire to be themselves, these heroes certainly went beyond 'ethos' and 'reason'. And if this is not proof enough, one need read Antipater's poem on the death of a peasant, written sometime during the second century B.C., to realize the clear insight which the Greeks had into the inner life of the individual, as well as the value they placed on it. This is the poem:

> A single heifer, and a sheep with woolly hair was the wealth of Aristides; by them he kept off hunger from his door. A wolf killed the sheep, and labour-pains the heifer, and the herd of poverty perished. And he, having twisted a noose to his neck with the string that tied round his wallet, died piteously by the cabin where there was no lowing.

Does not the poem convey clearly enough the value of an individual in his uniqueness? A candle, a single one, dies out and the whole world of man becomes darker and poorer.

GREEK, EASTERN, AND MODERN MAN

We have already seen that the type of mental development covered by the concept of personality is an historical phenomenon, which means it is conditioned by a complex of circumstances, social, cultural and psychological, characteristic of a certain community of people living within a certain period of time. The civilization of Attica was the very embodiment of this. It follows from this that the concept of personality can be applied only by analogy, or as a comparative term, to types of mental development characteristic of other cultures or other historical settings.

The idea that the mental development of the individual of

[1] Op. cit. p. 191.

eastern civilizations went in a different direction from that indicated by the concept of personality is suggested, and sometimes elaborated by many comparative historical or anthropological studies. At the very beginning of his famous 'Paideia', Jaeger feels the need to compare the Greek with the eastern type of mental development. While the former leads to the self-fulfilment of the individual, to 'a rational consciousness of selfhood', the latter leads to the negation of the individual. The idea of selfhood characteristic of Greek culture is in stark opposition to the self-abnegation of the pre-Hellenic Orient, which can be seen in the sombre majesty of Egypt's pyramids and the royal tombs and monuments of the east. The value of the individual is opposed by Jaeger to 'the oriental exultation of one God-king far above all natural proportion . . . and to the oriental suppression of the great mass of the people'.[1] The mass character of Eastern civilization is opposed to the development of human personality. The same basic idea is outlined by Misch in his often quoted work. The idea of individuality was according to him completely unknown in the pre-Hellenistic civilizations of Egypt, Babylon, Persia, and Judea. The extant autobiographical and biographical material demonstrates by its rigid adherence to a 'formalizing canon' the identity rather than the difference between various individual lives. 'In this monotonous narrative the individuals seem scarcely distinguishable from one another except in name and rank.' The individual's awareness of himself as shown by this material alternates between excessive self-glorification which is a sign of the individual's identification with a supernatural being, and self-abnegation to the degree of self-annihilation. Only in Greece did the individual gain self-awareness of himself as a rational being.

The relationship between the Greek individual and his environment is an articulate one; he differentiates himself from his environment, firstly, by a process of self-awareness, and secondly, by abstract thinking, i.e. by an attitude of disengagement. However, the Greek is never completely detached from his physical and social environment. The concept of 'nature' as an organic unity is fundamental to his attitude. The relation between the Eastern man and his environment is, on the contrary, inarticulate; he grows into, or rather merges into his environment. Hence his

[1] Op. cit. p. XIX.

basic tendency towards identification rather than towards self-emergence, or differentiation of any sort. Man's contact with things and events, his 'knowledge' of them, excludes *abstraction*; it is in fact based on his emotional identity with them.[1] By this attitude he grasps the 'sameness' and stability of his universe rather than its articulation in individualities, or its evolution in time. There is no history for Eastern man.

The relation between modern man and his environment is essentially dialectical, i.e. one of interconditioning by opposition and contradiction. The tension aroused by this kind of relation has in the long run prevented the human mind from developing within the organic unity of nature, and at the same time forced it to grow artificially according to an abstract, mechanical model. This complex idea has to be clarified.

The difference between the concepts of mental polarity and mental ambivalence is perhaps the best way of expressing the distinction between the Greek and the Western mind. While polarity connoted opposite forces within a basically integrated whole, ambivalence involves the idea of oscillation between extremes, and even that of split. One can say that the former concept applies more to the Greek personality structure, while the latter to the personality of modern man. This can be illustrated in more than one way.

On the social plane, the Greeks held together in a united structure the poles of individuality and of society. 'In the winning of his livelihood,' says Kitto, 'he was essentially individualist; in the filling of his life he was essentially "communist".'[2] A similar idea is expressed by Thucydides when he says that the Athenians regarded their bodies 'as expendable for their city's sake as though they were not their own; but each man cultivates his own intelligence, again with the view to doing something notable for his city'.[3] It was the Greeks, or, more precisely the Athenians, who created the model of the 'citizen', an individual who, according

---

[1] W. S. Haas puts this clearly: 'The Eastern man strives rigorously to prevent the discomposition of knowledge into elements of purely theoretical nature. He tries to keep it within the boundaries of man's manifest spiritual and natural needs.' Haas' distinction between the attitude of *awe* as characteristic of the Eastern mind and that of *wonder* characteristic of the Western mind is suggestive. *The Destiny of the Mind*, London. 1956. p. 50.

[2] Kitto, H. D. F.: *The Greeks*. p. 78.

[3] Op, cit, p. 51.

to Aristotle, 'knows how to govern like a freeman, and obey like a freeman'. Thus the Greeks had developed a form of social behaviour which combined harmoniously the poles of individual freedom and social order. Since the Athenian democracy this has seldom been realized again. What was polarity for the Greeks has gradually become ambivalence in Western civilization. The balance between individuality and collectivity—the terms have become 'individualism' and 'collectivism'—has so often been lost in modern times.

The Greek's feeling of proportion and his horror of ambivalence are visible also in the cultural field. Theory and facts, emotion and intellect, grow naturally from, and into each other. What a commentator of Thucydides writes is revealing in this respect: 'L'histoire—telle que la propose Thucydide—unit et fait servir l'un á l'autre deux caractères qui, semble-t-il, s'excluent: la plus grande exactitude matérielle et la plus grande généralité'. Nietzsche seizes upon the same general idea when describing the Greek mind as a harmony between Dionysian and Apollinian urges.

As has often been remarked, the Greeks had 'an innate sense of the natural'. This is a vague but nevertheless fitting description of the Greek mind. For the concept of the natural involves first of all proportionate, harmonious and wholesome development. Snell is suggestive on this point. 'The natural'—he writes—'first sees the light of day in the Homeric poems; its emergence involves an intimate connection between the life of man and the purpose of the gods. Because these gods do not use brute force and senseless terror in their contact with human life, it is free to unfold itself in accord with its modest principles.' To this one can add: In Greek civilization, particularly in its classical period, the same ease and intimacy is characteristic of man's contact with his whole environment, physical and cultural. In this lies the prime condition of the type of mental structure which has been described so far. In their historical evolution, the Greeks had created a type of mental organization which has remained as a norm and ideal for Western civilization. It is in this sense that one can say that the modern mind has its origin in Greek civilization. It must, however, be realized that the Greeks developed the type of mental structure covered by the concept of personality in a genuine and natural environment, physical, social, and spiritual. This means that their 'given' as opposed to created environment, contained the fundamental condition for man's spontaneous development as a personality. The 'given' environment in itself provided the Greek with a strong system of inner security. This explains the origins of his strong sense of the natural.

Modern man strives to achieve the same type of mental organization, and the same model of personality, under different conditions of life. His given environment, physical and spiritual (the Christian idea of God is particularly important in this respect) does not allow him a contact as friendly and intimate as that of the Greek. Therefore, if the same system of inner security and the same mental structure was to be achieved and preserved, the only solution would be to change and build up a new environment. Here lies the origin of a new attitude towards nature as a whole which has become more and more characteristic of modern man. This is both an aggressive and creative attitude. Modern man had to develop his environment artificially in order to build and maintain a mental balance which the Greek achieved spontaneously in his natural environment. He had to devise schemes and plans by which to organize his physical environment, his society and spiritual world; he had to manufacture his environment in order to get from it the same security and mental balance which the Greek found naturally. This points to the psychological origins of modern science, and particularly to the technological aspect of this. Nietzsche certainly put his finger on something when he said that at the root of such cultural development there lies an 'attitude of revenge' towards nature. It is obvious now that the Greeks did not develop science in the modern sense because they did not need to manufacture the medium of their mental development. The difference between the creativity of the Greek mind and that of the modern mind is essentially a qualitative one: the Greeks created human personality, i.e. the model of mental and spiritual order, while modern man has created the machine, i.e. the model of mechanical order.

V

THE ORIGINS OF ENGLISH
CHARACTER: I

The Great Interlude

Thus my mother was big with such fear that she brought
twins to birth, myself and fear at the same time.

THOMAS HOBBES

INTRODUCTION

THE aim of this chapter is to analyse the formative
stage of the English national character rather than to
present a full description of it. Moreover, its principal
purpose is to demonstrate a specific type of research in historical
psychology rather than to solve a psycho-social problem in all its
complexity, therefore the phenomenon of national character is
viewed from a relatively narrow angle. We are chiefly concerned
here with a type of mental organization or personality structure
more characteristic of members of the modern English community than of members of other Western European ethnic groups.
The question to be answered is: what were the main conditions,
physical, cultural and particularly, psychological, of the formative
field of this type of personality?

The basic assumptions here are, firstly that there is a modern
English character and that it can be identified in some of its main
traits from the end of the sixteenth century onwards. To go a
step further, there are grounds for saying that the mental organ-
isation of the individual of the modern Western world was created
in England. Since the beginning of the modern era the English-

man's personality structure has been in some important respects the prototype of personality structure in modern Western civilization. It is rooted in a secular system of security; a self-centred personality characteristic of individuals with a high degree of self-awareness, self-integration and self-control; a personality which emerges from, and by virtue of a psycho-social cycle leads to, an individualized social order.

This cannot be taken as a value judgement, nor is it meant to imply that other communities have not produced their own personality type. Nevertheless, in any analysis of the basic personality type in modern Western civilization, that of the modern Englishman has a relatively large significance.

THE FORMATIVE FIELD

The term 'formative field' is used here metaphorically to emphasize from the very beginning the complex, and at the same time dynamic, character of a specific psycho-historical situation. This situation comprises, broadly speaking, the totality of life conditions characteristic of the English community during the sixteenth century, and the beginning of the seventeenth century. A psycho-historical situation cannot be confined within chronological limits without obvious difficulties, so arbitrariness and artificiality are, to a certain extent, unavoidable. For the only possible way of circumscribing such a situation is to cross-section the historical process within a certain community of people, and to analyse its components as if they belonged to a static situation. This analysis will show those socio-cultural factors, as well as their inter-relations, which shed light on the formation during this period of a specific type of personality. The intention is, therefore, to present a climate of individuation rather than describe an historical period.

Why has the sixteenth century been chosen for this analysis? Because during this century, particularly in the second half, one notices most clearly the emergence of a new psycho-social climate leading to the formation of a new type of personality, which embodies the main traits of English national character throughout the modern era. For this reason this period in English history could be described as revolutionary in a psychological sense, or, as a period which saw a radical change in the organization of human personality. This does not mean that the sixteenth century can or should be isolated from its preceding or succeeding periods. Some events and circumstances which contributed to the moulding of the modern English character existed both before and after the sixteenth century. Some of these, such as 'race' and 'climate' are super-historical, or almost so. However, nothing will be said here about the racial factor, despite the fact that many existing studies of English character start from here.[1] The reason for this is that race is psychologically a confused and confusing term. As regards the part played by climate, the position is slightly different. A few remarks on this point were made in a previous chapter when dealing with the formation of the Greek mind. The northern climate, the landscapè, the quality of the soil characteristic of the British Isles, have had, directly and indirectly, very much to do with the formation of the English character. Important traits of this character, such as aesthetic sensibility as expressed in art, have rightly been connected with the specific quality of light, and with the landscape in this country.[2] Though all this has important bearings upon the formation of the typical personality of the modern Englishman, it can be only mentioned superficially in the present study. The reason is that there is no evidence of any considerable change in this factor in the period between the medieval and the early modern era of English history. Therefore, in order to account for the change in personality type noticed in the sixteenth century, truly historical factors must be considered first.

'THE SEETHING CAULDRON'

The sixteenth century can in many ways be regarded as the period in which the English community underwent a process of radical change resulting in its emergence as a modern nation. We will look now in more detail at this agitated period, paying special attention to sources of social and cultural tension, and to changes in the community's institutions, particularly (a) political, (b) economic and (c) religious, which are important to the understanding of changes in people's behaviour.

(a) Though the ascendancy which the Crown had won over the

---

[1] Ernest Barker: *National Character and the Factors in its Formation.* London.
[2] Dagobert Frey: *Englisches Wesen in der Bildenden Kunst.* Stuttgart. 1942.

Church had reached a certain definite stage by the fifteen-thirties, the conflict and tensions involved in such an important transfer of power persisted throughout the century and even outlasted it. To start with, this aroused a strong reaction from the forces associated with the old faith, on the one hand against the State, and on the other against the representatives of the new faith. The State itself became a bone of contention in the struggle between the old and the new faiths. Interferences from abroad intensified this internal strife even more.

The growth of the new Church constituted in itself a focus of social tensions. It is enough to mention the struggle for political power starting with mild attempts during the early Reformation and culminating with the violent Puritan upheaval in the first half of the seventeenth century. Most significant also is the meandering line followed by the crystallization of the reformed faith which finally led to the conflict between conformists and nonconformists. Though having an important political implication, this point will be more adequately dealt with in a later section.

The emergence of a centralized political power in sixteenth-century England produced similar effects. The early Tudors had succeeded in building up a powerful State, a young Leviathan, by putting an end to the previous feuds over the Crown. However, this was not achieved without creating new tensions. The question of who represented the State was still waiting for an answer. Thus the sixteenth century saw the growing despotism of the Crown, on the one hand, and the growing ambition and strength of the Parliaments on the other. This contest for power grew stronger and stronger until in the following century it came to a violent climax, which shook the very foundation of society.

The sixteenth century was also a period of great changes in the class structure of English society. The Tudors themselves were responsible for 'blurring the lines of social cleavage to a far greater degree than any of their predecessors'.[1] As compared with the previous century, the power of the aristocracy was considerably reduced; the role of the aristocracy was transformed from one of contestant for, to one of obedient servant to the Crown. No less a change took place at the bottom of the social pyramid. The dissolution of the old medieval order went deeper

[1] Bindoff, S. T.: *Tudor England*. Penguin. p. 26.

here than in any other section of society. The villeinage was rapidly declining, attacked both from above and from below. Henry VIII struck a powerful blow at it by dissolving the monasteries. On the other hand, one of the main demands of the rebellious peasantry of 1549 was 'that all bondmen may be free'. By the end of the century there were few such people left. This upward pressure was somehow transmitted to the middle strata of the population, to the simple 'tenants', to the 'yeomen' and particularly to the 'gentry' who throughout the century kept the Heralds very busy with their demands for patents of arms.[1]

Nothing can illustrate the measure of change in the structure of English society better than the growth of the urban population. By the middle of the century, one in every ten inhabitants of the country was a townsman. The striking growth of London—though an isolated case—is indicative of this process. Its population of about 75,000 in 1500, swelled to 200,000 in 1600, and to over 300,000 in 1634. (The population of the country throughout this period varied between 2½ and 4 million.) Though the difference between town and country was much less marked then than today, the history of sixteenth-century England as a whole would have been much different had London remained what it was at the beginning of the century.

But the development of London was only a symptom of the development of new strata in English society. The sixteenth century was the period of the spectacular rise of the middle classes. Though this was in essence an economic phenomenon and as such will be dealt with in the next section, its political consequences were such that it deeply affected the whole social order. Firstly, the prosperous businessmen, merchants and industrialists, as well as some members of the professional classes who succeeded in thrusting their way upwards, brought about a considerable change in the character of the upper classes. Secondly,

---

[1] A bitter controversy is going on at present regarding the fate of the gentry during the sixteenth and the beginning of the seventeenth century. Tawney speaks about the gentry as a rising class made up of owners of estates of middling size, while Trevor-Roper speaks about a declining gentry. However, the following positive points seem to emerge from this controversy: The decline—economic and military—of the great landlords group taking place throughout this period created a power vacuum which was filled by the prosperous gentry (Tawney), or by an embittered gentry during the seventeenth-century revolution (Trevor-Roper). The result was the same, a 'rearrangement of social forces'. See J. H. Hexter: 'Storm over the Gentry.' *Encounter*. May, 1958.

the middle men as a group had made an impact upon all other strata of society. They were responsible for the development, not only of new economic practices, but also of new ways of thinking, and, on the whole, of new patterns of behaviour. This penomenon alone would have been enough to make the sixteenth century a period of great social and political change, a period of 're-arrangement of social forces', as Tawney very suggestively puts it.[1]

(b) A mounting tide of economic change was one of the most impressive features of sixteenth-century England. Nothing can illustrate this better than the rapid increase of foreign trade. The fact that round about the middle of the century no less than half of the population was living, directly or indirectly, upon trade with the Netherlands, gives some idea of the impact economic development had on people's lives.

The economic history of the period leaves no doubt that England was far ahead on the road towards breaking away from the traditional medieval economy and entering a new economic age. The growth of commercial and financial capital contributed greatly towards the new economic development. Since foreign trade was almost exclusively based on the export of woollen cloth, a rapid development of the cloth industry was another feature of the economy of sixteenth-century England. This industry was extended from town to country; almost every village became an industrial, as well as an agricultural unit. This had a twofold consequence: On the one hand it increased the homogeneity of English society by reducing the difference between town and country. On the other hand, it created new social tensions by intensifying the competition between rural and urban manufacturers. Another consequence of the development of industry was the larger number of industrial employees, i.e. of people depending for their living on industrial establishments. Even before the middle of the century there were industrial organizations such as Abington Abbey which occupied 'daily 500 of the King's subjects of all sorts'. This, obviously, created new social roles and new forms of human relations. Even the problem of rational organization of production was somehow in the air.

The second half of the century saw another spectacular development in the economic field which contributed, in the long

[1] Tawney, H. R.: *Religion and the Rise of Capitalism*. London. 1926.

run, more than anything else to the emergence of the modern English nation. The seas were opened to English trade. It was the period of Francis Drake's exploits, when people like John Hawkins opened new markets for English-manufactured goods by exchanging them for Negro slaves from West Africa. The dawn of England as a commercial power was well in sight.

Such developments could not have taken place without a certain amount of disturbance. Some historians speak about this period as a 'crisis of growth'. Most remarkable was the effort made by England to organize herself internally as a commercial and industrial unit, and at the same time, to adjust herself to the changing demands of an international market. Naturally, this involved her in a series of difficult problems such as those arising from insufficient organization of labour and production, of over-production and unemployment. The question of prices caused particular concern. Frequent measures of currency depreciation, of 'debasements' as they were then called, which took place during the early Tudor period, are proof of this.

As one consequence of these developments the growth of the commercial spirit is particularly important. This was shown by the extent of land speculation which was a characteristic phenomenon of the period, caused primarily by the prevalent drive among prosperous members of the middle classes to invest capital in land. The dissolution of the monasteries in 1536 offered a unique opportunity for such an enterprise. On the other hand, the land-lords themselves were not slow to grasp the spirit of the age; they were only too eager to take advantage of leasing their demes-nes to capitalist farmers. The spirit of the middle classes spread rapidly upwards, as the lords were gradually turning 'asute businessmen'.[1] This sums up the most remarkable cultural phenomenon of the period, which was the expansion of the middle classes and the emergence of new values among members of the English community as a whole.

These phenomena gave English society a degree of mobility often verging on instability. The upward movement of the middle classes brought about a general change in the system of social obligations as well as a considerable growth of status anxiety on the part of almost every member of society. The same phenomena, and particularly the policy of 'enclosures' and price fluctuations,

[1] Tawney, H. R. Op. cit.

aroused insecurity and incited revolt among many members of the community, particularly among the peasants. In the words of one historian, sixteenth-century England was a 'cauldron seething with economic unrest and social passion'. On the whole, this was a period of transition in which old forms of life were crumbling and new ones were in sight. The mood of reform was the only factor which gave this period any continuity.

(c) If change was obvious in the social, political and economic spheres of life, it was even more so in the sphere of beliefs. The effect of the Reformation, which was undoubtedly the chief event of the period, amounted in the long run to a radical change in this particular field of life. Of the many causes of the Reformation the following are usually mentioned: the growth of formalism and superstition within the old Church, the corruption of the clergy, the growing ambition of the English monarchy for absolute power, a mounting feeling of nationalism, and finally the most complex of all, the rising middle classes. Admittedly, all this formed part of the historical background of the Reformation. But something which lay nearer than any of the above factors to the origins of the English Reformation was the decline of faith among most members of the English community of the time; the decline of religious faith in general, not merely of a particular faith expressed by the dogma of the old Church. This state of mind is vividly evoked by an historian commenting upon the reaction of the people to the Henrician Reformation: 'The faith which had once moved mountains had been corrupted by the life of the plains: a clergy which had growing difficulty in leading the flock looked in vain for leadership from dignitaries who set their dignity before their duty, and their duty to Caesar before their duty to God; and a Church which had ceased to stand unmovable upon the rock of principle was betrayed among the shifting sands of a delusive expediency. The trumpet gave an uncertain sound and there were few who prepared themselves for the battle.'[1] Opinions about historical details of this situation may vary, but the fundamental fact remains that faith had subsided as a result of a long conflict within the individual between aspirations and possibilities aroused by newly developed conditions of life, on one side, and old values and patterns of behaviour, on the other.

The Continental Reformers, Luther and Calvin in particular,

[1] Bindoff, S. T. Op. cit. p. 99.

destroyed and built up at the same time; a stronger and purer faith was their avowed goal. There was nothing comparable to this in England. Here the first Reformers were primarily concerned with political and social 'reforms'. Whether out of personal or general political reasons, Henry VIII's first aim was to promote the Crown to the supreme headship both of the State and of the Church, and to reorganize society in such a manner as to eliminate as much as possible the influence of the latter. The theological element of his Reformation was conspicuous by its absence. As Luther said, Henry VIII needed an article of faith for himself. In England the new faith was slow in crystallizing. The first Reformers remained within the old faith either out of expediency, or because they had no fresh religious need to satisfy. Moreover, the manifestation of the new faith was discouraged not because it was against the old faith, but rather because it sapped at the foundation of national unity by its fanatical and extremist character. This political and social—therefore secular—purpose persisted in various forms throughout the English Reformation. In their religious policy the Tudors endeavoured to create a *via media* in religion by relying on moderate elements from both sides, the old and the new faith. In other words, they relied on people who were little, if at all, inclined to put the salvation of their souls above other matters regarding their own and their community's life. Thus, they cultivated neutrality, the sense of compromise and tolerance, rather than fanatic faith in the field of religion.

It would, however, be inadequate to describe the weakening of faith which contributed to the rise of the Reformation only in terms of moderation and common sense. The Reformation became, to a considerable extent, an expression of dislike for, and even hostility towards things religious for many members of the English community. Thus, freedom from religious dogmas and values remained as one of the permanent aims of the Reformation. This is normally attributed to a more or less perennial English dislike of formalism and mysticism, to a mounting feeling of nationalism, and particularly to the practical sense of the middle classes, who had for a long time been frustrated in their economic persuasions by the irrational character of religious beliefs and dogmas. But, whatever its causes, the fact remains that, during certain stages of the Reformation, the tide of revolt against the old Church ran so high as to make one suspect that it was 'irreligion' which guided the people's mind rather than a passionate search for salvation. This was epitomized by the second phase of the Edwardian Reformation with its violent attack on clericalism and its repudiation of some basic religious values. It was this kind of attitude which led gradually to a sort of man-made religion, i.e. to a religious faith and doctrine which could be adapted to the values of man's worldly life.

The sixteenth century in England was therefore a period of transition in the sphere of religious beliefs, and even on these grounds only it could be described as an interregnum period. This can be ascribed particularly to the time interval between the dissolution of the old faith and the complete crystallization of the new one, which was considerably longer in England than in most other countries which broke away from the Roman faith.

This period of interlude has psycho-historical significance. A 'neutral religious consciousness' and 'hostility to religious values' are terms which cover only one aspect of it. If not seen in context, such terms can be misleading for they may give the impression that the people of the period were entirely ready to dispense with religious beliefs in their adjustment to the world. There was, however, another aspect which was in many ways opposed to the previous one, and which becomes apparent only if one takes into account the fundamental historical fact that the people of the period were in the process of transition between two systems of religious belief. Their situation must have been very near what one can describe as a 'disoriented faith'. The sources of their faith were, therefore, not dried up but rather blocked by lack of direction in a world of unsettled values. On the psychological level, the situation was characterized by an outburst of primary mental energy—instincts and wishes—which escaped the moulding and repressing influence of traditional values and patterns of behaviour. People passed through a period of reorientation of their mental structure, and particularly of their conscience. It would perhaps be appropriate in this case to speak about a period of interlude in the human conscience in the sense that the conscience articulated by the old world of values was weak while the new was not yet framed. Thus, the period was one of mental freedom verging on inner anarchy.

The results of this psycho-historical situation created by a shift in the system of beliefs will be discussed in some detail at a later stage. One of its main symptoms was the dynamic rhythm and the sense of adventure characteristic of the Tudor period in general. The growth of imagination and the sense of greatness which made the Elizabethan period unique in the history of England were also results of this freed mental energy. It is worth noting that this period is normally referred to as a period of 'spontaneity', of 'youth' of 'merry England'. But the same psycho-historical situation manifested itself as confusion, ambiguity, and contradiction in the world of values. Virtues and greatness were not clearly defined; virtues and vices were separated only by a thin wall. In this lies the most important symptom of the inner anarchy. Lacking a stable world of values, many individuals were inclined to take their own instincts and passions as the only guiding standards of behaviour. It is commonly accepted that the Reformation was followed by a wave of wickedness. Once the outward expression of conscience, that is to say, the dogmas of the old faith and the spiritual power of the priest, was weakened, the unrestrained human instincts came freely into the open. People living during the period of interlude could not help becoming increasingly attracted by new goals in life which were incompatible with their religious conscience. Not only were they becoming more and more prepared to admit that their minds were often activated by primitive egoistic impulses, but also that this should be so. Thus, a new way of evaluating human feelings and action was dawning. It is significant to note that while dealing with 'heretics' Elizabeth constantly proclaimed that 'she had punished and would continue to punish only those whose actions threatened the State'. It was round about this time that the principle of 'reason of State' was coined and began to be applied. 'Reason of State' involved motives and values not included in the traditional religious conscience. However, one cannot say that complete adherence to secular values was a characteristic of the period of interlude. What was characteristic was an ethical inconsistency, and an oscillation between the extremes of religious and secular morality. It was this wavering and search for guidance in life that led to the articulation of the new faith in Puritanism. As will be shown, Puritanism was both an extreme reaction to the state of disorientation, and an attempt to establish a new balance between sacred and secular values.

To go back to the general description of the period, we have said so far that culturally the sixteenth century was a period of interregnum in the sense that the people's detachment from the traditional ideas and beliefs was growing so fast that their new ideas and beliefs were neither clear nor strong enough to fill the gap.

In its main features the cultural climate of the sixteenth century is typical of most periods of rapid social and cultural change.

THE PUZZLE OF LIFE

Perhaps the most striking trend of this cultural climate consisted in an unusually intense concern with what a philosopher or theologian might call the ultimate meaning of life. Psychologically this can be described as the need of an individual or a group of individuals for a stable frame of reference for their behaviour. At the cultural level, this need was manifested by a specific inclination in the people of the sixteenth century to explore the foundations of their beliefs and assumptions, to question them, and if possible to re-formulate them. This they did either by means of conceptual analysis or by the means of their emotional experiences, or by both. There is no lack of evidence for this. We have only to look at the fate of the basic beliefs and assumptions regarding the nature of the universe. The influence of Copernicus upon this period can easily be underestimated. For, though it is generally accepted that 'the educated Elizabethan had plenty of textbooks in the vernacular, instructing him in the Copernican astronomy', it is, nevertheless, often said that this had relatively small effect on the sixteenth-century picture of the world, which, according to the most popular works of cosmology or literary fiction, continued to be medieval in its main traits.[1] But from a psychological point of view the relationship between the Copernican theory and the culturally articulated picture of the world prevailing in the sixteenth century is of secondary importance. It is the relationship of this theory with the deeper strata of the mind that matters most. From this point of view the existence of a considerable number of textbooks dealing with this matter is in itself a proof of the readiness, conscious or unconscious, of sixteenth-century people to question their fundamental beliefs and

[1] E. M. W. Tillyard: *The Elizabethan World Picture*. London. 1943. p. 6.

assumptions about the structure of the universe. And it is this mental readiness that constitutes a primary historical factor, for it contributed in the long run, not only to the general acceptance of a specific theory of the physical universe, but to the reorientation of human life as a whole. Few people today would not agree that the significance and importance of atomic physics for twentieth-century man cannot be confined to the actual influence these discoveries had upon the cosmological theories of this period. It would, therefore, be equally wrong to estimate the significance of the Copernican theory for the sixteenth-century Englishman only, or mainly from the direct knowledge of this theory, or from its influence on cultural expression.

In no other field was the eagerness of the sixteenth-century man to get down to fundamentals greater than in the field of religion and ethics. The above remarks on the development of the Reformation indicated clearly that the sixteenth century, and particularly its second half, was a laboratory in the field of religious experience. This phenomenon had a strong influence on the society and culture of the period. Any vacillation and confusion in this field was liable to affect directly all the main spheres of social life. This is illustrated by the amount of disorganization in schools produced by secularization and by frequent changes of catechism as the wind blew towards Catholicism or towards the Reformation.[1] A laborious effort was being made towards establishing a new relation between church and society, church and individual, as well as between church and state.

The nature of the individual's relation with his society was also subjected to this attitude of inquiry. The conflict between the canon and civil law was a good example of this; it was vitally important to people of this period to decide which of the two lay at the basis of their social behaviour. It was during this period that the limits and shortcomings of corporate morality were clearly revealed. As has often been pointed out, one reason for this was the rise of the middle classes, whose economic practices could no longer be carried out within the framework of the traditional morality based on the concepts of brotherhood and charity.

[1] This point is discussed in A. Leach: *English Grammar Schools at the Reformation.* London. 1895, and F. Watson: *The English Grammar Schools to* 1600. Cambridge. 1908.

At the beginning, the Reformers themselves oscillated considerably in their ethical attitudes; they tried to balance the norms of commercial practice with those of charity, or the individual's drive towards prosperity with his social obligations. There was therefore a tendency on the part of many individuals and groups of the period to forge for themselves a new social consciousness.

A considerable amount of vacillation was apparent in the field of scientific knowledge—if this term could be applied here. There was a 'strange world of science', as L. Wright very accurately puts it; a world which contained enough room for Bacon and Harvey, as well as for Antonio da Torquemada; a world which showed a strong interest in applied science dealing with 'the profitable art of gardening', or with the utilization of coal, and at the same time, trying very hard to discover 'how to turn water into wine'.[1] The confusion resulting from the swing between a naturalistic and a religious mystic approach to nature must have been considerable.

The cultural climate of the interregnum period discloses a deep spiritual crisis in the life of the community. It was in fact a 'split' culture, and this was manifested primarily in the tendency of the people of the period to swing to two extremes with regard to their general attitudes and values. There is much truth in the opinion according to which the central motive of this many-sided process had found its final expression in the clash between religious and secular ethics. 'An increased distance' between the transcendental and the imminent world was certainly a specific trait of the interregnum period, to use in a slightly different context one of Max Weber's well-known expressions. It ought, however, to be pointed out that 'increased distance' meant, at least during this period, 'increased tension', i.e. strong inner conflicts. Thus, a genuine need for a stronger and purer religious faith grew side by side with an increasing adherence to more secular values. While the Puritan revolution was in full swing, the clown Tarleton thought fit to amuse his audience by advising them to pull down the church and to set up the ale-house. It is likely that during this period religion had an ambivalent meaning; a negative one derived from the old traditional church, and a positive one, attached to a new kind of faith which at the time was

[1] Wright, L. B.: *Middle Class Culture in Elizabethan England.* Univ. of North Carolina. 1935.

not fully crystallized. The mind of the people was swayed between two opposite poles.

A split feeling had crept into more than one aspect of the sixteenth-century cultural climate. An all-or-none attitude was noticeable towards the State, the community, authority, conformity, and freedom. In a quick succession, the State, for instance meant either an 'organism', 'our Jerusalem', or a matter of convenience for individuals; a Saviour or a monster. The point might be raised that these two views were held by different people, and that they indicated merely a clash between two social groups or two ideological trends. But on the other hand, the change in attitude was too quick, and the position taken too radical not to make one suspect the presence in many members of the community of a considerable amount of ambivalent feeling, which they alleviated by identifying themselves with one of the extremes, or in some cases with both extremes in turn. It is this mental polarity which is responsible for the black and white picture of the cultural world as well as for the individual's swing between two extreme attitudes towards the basic problems of life. The degree reached by this mental and cultural polarity is shown by the swift change in the concept of human nature which took place towards the beginning of the seventeenth century. In opposition to the traditional concept according to which 'nature' meant charity and brotherhood, that is to say, restraint upon self-interest, in the seventeenth century, 'human nature had come to connote not divine ordinance but human appetites.'[1] It ought to be emphasized again that this was not a simple theoretical contradiction which was solved by the passing of time, but rather a polarity of attitudes towards human nature. The basic elements which were closely integrated in the structure of western medieval culture had, during this period, fallen apart. Thus, what was previously a homogeneous and almost monolithic structure became during this period a split, or at any rate bipolar, structure. Typical of this was the relationship between state and individual as expressed by Hobbes. One term is the absolute negative of the other. This stage is of paramount importance for the development of modern culture and type of personality. For, as opposed to the monolithic character of medieval culture, modern culture contains a double set of values. Consequently, the basic process in the

[1] Tawney, H. R. Op. cit. p. 180.

individual's adjustment to his environment is not one of identification, but one of choice, deliberation, and balancing between contradictory aspects of this world. Integration becomes more and more dependent on the individual's conscious effort.

What Lucien Febvre considers as the most general characteristic of the French sixteenth century can, on the whole, be applied to the English sixteenth century. Febvre attacks both the view that the sixteenth century belongs to the modern rationalist era, and the view that it still lingered in the trail of the Middle Ages. Sixteenth-century culture was a culture of transition between the medieval world of firm faith and the modern world of critical mind. Though overstressing the lack of rationality in people of the sixteenth century, Febvre is right when he calls the mentality of this period essentially religious: it was '*Un siècle qui veut croire*' he writes.[1] By this he had summed up perfectly one of the main features of mental orientation in sixteenth-century France, and one which was even more in evidence in England. This can be explained as follows.

The approach of sixteenth-century man to his environment was based on faith. In this respect he was still inheritor of the Middle Ages. Consequently, he was inclined to look upon any new doctrine, any new philosophy, and any new form of knowledge with the eagerness of a believer. Since Christianity was still the centre of his beliefs he persisted in his effort to organize all other beliefs round it. But, for reasons which are obvious, the chief being the rapid rate of change in the sixteenth-century world, he could not for long be successful in this enterprise. There resulted from this two attitudes of mind which could be considered as two characteristic mechanisms of adjustment to the sixteenth-century world, and to a great extent, to any period of crisis. The first attitude can be called, after Febvre, though not entirely following his use of this concept, the Lucianic attitude. This consists in the individual's ability and inclination to accept other fundamental beliefs side by side with his Christian faith, and consequently to try to see the world on the assumption of a plurality of beliefs. On the whole, Lucianism implies a certain amount of tolerance and even cynicism, though not necessarily a rational attitude towards religion and towards the world. Now, it is true that such an attitude can be detected before the sixteenth century on the

[1] Op. cit. p. 489.

Continent and in England. Erasmus is a famous example. But it was during this period that it reached a peak. This had much to do with the rise of the religious Reformation.[1]

The second attitude formed in the sixteenth-century cultural climate is closely related to what has previously been described as 'disoriented faith'. Febvre speaks of a *'oui dire'* attitude as characteristic of the period. He seeks to explain by this the credulity rather than scepticism of the people at this time. This credulity was in itself a sign of the weakening of the central faith. Hence their need to search in more than one direction for a central point in their beliefs. This was a period of a strange combination of attitudes and beliefs, Christianity on the one side, and the revival not only of ancient philosophy, but of the classical cult of the hero, on the other. There was a general inclination to believe in any confused theory and doctrine. Even the exceptional thirst for knowledge which Louis Wright, among others, considers a characteristic of the rising middle classes in England, was rooted in the same need for a central point of reference.

Febvre's remarks throw considerable light on the mental structure of sixteenth-century man. He had on the whole a fluid and almost shapeless mind. Ideas, beliefs, doctrines, and theories abounded, but they could not be organized into a whole. This was mainly because of the lack both of a strong central faith, and of a rigorous and consistent method of thinking. The people of the period were coming out of the medieval world of faith without possessing a rational, critical mind by which to regulate their contact with the world; they were leaving a monolithic world, being not yet prepared for a pluralist one. This takes us back to the central idea of this section, the impact which the lack of a stable frame of reference had upon the individual's mind. Since the characteristic personality type of the modern English community has been formed by a reaction to this state of affairs, it is important to look more closely at its psychological implications.

---

[1] According to H. Berr 'Lucian', 'Lucianist', or 'Lucianique' are words which were applied towards the mid-sixteenth century *'à tous ceux qui pensaient un peu hors série, ou on s'en donnaient des aires'*. Quote from: *Psychologie Collective et Raison Individuelle,* introducing Febvre's book, p. xix. L. Febvre characterizes such an attitude in paradoxical terms *'une sorte de opportunisme timide et audacieux'*, which is characteristic of the adjustment to a period *'dominée par des religions rivalles mais également officicelles'*. p. 360.

THE DISSOCIALIZED MIND

The impact of the cultural climate of interregnum upon the human mind showed itself in a low degree of unity in the structure of human personality. The concept of a socio-psychological cycle is relevant here. What should, in order of determination, be considered first, the lack of unity in human personality, or the critical state of the cultural climate? This is a difficult problem which cannot be dealt with here. However, it is important to note that a classical concept of causality does not fit well in this context. The two levels of human life condition each other.

It is often said that medieval man had an integrated personality structure because he lived in a relatively stable, well organized world. If this is so, when did disintegration start, what were its forms of manifestation, and what degree had it reached by the ·immediately post-medieval period?

That human nature is unstable and inconsistent was a most common belief, and a cause for complaint among people of the sixteenth century. One can easily object that this kind of belief and complaint are common to many other periods. It would, however, be wrong to leave the whole matter here, without at least trying to indicate how strongly motivated were these beliefs in individuals belonging to English sixteenth-century culture. Such beliefs were roused by the individual's increasing awareness of the gap and contradiction between 'real' and 'ideal' behaviour as represented by Christian ethics. They were aroused and accentuated by his daily awareness of the clashes and struggles in the social field of his time: the ideals pursued by some social groups were not those pursued by others. The same beliefs could have come from the clash between fundamental creeds and doctrines particularly after the advent of the Reformation. However, lack of united social purpose is only a general symptom of the lack of personality integration characteristic of this period; it does not indicate the depth reached by this process. The opinion of human nature of a social psychologist of the period, a moralist who had considerable influence upon the people of his time might be indicative if not entirely convincing: 'No man,' he says, 'continues to wish and design the same thing two days together ... Thus we shift our character each moment and act as thousand several parts.' And again: 'Most part of our actions do not arise from steady thought but are sudden starts and sallies, the effects of accident and impulse, and look like shreds of several stuffs patched up, and sewed together.'[1] We are told that the main reason for this lies in the fact that human nature is influenced by 'the motion of time and seasons'. Two ideas are contained in this statement: a particular awareness of time and change and the awareness that human nature is conditioned by the empirical rather than by the eternal order of the universe. In a different order of ideas, the individual's moods are stronger than his reason.

Some attempts made to construct what might be called the 'Elizabethan Psychology' fully confirm the ideas mentioned above. Ruth Anderson, for instance, stresses the general inclination of the Elizabethan writers to represent life as 'a series of conflicting purposes and inexplicable actions'. Thus, in contrast with modern psychology which 'finds unity in human behaviour, Elizabethan thinking emphasizes variability and even inconsistency in conduct'[2] In conclusion she goes as far as to say: 'the Elizabethan did not search for unity in human behaviour'— probably because he knew that it was not there.

The revolutionary ideas about human nature formulated during this period illustrate this in a striking way. It was the period of Machiavelli—sometimes called the father of modern psychology —for whom human nature, and therefore, the ultimate source of human conduct consisted of primitive impulses and passions. For an outstanding writer to think in terms like these suggests a degree of disintegration of human personality verging upon anarchy. For, in such a conception of man, nothing can be taken for granted except the individual's striving towards the gratification of his impulses and passions. Society, morality, principles, and all that defines human conscience are for such an individual simply super-structures. Moreover, the man described by Machiavelli makes intellect and will the allies of his instincts rather than of his conscience. Lord Acton points to this very phenomenon when he describes the implication of Machiavelli's doctrine for the political practice of his time: 'It appeared to him' (Machiavelli)—Lord Acton writes—'that the most vexatious obstacle to intellect is conscience, and the vigorous use of

---

[1] Pierre Charron: *De la Sagesse*. Bordeaux. Quoted by Ruth L. Anderson: *Elizabethan Psychology and Shakespeare's Plays*. University of Iowa, Studies. Humanistic Studies. Vol. III, No. 4. 1927.   [2] Op. cit. pp. 174 and 175.

statecraft necessary for the success of difficult schemes would never be made if governments allow themselves to be hampered by the precepts of the copy-book.'[1]

Since 'modern psychology' has been mentioned in this context, one is tempted to use a more modern vocabulary for the description of this state of affairs. The individuals to whom such a conception refers, tended to see life and to adjust themselves in terms of their 'id', which is a primitive structure of the mind made of instinctual drives. Their conscience had been weakened as a result both of strong conflicts with the 'id', and of a series of inconsistencies in the value system of their culture. To speak about personality integration in such circumstances is difficult, if not impossible, for the 'id' is anarchic in itself. The organization and stability of human personality results mainly from the repression and moulding of the 'id' by a later developed structure of the mind which can be called the 'superego', 'internalized society', or simply conscience. The man described by Machiavelli was the man of the interregnum period in whom the structure formed by the norms of traditional religious society was in the process of dissolution, while no other norms were internalized. The result was that his behaviour was predominantly determined by the forces of the 'id', by egotistic pleasure, by need for personal power, or simply need for aggression. Lord Acton realized the psychological connection between Machiavelli's teachings and the increase in the absolute power of the sixteenth-century monarchs when he wrote: 'Machiavelli's teachings gave an immense impulse to absolutism by slicing the consciences of very religious kings, and made the good and the bad very much alike. Charles V offered 5,000 crowns for the murder of an enemy. Ferdinand I, and Ferdinand II, and Louis XIII, each caused his most powerful subjects to be treacherously dispatched. Elizabeth and Mary Stuart tried to do the same to each other.'[2] All this discloses 'a studied philosophy of crime', that is to say, the morally anarchic 'id' associated to itself the intellect and the will.[3]

Admittedly, Machiavelli represents an extreme example more characteristic of some Italian communities of the Renaissance.

---

[1] *The History of Freedom*. Macmillan Ltd. 1907. p. 40.

[2] Idem. p. 41.

[3] The reader is asked to notice that the terms 'id' and 'super-ego', as used in this study have a broader meaning than that attributed to them by Freud.

On the other hand, it is not easy to establish the influence of his conception upon English sixteenth-century thought. Hobbes who obviously moved in the same direction in his conception of man, does not acknowledge any such influence. But in this case, the question of ideological 'confluence' is more relevant than that of a direct ideological influence. Indeed, a series of phenomena of sixteenth-century and the early seventeenth-century England suggest the same anarchic state of human personality.

To start with, the period as a whole gives the impression of a culture based on 'pathos' as opposed to 'ethos'. Though there is a considerable amount of disagreement as to the use of these terms, from the point of view of social psychology, this has a specific implication. In a culture based on pathos, the individual's drives, feelings and values can no longer conform with the existing canons of behaviour of his society. Culturally this is a form-free period, a period lying between a dying and a rising style. Psychologically, this is a period in which the individual's behaviour undergoes a process of 'dissocialization'. As a result of this the individual's drives and feelings lose their purpose and meaning, and a great deal of their shape. The individual experiences his drives and feelings in a form-free climate; hence the destructive and anarchic character of such experience. One or two examples will illustrate this.

There are grounds for believing that the Elizabethans were acutely aware of the destructive character of love. Comments such as the following were not untypical: 'Love is a little better than mere madness,' or, '. . . the beginning, middle, and end of love is nought else but sorrow, vexation, agony, torment, irksomness.' Love was considered as a 'torture', or a 'plague' says R. Anderson, from whom the above quotations were taken.[1]

Though the temptation is strong, it would be inaccurate, if not completely wrong, to explain this attitude in terms of religious asceticism only. Behind it lies in fact an increased awareness in the individual that the feeling of love arouses anxiety verging on the fear of self-destruction. This is certainly closely related to the 'dissocialization' of behaviour which has just been mentioned. As a result of this, the individual's drives and passions escape the control and the moulding influence of social conventions; the individual's 'internalized society' no longer functions

[1] Op. cit. pp. 130 and 129.

in this sphere of life. In such mental condition lies the origin of romantic love, a kind of emotional experience which owing to its intensity causes a conflict between the individual and his society. In other words, it causes the breakdown of the integrating structures of his personality. The feeling of death is often associated with such a passion.

It is not intended here to prove that the sixteenth century means the beginning of romantic love in English society.[1] However, in the light of what has just been said about the process of dissocialization, it would be reasonable to assume that this was a period in which the formation of such an attitude was not only possible but even probable. After all, this was the period in which *Romeo and Juliet* was created.

A curious psycho-social phenomenon may throw considerable light on disintegration of human personality during that period. There are grounds for suspecting a certain confusion and even inversion of two basic traits of human personality, masculinity and femininity. Unmistakable signs of this can be found in two pamphlets published towards the beginning of the seventeenth century, namely: (a) *Hic Mulier: Or the Man Woman: Being a Medicine to cure the cottish Desease of Staggers in the Masculine-Femenines of our Time;* and (b) *Haec Man, or the Womanish Man.*

[1] Some speak of a much earlier period in which such an attitude could be detected. (Paston Family.) A great deal depends, of course, on the definition of such an attitude. Generally speaking an investigation into the connection between a romantic attitude to love and 'dissocialization' can be rewarding from the point of view of social psychology. As this attitude has come to be known in Western Europe it would be right to assume that it is rooted in a process of dissocialization, the result of which being that the individual takes his primitive self as the only point of reference of his feeling towards a member of the opposite sex. Thus, the rapid growth of a romantic attitude to love which took place towards the beginning of the last century, went hand in hand with a revolt against the social institutions concerned with this feeling, such as marriage and family, as well as against the whole social order. In fact this was part of an anarchic psycho-social climate. This implies, of course, anarchic personality structure, and anarchist social movements. It is enough to mention in this respect names such as George Sand, Alfred de Musset, Bakunin, Lord Bryon, and the groups to which they belonged. On the other hand, well-integrated societies which produce a strong socialization of the individual's behaviour discourage and even destroy romantic attitudes to love. In such cases the personal meaning of love is lost: its emotional contents are confined to its social functions. Typical examples of this are the Soviet and medieval societies. It is interesting to note that, according to Werner Sombart, the beginning of romantic love was as early as the thirteenth century in Italy. He refers to the secularization of love in somehow similar terms to those used here with reference to 'dissocialized love'. (See W. Sombart: *Luxus und Kapitalismus*. Leipzig. 1923.)

The first is an indictment of the masculine tendencies in women's dresses, and manners, such as the wearing of men's hats, going to the barber, short hair, face painting, extravagances in dress. The second defends woman's right to personal freedom, and attacks feminine trends in man's behaviour. 'The Womanish Man is a fop dressed in new-fangled garments.'[1] Obviously, this tendency towards the confusion and inversion of the two basic 'roles' cannot but be a result of the great social and cultural 'rearrangements' of the time. This must, in its turn, have caused a considerable amount of dislocation and reversal within the structure of human personality.[2]

The most comprehensive proof of the low degree of personality integration can be obtained from psychological analysis of the main characters created by dramatists of the period. Unfortunately, the so-called 'content analysis' which has proved to be a useful method of investigation into national character, cannot so easily be applied here. The difficulty is a twofold one: the dramatic output of the period under consideration was unusually high; it is reckoned that the number of plays produced between 1557 and 1642 exceeded two thousand. Of these only one quarter is extant. Secondly, though a considerable amount about public taste during the Elizabethan period is known, it is still hard to assess the degree of popularity enjoyed by various plays or playwrights. However, a study of the drama of the period is by no means unrewarding, and there is no better dramatist to start with than Shakespeare.

A great part, perhaps the most characteristic part, of Shakespearian drama can be viewed in terms of inner disintegration of the human mind. The sources of tragedy in human life are closely related to, or are better revealed by the unsuccessful effort made by outstanding individuals to act, or to live as harmonious personalities, that is to say, to live according to a general purpose, which is enlightened by a clear reason, executed by a strong will, and, to complete the Elizabethan picture of an harmonious mind, assented to by a sensitive heart. Ruth Anderson describes the

---

[1] Quote from L. Wright. Op. cit. pp. 494, 495.

[2] Though inequality of the sexes was characteristic of Tudor England, an increasing interest in women's education as well as an increasing number of independent women traders were obvious trends towards a change in the status of woman. In the second half of the sixteenth century there existed a kind of feminist movement.

common trait of the principal Shakespearian heroes as disharmony of the mind. This condition is created either by 'one-
sidedness', i.e. the omnipotence of one impulse or passion, or by
'conflict' between the main faculties of the mind. Thus Anthony's
tragic condition is determined by his inclination to 'make his will
lord of his reason'; Coriolanus' tragedy comes, on the other hand,
from the fact that 'his heart is his mouth', i.e. his emotions are
stronger than his reason. The list of the tragic victims of the
heart is impressive: Othello is overcome by jealousy, Romeo by
love, Lear by vanity; Tarquin confesses: 'Affection is my complaint.' And finally, even Hamlet joins in for he . . . 'is a noble and
vigorous character, but he possesses a tragic weakness, the
tendency of the heart and the imagination to blind the intellect.'[1]

Needless to say, this idea contains little if any novelty, and
indeed little of what has not been expressed directly or by implication in some classical views on the nature of the tragic hero,
either the Aristotelian concept of 'hamartia' or the Hegelian
concept of one-sided perfection, i.e. perfection without wholeness.
But the sources of mental disharmony in Shakespeare's heroes,
and their consequent tragic condition are deeper than any of these
views, which are based on the rationalistic interpretation of the
human mind, indicate. Shakespeare might have talked the language of rationalistic psychology, according to which any inner
conflict takes place at a conscious level as a conflict between
faculties or between ideas, but his insight into the human mind
certainly went deeper than this. And in this lies the great relevance
of his heroes to the human condition of his time. One can see in
some of his principal heroes the prototype of modern man at the
most critical stage in the formation of his personality, i.e. a man in
search of a new soul. This constitutes, in a way, the beginning of a
drama which has never ended for the individual living in the
modern era.

The man described above is the man *who cannot integrate*; he
cannot integrate either because he does not know his mind, or because he does not know the mind of others, i.e. he does not know
his society, or, if he knows, his knowledge is too wide and too
ambiguous. This explains two main traits in the mental structure
of this man: firstly, his exaggerated need to change, to hesitate, to
deliberate and choose, secondly his strong inclination to fall

[1] Op. cit, p. 159.

either into the extreme of blindly following one impulse or passion, or into the extreme of reflection and doubt.[1]

In the light of this, Hamlet is neither a 'noble' nor a 'vigorous' character, though he has many noble as well as vigorous passions. He has, in fact, too many and too divergent passions and ideas, and in this lies the root of his tragic condition. If he has a character this can only paradoxically be defined as the character of a man who 'cannot make up his mind'. Though he has a vivid and far-reaching intellect and a deep and varied emotionality, just because of this mental richness, his personality is ridden by insoluble self-absorbing conflicts. To say that this psychological situation accounts fully for his introspection, for his wavering, for his depression, and finally for his desperate lack of purpose, is to say little more than the obvious. The main point is to know how this psychological situation was created. A purely psychological or psycho-biological explanation is not enough. According to a well-known opinion, Hamlet's character was determined by his early eroticism; owing to early circumstances in his life he remained with ambivalent feeling towards his parents. Here lies the root of his inner conflicts and his lack of determination. The main fault of such an explanation is that it is, in this particular case, far too speculative. The little that is known about the cultural climate in which the character of Hamlet was created exceeds by far what is known about his childhood, therefore Hamlet's mental condition can more adequately be described in psycho-cultural terms.[2] Thus, the basic trait of his personality derives from the fact that he lived and formed his personality in a cultural climate of conflicting social and moral ideas. In a penetrating study of Hamlet's character, Peter Alexander expresses this fundamental truth very clearly. In his opinion Hamlet embodies, or tries to embody in himself, not less than three ideals of man: the soldierly ideal belonging to the bygone era of his father; the

[1] The point should, however, be stressed that Shakespeare describes modern man at a very early stage in his development, i.e. before he formed special structures in his mind which would enable him to adjust to a changeable world or which would orient his deliberation and choice in a varied and pluralistic world. This explains even more his incapacity to integrate.

[2] Admittedly, the expression 'the cultural climate in which the character of Hamlet was created' is 'ambiguous'. It refers to the cultural climate of the twelfth century in Denmark and at the same time to the mental climate in which Shakespeare created such a character. Though from the genetic point of view the latter climate is more important, for obvious reasons the above can be applied to both climates.

scholarly ideal belonging to his generation, and the ideal of honesty and justice. This is an explosive mixture. Developing this point, Alexander writes: 'To what may be called *the instinctive wisdom of antiquity and her heroic passions*, represented so impressively by Hamlet's father Shakespeare has united the *meditative wisdom of later ages* in Hamlet himself.[1] From here he goes straight to the core of the matter: '. . . the idea of drama'—he writes—'comes from the impact of new circumstances upon the old forms of feelings and estimations; there is a conflict between new exigencies and old pieties, that have somehow to be reconciled.' But again, the point should be made that Hamlet cannot reconcile within himself these 'old forms of feeling' and 'new exigencies'; his personality is at a crossroads; hence his greatness, and at the same time, his tragedy. Alexander reaches essentially the same kind of conclusion when he uses the idea of 'complete man' as a possible clue to Hamlet's tragedy. The term of 'complete man' can grossly mislead if applied directly to Hamlet's personality. For, obviously, Hamlet is not the 'complete man'. In a way which is essential to Shakespeare's drama, he is the very opposite; he is a brave effort towards such an ideal, and a tragic failure at the same time. The ideals, virtues and the patterns of life belonging to various ages and generations, though present in his intellect and sensibility, could not be fused in a united structure. Thus the basic trait of his personality can be expressed in the words which Goethe, who lived in not dissimilar psycho-cultural circumstances applied to himself: '*Das traurige Gefühl für Harmonie*.'

Hamlet symbolizes the tragedy of over-consciousness; he knows and senses too much, and too much light thrown on himself and on his world blurs the shape and design of his perception. In *King Lear*, the tragic element, though having substantially the same meaning, springs from more obscure regions of the human soul. It is just the opposite of the tragedy of over-consciousness. If the source of tragedy in this play, often considered as Shakespeare's greatest work, can be summarized in a sentence, this consists in a clash—a clash with disastrous results—between human beings guided by nothing but blind libidinal forces. Human action is almost completely devoid of any rational and moral character; whence so much *naïveté* and unconscious directness, on one side, and so much ingratitude, selfishness, and brutality, on

[1] Peter Alexander: '*Hamlet*', *Father and Son*. p. 184. Italics his.

the other. If most Shakespearian tragedies contradict the 'cheap moral',[1] 'that Truth and Virtue shall at last succeed', *King Lear* is no exception. The point is, however, that his 'cheap moral' is the basic feature of conscience and the superego, and if flatly contradicted, the probability is that man, like an animal, will take his primitive impulses as the sole guide for his actions. As Lear himself proclaims: 'Thou art the thing itself: unaccommodated man is no more but such a poor, bare, forked animal as thou art.' A. C. Bradley mentions as 'a very striking characteristic of *King Lear*— one in which it has no parallel except in Timon—the incessant reference to lower animals and man's likeness to them'.[2]

It would, however, be wrong merely to repeat yet again that Lear is a tragic hero because he never knew himself, or his world, and when he comes to know them it is too late. In fact, he knew both himself and the world, but his knowledge was founded on the narrow basis of his libidinal drives; his relations with others were based on totalitarian impulses and feelings, on absolute power, absolute love, and naturally, on expectations of absolute gratitude. Thus, he is guided in his life by 'flattery', by the pleasure principle, as the psychoanalysts would have it. He yields to flattery, he acts to get it, he justifies it. The tragedy of Lear is the tragedy of a man who, though at an old age, and after living in a complex world still remains dominated in his conduct by the vague imageries of the 'id'.[3] From the idyllic infantile mental climate of the beginning of the play, he swings to the no less infantile climate of the end in which the whole world crumbles under the feet of his volcanic rage. In this sense he represents yet another failure of personality integration, i.e. the failure of an individual to form an integrated system of control of his primary impulses, and at the same time, the failure of culture to provide the individual with a well established and unequivocal purpose in

[1] The expression belongs to A. C. Bradley: *Shakespearian Tragedy*. Macmillan Co. Ltd. 1957. p. 205.

[2] Bradley. Idem. p. 218.

[3] In the very midst of his misfortunes his child-like dream of perfect happiness is still with him when he says to Cordelia:

> 'Come let's away to prison:
> We two alone will sing like birds i' the cage,
> When thou ask me blessing, I'll kneel down.
> And ask of thee forgiveness: we'll live,
> And pray, and sing, and tell old tales, and laugh
> At gilded butterflies . . .

life. Lear, like Hamlet, expresses the same 'tragic strife for integration'.

THE BAROQUE MIND

The man portrayed by the main Shakespearian heroes is man escaped from the morally rigid medieval world, and not yet integrated with another world. Consequently, he is a man with liberated instincts, with explosive vital energy but without unity of purpose. This lack of unity of purpose is expressed at the psychological level both by a basically weak ego, and an incoherent super-ego. The weakness of the ego is easy to understand when one takes into account that Shakespearian man did not live in an individualized world; the ethics of self-interest were not yet worked out and internalized. The incoherent character of the super-ego and its consequent weakness, were primarily caused by the rejection of the traditional system of values, and by the disorganization and ambiguity in the world of values which resulted from this. Consequently, the man portrayed by Shakespeare's heroes is one whose 'id' could easily break through his ego and superego, or, in more commonly-accepted terms, through the rational and ethical structure of his personality. Here lie the sources of his depth and greatness. For his impulses, desires and aspirations, in other words, his imagination, go far beyond his sense of reality, or his logically and morally organized world. In this sense one can say that he is larger than life. But here lies also his tragic condition, his inner anarchy and his gigantic and often vain efforts towards self-integration and self-realization.

The phenomenology of inner anarchy presented by Shakespearian drama is rich and varied. Sometimes it appèars directly as a mental structure centred round an insatiable need for destruction, as a psychopathic personality, as modern psychology would have it. Shakespeare is still unsurpassed in his ability to evoke the power of destruction and death. At other times man's inner anarchy appears in a disguised form. It appears, for instance, as an escape into a bucolic, quasi-fantastic world. This can be called a form of 'retreatism', an avoidance of anxiety aroused by inner conflicts. The escape into the ancient past, as in the cult of the ancient hero, can also be considered as a symptom of inner anarchy. Psychologically this can be understood as a regressive form of behaviour aroused by the need to cope with anarchic impulses.[1] It should also be added that this has a strong cultural determinant. The tendency to graft on to the individual's mind a Greco-Roman super-ego was strongly stimulated by the Renaissance and was noticeable in the behaviour of the English upper classes of the time. But the most obvious symptom of inner anarchy is displayed as depression, lack of will, and sometimes as a feeling of nothingness invading the human soul.[2]

At this stage one can go a step further in the psychological analysis of Shakespearian drama by making an attempt to establish some general traits characteristic of the whole period. The character structure, and, on the whole, the mental climate outlined above, suggest strongly what some literary critics have described as the 'baroque' character of Shakespearian drama, and to a certain extent of Elizabethan drama as a whole. Admittedly, the term 'baroque' is vague. Nevertheless, it can be a useful conceptual tool for the analysis of a complex psycho-historical situation.

In trying to establish 'some general principles' observed in the construction of the Elizabethan tragic heroes, one of the critics referred to above writes as follows: 'In the main there are three of them. The common root is the tendency to be—in the words of the painter in *Timon of Athens*—"livelier than life". First of all there is the striving after heightening the figure of the hero by extraordinary intensification of the emotion, there is secondly, a predilection for what in Elizabethan language is termed the "fantastical", namely, eccentricity, extravagance, or oddity which could be summed up as the bizarre, and there is thirdly, owing to a partiality for the majestic, an inclination to favour the representation of a certain self-exalting attitude.'[3] This condensed

[1] The same tendency was noticeable in France particularly towards the midseventeenth century. La Rochefoucauld, for instance, spoke about a man endowed with 'pagan virtues'.

[2] The famous 'Elizabethan malady', melancholia, is a conspicuous symptom of personality disintegration. The interest manifested by the literature of the period in a kind of schizoid 'retreatist' personality cannot be denied. It would, therefore, be reasonable to assume that this interest was aroused by the existence of such inclinations in many members of Elizabethan society. An analogy with the period round the beginning of the nineteenth century in Germany and France can be drawn. Both the 'Elizabethan malady' and '*le mal du siècle*' are symptoms of a low degree of integration of human personality.

[3] Shücking, L. L. The Baroque Character of the Elizabethan Tragic Hero. *Proceedings of Brit. Acad.* 1938. p. 110.

characterization—in which one can easily understand what the main features of the literary baroque were—is illustrated by a brief analysis of the main heroes of Marlowe, Marston, Kyd, Jonson, Chapman, and Shakespeare. Thus, Marlowe's Tamburlaine, one of the most influential figures of Elizabethan drama, exhibits 'monstrous pride', 'wilfulness', 'rashness', 'cruelty', and 'love of display'; Marston's Antonio displays melancholy which 'frequently borders on hysterical derangements'; Jonson's Sejanus and Catilina are, in their 'hyperpathetic craving for destruction', monsters who cannot be measured by human standards; Chapman's Byron shows 'abnormal self-assertiveness' and 'insatiable ambition'. Similar character structure is revealed in Shakespeare's heroes. Thus, Hamlet's melancholy leads through its intensity to madness; Othello behaves as if he has 'epileptic fits'; Lear gives way to 'volcanic outbursts of rage'; Macbeth 'loses his nerve and sees hallucinations in the air'; Titus Andronicus 'overshoots the mark', and Coriolanus is an 'absolutely self-centred individual' completely blind to the feelings of others.

Speaking of the Elizabethan tragic hero in general, the same critic uses terms such as 'inclination to deviate from the ordinary', 'pathological ecstasy', and 'bizarre element'. Most relevant is the inner contradiction within the mental structure of this hero. Shakespeare in particular builds up characters 'with strongly marked mixture of qualities of which the one seems almost to preclude the other'. Macbeth is given as an example of this: he is a moral coward, and at the same time, a lion on the battlefield. Bearing in mind what has been said earlier about Hamlet, he presents an even better example of a mixture of contradictory qualities.

The conclusion is that these heroes portray a personality structure with a low degree of integration. This is clearly demonstrated by their heightened emotionality, and by their stupendous vital energy which overwhelms not only their intellect but also the pressure of social convention, and even the pattern of Nature. These heroes live beside themselves as if exploring new human modes of being. If they achieve any kind of unity it is highly tense and precarious, for it includes in itself more than human reason can organize, and more than society can allow. Hence the fantastic, and bizarre, or irrational element in their characters.

'Irrational' is the key word here as it points directly to the sources and nature of the chief characteristic of the mental structure of the Elizabethan tragic hero, his heightened emotionality. For what is this heightened emotionality if not an upsurge of primary libidinal forces disrupting any inner and outer controls. Two forms of heightened emotionality in particular show the anarchic libidinal condition of the hero's mind, aggression, and egocentricity. As has often been said, this hero lives according to the motto: *rage has the privilege.* On the other hand, he often indulges in such fits of self-glorification that he may give the impression of mental infantilism, of not being fully aware of the limits of his personality, and of taking for reality his dreams of power and self-assertion.

How can one account for the genesis of this kind of personality structure? Naturally, the first answer that comes to mind is that it is the product of the imagination of a particular writer. This is, however, not the whole truth. A psycho-historical study such as this is meant to show that all these characters have a strong socio-cultural determinant. From what has been said so far the mental structure exhibited by the Elizabethan tragic hero fits well into the psycho-historical situation created by the interregnum period. This type of personality structure is characteristic of individuals living in a period of disruptive social and cultural change, when old values and patterns of behaviour are discarded, and new ones are not completely formed, when the old super-ego disintegrates, and the new one is in the process of growth. It is in this specific sense that one can describe the mental structure of the Elizabethan tragic hero as 'dissocialized mind'. This explains the hero's self-centredness, and particularly the explosive state of his libidinal energy which flings up his personality above the level of reality where greatness and tragic failure merge into each other.

It is reasonable to infer from this that the Elizabethan tragic hero exhibits in a heightened form a kind of behaviour which can be found in various degrees in many members of the sixteenth-century community. Thus he can be considered a psychological representative of his period. A detailed study of every-day life in Elizabethan England might yield considerable evidence in support of this. This is, however, too complex a matter requiring a separate treatment. But even a brief look at the behaviour of the theatre audiences of this period shows firstly that the atmosphere was such as to induce as quickly as possible a state of heightened emotionality in the audience. This was done by ornate display, gaudy costumes and pompous processions, in short, by an atmosphere of magnificence which appealed to the spectators in every possible way. This was precisely what the average Elizabethan spectator expected, for he went to a 'show', and liked 'to be dumbfounded, to feel flesh creep, to shudder . . .'[1] Secondly, it shows the explosive state of libidinal energy characteristic of the Elizabethan audience. Any public spectacle, in any country and in any century, appeals to the repressed libidinal drives of the individual. But seldom has this been more obvious and more intense than at an Elizabethan 'show'. There, Eros and Thanatos —to use a Freudian formula for the libido—were absolute masters over the audience's mind. And this was not only the result of the play itself, or of the contamination of the audience by the behaviour of the characters on the stage. It was the kind of behaviour expected in the London playhouses where—as a contemporary says—'it is the fashion of the youths to go first into the yard, and to carry their eyes through every gallery, then like unto ravens where they spy the carrion thither they fly, and press as near to the fairest as they can'; and where, before the play started the audience show 'such heaving and shoving, such itching and shouldering to sit by women . . .'[2]

The other aspect of the libido, aggression, was well in evidence, for rare were the 'shows' without fights and abusive behaviour towards the actors.[3] A contemporary dramatist seizes upon this specific mental condition when he describes the London audience as being made up of people who 'in the afternoon being the idlest time of the day . . . do wholly bestow themselves upon pleasure, and that pleasure they divide either into gaming, following of harlots, drinking or seeing a play'.[4] With a remarkable insight the

[1] Schücking. Idem. p. 81.

[2] Stephen Gosson: *The Schoole of Abuse*, and *Playes Confuted in Five Acts*. Quot. by John Dover Wilson in *Life of Shakespeare's England*. pp. 214 and 215.

[3] This kind of behaviour is not entirely peculiar to sixteenth-century English audiences except, perhaps, in its intensity. Similar behaviour was exhibited by audiences in Spain, France—Hotel de Bourgogne—and particularly in Italy. This, of course, does not invalidate our argument, for the causes of such behaviour may have been the same. For a comparative view see: H. A. Rennert: *The Spanish Stage in the Time of Lopez de Vega*. 1909.

[4] *The Actors' Remonstrance*. 1643. Quot. by J. D. Wilson, Op. Cit. p. 233.

quoted dramatist suggests that a 'show' is primarily meant to discharge a kind of repressed primitive energy which otherwise would go into debauchery, crime and even revolution. It is again the 'dissocialized mind' that makes itself conspicuous in the behaviour of the audience as well as in that of the dramatic hero of the time. This becomes even more apparent if one looks at it in its historical perspective; for instance, if this kind of behaviour is compared with that of an audience at a medieval morality play or at a contemporary play.

It is fitting to conclude with a few general remarks about the social psychology of the baroque and the social psychology of tragedy, as they pave the way to an important field of research in historical psychology.

There is a widespread tendency among art and literary historians to regard a style as primarily a classificatory concept and consequently to define it through a series of formal qualities. The baroque is characterized by big design, by irregularity and amplitude of forms, and by a combination of contradictory elements. Sometimes the formal qualities are of a more or less psychological nature, or at least expressed in psychological terms. In this case one speaks about the feeling of movement, about the impression of statelessness and of the fantastic, and above all, about high emotional tension. This view seems to be rooted in, and to lead to, the conviction that a style is ultimately a cultural technical phenomenon, i.e. a more or less coherent set of rules consciously or unconsciously observed by a number of artists belonging to specific ethnic groups, or to a specific period. Thus, Rubens' paintings, Shakespeare's characters and Vivaldi's or Albinoni's music were to a high degree the result of a certain artistic technique, of certain attitudes and modes of perception, and of a certain conception of man. It is all this that defines their style, be it called baroque or otherwise. Now this is obviously true, but as it is, it does not answer a basic question concerning any cultural phenomenon, the question of its historical character. And it is precisely this question that constitutes the main concern of historical psychology.

In the present study, an attempt has been made to go beyond what may be called the formative field of such a phenomenon. Thus, it has been suggested that the baroque is the expression at the cultural level of a specific mental structure resulting from the psycho-historical situation of the interregnum period. The implication of this is that there exists such a thing as a baroque mind which is the source of specific artistic techniques, specific attitudes to life, and a specific conception of man. In other words, the baroque can be spoken of in terms of a basic personality structure. Thus, irregularity and amplitude of forms, inner contradictions, the feeling of statelessness and of the fantastic are so many expressions of a personality structure with a low degree of integration. The big design, the tense feeling of form, the impression that the 'apotheosis' of artistic achievement lies outside itself, the movement and the heightened emotionality seems to suggest both the anarchic libidinal state and the complementary effort towards inner integration characteristic of the basic personality type of the interregnum period.

It must, however, be stressed again that the intention here is to indicate a new approach to the phenomenon of style rather than to provide a psycho-social definition of it. For a more adequate psychological understanding of this phenomenon we have to take into account, among other things, the fact that the baroque in visual art as well as the literary baroque arose towards the end of the interregnum period, that is to say, at a time when the anxiety created by the disintegration of the old world, of the old super-ego in particular, began to subside, and when the shape of the new world was well in sight. Thus, the baroque conveys more confidence than the mannerism which preceded it, in spite of, or just because of, the inflated formal character of the latter. The baroque expresses a state of inner contradiction and anarchy in the depth of human existence, and at the same time a daring and vigorous formative urge; as an artistic expression it combines the highest degree of freedom with a gigantic effort towards a new kind of integration. This leads to the second point to be considered here, the social psychology of tragedy.

First of all it is important to note the sociological fact that tragedy, as a literary genre, arose in periods of transition to an individualistic society. The fifth century in Greece, the sixteenth century in England, and the seventeenth century in France are almost identical from this specific point of view. This strongly suggests that the psychological pattern of tragedy is rooted in the same psycho-historical situation of interregnum. Thus, to put it briefly, tragedy expressed the existential situation of what has been called 'l'homme désaxé'. It expresses both the anxiety and the joy of a man escaped to freedom from a rigidly organised society; it expresses the relief of a man whose instincts have escaped from a rigid super-ego based on external, mainly religious, authority. In this specific sense, tragedy represents man's struggle against the gods, or against destiny. But at the same time, it portrays the adventures and the greatness of a man in search of a new meaning of life and of a new order in his universe. It seems that the final fall of the tragic hero is inscribed in the human condition, for the individual alone cannot find any final meaning of life, and any stable order in his universe. Tragedy expresses both the virtue and the sin of individualism. That is why there is no tragedy in a patriarchal or a totalitarian society.

VI

THE ORIGINS OF ENGLISH CHARACTER: II

The Creative Reaction

His conscience and his character compound matters very amiably.

HAZLITT

INTRODUCTION

THE first part of this chapter was concerned with the description of a specific set of conditions in the life of the English community determining by a system of reactions and counter-reactions the emergence of a new type of personality structure. The second part will deal with the main aspects and stages in the development of this personality structure.

The experience of anarchy resulting from the collapse of the medieval world seemed to have been more intensive in England than in other parts of the Western world. The reason for this was twofold. Firstly, the process of dissolution of the medieval religious institutions went, in England, deeper than in most countries of the West. This is borne out by the strong secular character of the Reformation, and the length of the period of disoriented faith resulting from it. Secondly, the rise of the middle classes as well as the process of urbanization took place in sixteenth-century England on a larger scale than in other communities of the period. Consequently the number of individuals who, as a result of a new way of life, cut themselves off from traditional beliefs, was considerably greater in England.

The psychological origin of the modern English character lies not only—as is often believed—in a reaction from the medieval world, but also in a reaction to the period of anarchy created by the dissolution of that world. In other words, it is a reaction from a type of mental structure dominated by the super-ego or by the individual's need to identify himself with a world of social and ideal values, and at the same time, a reaction to an opposite mental structure dominated by the 'id'. This situation allows the first insight into what one might call the matrix of that mental structure which defines the modern English character. This is a flexible mental structure compromising between the inner drives of the individual and the demands of cultural environment.[1] The state of anarchy created by social changes and particularly by the disorganization of the individual's system of beliefs is a classic case of an anxiety-rousing situation. Such a situation normally leads to an increase in the individual's self-awareness. A detailed explanation of this kind of phenomenon has been given elsewhere. What ought to be emphasized here is the fact that this anxiety and the increased self-awareness resulting from it, can be considered as preliminary psychological conditions for the emergence of a self-centred personality structure in the cultural climate of six-teenth-century England. The disintegration of the traditional patterns of behaviour, on one hand, and increased self-awareness, on the other, aroused in individuals of that period the need as well as the ability to make a new kind of adjustment to their environment. In other words, their task was to build up a new frame of reference for their behaviour and a new system of values which had as a starting-point the individual's perception of them-selves as individuals.[2]

One can easily recognize from this the psychological prere-quisites of what has come to be known as modern individualistic

[1] One would like to stick to the vocabulary used so far and to call this flexible and compromising structure the 'ego', and to describe the mental structure of the modern Englishman as strong ego personality. But this raises important difficulties. As will be seen later, one of the characteristics of the basic English personality structure consists in a small distance between the ego and the super-ego and in their inter-convertible character.

[2] Similarities between the sixteenth-century personality structure and that of the twentieth century can be seen in the ambiguity and subjective character of values, i.e., in the individual's feeling that there is nothing outside himself to support his pur-pose in life. It is expressed today by existentialism in the concept of *choice*. In seven-teenth-century France, Pascal expressed a similar condition by his concept of *ennui*.

civilization which was for the first time, and perhaps in its purest form, realized in England.

This is one of the many occasions on which one has to recognize that psychological description is not adequate for the understanding of complex socio-cultural phenomena. For the questions arise of why the individuals of the sixteenth-century English community changed their pattern of behaviour in this particular way; and why they started to stress their own individualities in their adjustment to life. The increase in their self-awareness as a purely psychological phenomenon cannot answer these questions. However, although a definite answer is beyond the purpose and possibilities of this study, a way towards one can be found if we view the problem from a sociological as well as a psychological angle. It must be emphasized again that these individuals belonged substantially to the rising social group of the middle classes. They can generally be described as displaced individuals in the sense that, owing to their interests and practices, they detached themselves from the traditional way of life. They had to build up new types of community for which they had no pre-established norms of human relations. Consequently, each individual had to work out his social adjustment for himself. The important features of the economic practices of these individuals were private means of production, private initiative and freedom of action in the economic field. All this strengthened in them the need to adjust themselves to life as individuals, and at the same time, to build up an individualized society.

Here the socio-psychological cycle can be followed. This type of adjustment required, and at the same time determined, a new inner organization of the individual's mind or a new personality structure. And the next question is how this was achieved.

NEW VITAL EQUILIBRIUM

Two main aspects of the way in which the English, particularly the middle classes, reacted to the state of inner anarchy resulting from the psycho-historical situation of the interregnum period can be distinguished, (a) a movement *against* the inner sources of anarchy, and (b) a movement *towards* these sources. Naturally, these two complex psycho-historical processes are often intermingled in their development.

(a) The movement against the inner sources of anarchy is, broadly, demonstrated by the development of Puritanism. Admittedly, no reductionist view, be it economic, sociological, or psychological, can account for the advent of this phenomenon. However, in a study of historical psychology it seems pertinent to start with, and even to emphasize, its mental background. As a mental process, Puritanism was a reaction from a state of disoriented faith. As such it can be understood as the outcome of growing need in a group of individuals to deal with a state of inner anarchy by a movement in an opposite direction, that is, by a rigid organization of the inner life. The same situation can be expressed in religious terms. In this sense, Puritanism was a reaction to the unconscious fear of damnation produced by the separation from the old faith, or a reaction to the state of 'irreligion' heightened by the Reformation. This is borne out by the dominance of the *motif* of fear, and by the stronger sense of original sin, as well as by the desperate need for salvation and purity of conscience which were so obvious in the behaviour of the first Puritans. The intensity with which a new formula of salvation was needed was proportionate to the length of the period of disoriented faith. Round about the beginning of the Reformation, the Bible was 'disputed, rhymed, sung, and jangled in every ale-house and tavern', while at the turn of the century the athletes of the new faith dominated the whole society.

In terms of depth psychology, the basic psychic process determining the rise of the Puritan mind, was that of reaction-formation. Thus, a state of low degree of integration in human personality was compensated for by rigid organization; the dominance of emotional factors in the structure of personality was counteracted by a severe rationalization of life; from a state of confusion in the world of values, and lack of united purpose in life, a leap was made into a new world dominated by the belief in the individual's fixed calling in life and in the predestination of his soul. Finally, from a personality structure with a weakling super-ego the reaction was towards a personality structure with a super-ego more rigid and more intolerant than the medieval super-ego. In this specific sense Puritanism can be described as a reaction-formation motivated by the inner anarchy of the interregnum period rather than a reaction from the rigidly organized medieval personality type and society. As such its immediate outcome was not a more relaxed mental structure and a more flexible society, but the very opposite: a monolithic mental structure predisposed towards a quasi totalitarian social order. The model of a theocratic tyranny was very much present in the social behaviour of the first Puritans.

However, Puritanism cannot be regarded as a purely endo-psychic affair. Its socio-cultural determinants are only too obvious. It has, nevertheless, to be said that the part played by these determinants has sometimes been exaggerated with the result that the rise of Puritanism was often too closely linked with the spread of the Calvinist doctrine in England, or with the growth of the specific culture of the English middle classes. Admittedly, Calvinism played an important part in the development of Puritanism, but the important fact remains that at the time when it was introduced into England, the psycho-genetic conditions for such a development were obvious. This explains at least why English religious exiles to the Continent had a particular affinity for such a doctrine. And it was these exiles who imported and spread Calvinism in England.

Any search for the cultural and social genesis of Puritanism has to take into account that the sixteenth century English community, particularly its middle classes, worked out their religious problem in a specific psycho-historical field. Firstly, their religious need was heightened by a relatively long period of crises of spiritual authority. This determined in them an acute religious conscience as well as an inclination towards a more rigorous practice of faith. Secondly, they worked out their heightened religious need within a culture with relatively strong authoritarian traits in the political sphere, and relatively strong disciplinarian habits in the field of education. What L. Febvre said about the God of the French Protestants can, perhaps, be applied here: it was a God created after the image of an absolute monarch. It is only reasonable to assume that the disciplinarian attitudes and habits were easily transferred from the political and educational into the religious field. Thirdly, most members of the English community worked out their awakened religious need in a period of increasing interest in material values, on the one hand, and of rapid growth of national consciousness on the other. This in itself had a considerable influence on the crystallizing of the new faith. For, the new Christian, though possessing a strong faith, was on the whole more tolerant towards human worldly needs than the man of the old faith. Civic discipline and morality became the touchstone of his religious faith. The virtue he praised and cultivated most was that of being a good citizen, an industrious and productive member of his society.

It follows from this that a series of specific factors in English culture contributed more than the Continental doctrine of Calvinism to the rise and development of Puritanism. This is obviously true, but one has to take into account that these two sets of cultural determinants had in common the specific culture of the rising Western middle classes. And it was this culture that contributed an important element to the crystallization of the Puritan mind. Above all, the Puritan super-ego was greatly determined in its contents and functions by the specific values of the middle classes.

One last point regarding the genesis of Puritanism has to be clarified. It would be a mistake to confine the psychological aspect of Puritanism to a reaction against the period of interregnum. This would stress too strongly the authoritarian character of the Puritan mind and culture. In fact Puritanism was also a reaction to the medieval faith, and civilization in general. In this sense it included, within itself, all those drifts towards a less sacerdotal and formal religion found in the English mystics of the pre-Reformation time who 'stressed personal rather than corporate religion, the inner life rather than the ecclesiastical practice'.[1] Indeed Puritanism was also an expression of the *Devotio Moderna*, and as such was the very opposite of medieval Christianity.[2] As against the formal and corporate authority of the Church, the Puritans stressed the authority of inner evidence. The Puritan faith and God were in essence internalized faith and God, however rigorous and authoritarian they may have been. Thus, religion became more and more a matter of personal feeling; even salvation and damnation came to connote the individual's awareness of the presence, or absence of God in himself. In this sense, Puritanism was also an expression of the growing spirit of individualism, a fact which seems to contradict what has been said about the totalitarian traits of the Puritan mind. The contradiction was real and reflected the spirit of the age in which

[1] A. R. Myers: *England in the Late Middle Ages*. Penguin. 1956. p. 161.
[2] Thomas Kempis: *De Imitatione Christi* was popular in fifteenth-century England.

Puritanism arose, For Puritanism was both a reaction to the anarchic world of the interregnum, and as such an outcome of the fear of freedom, and at the same time a reaction from the authoritarian religious society of the middle ages, and therefore an outcome of the need for freedom. One can discern in Puritanism the beginning of a new personality structure based on a new balance between the individual and society.

This sheds light on the part played by Puritanism in the formation of the modern English character. Puritanism can be considered as an early attempt to integrate and organize in a living whole the conditions of life characteristic of the English community at the beginning of the modern era. The main result of this was a new personality structure. In it could be seen the first outlines of what was going to be the English national character. It was, however, a rough and not altogether coherent structure which underwent serious changes in the course of time. The inner balances were not strong enough to eliminate the possibility of falling into the extremes of emotionality and rationality, of individualism and authoritarianism. But gradually the terms of these contradictions were brought together into a flexible and resistant structure. Thus, the modern Englishman has gradually realised himself as a practical sentimentalist, and a law-abiding individualist.

A movement away from and against the inner source of anarchy can be detected also in the rise of the naturalistic spirit in politics so characteristically expressed by Hobbes. We said earlier that Hobbes mirrored in his doctrine the state of anarchy—inner and outer—characteristic of his time. So overwhelming was his awareness of the anarchic character of his period that he had no doubt in assigning it to human nature in general. Thus, according to him, man was naturally 'brutish', 'insolent' and given to self-destructive aggression. And it was the very intensity with which Hobbes realized this which turned his mind in the opposite direction, so that he became acutely aware of the necessity of order and discipline in human life. In this Hobbes expressed the natural reaction of his contemporaries to a state of anarchy by an inflated need for order and authority. Here lies the origin of the authoritarian and gigantesque character assigned to society and state by Hobbes, and perhaps by many of his contemporaries who did not articulate their feelings and thoughts within a theoretical framework. Thus, the psychological root of the Leviathan lay in an excessive reaction against a state of inner anarchy. Is it not revealing that Hobbes, with his naturalistic insight, considered *fear* as the basic socializing, and indeed civilizing force in man? And since the need for society was rooted in the fear of anarchy and death, only a strong society could satisfy such a need. The basic purpose of political order was to provide the individual with security and peace, i.e. with remedies for fear and destruction. Like Machiavelli before him, Hobbes considered stability as the quintessence of a good state.

The early political naturalism was, like Puritanism, an attempt towards the formation of a personality structure capable of overcoming a state of anarchy. And like Puritanism again it was considerably changed during the course of time. The evidence for this can be seen in the later development of political naturalism in England. A prominent feature of this development seems to be that society, state, and order in general have become less and less terrifying necessities, less and less opposed to the basic nature of the individual; they have been gradually tamed and internalized. However, the early reaction-formation left its impact on the formation of modern English character. As will be shown later, a strong feeling for order, as well as a strong belief in the value of social conditioning, are important features in the personality of the Englishman. That the individual's mind is a compound of habits imposed upon him particularly by his social environment, has been a basic tenet in English philosophy throughout the modern era.

(b) It is obvious by now that the response to the state of inner anarchy was not only a negative one, or one of reaction-formation. Had this been the case, the 'puritanic' and the 'authoritarian' elements in the English character would have been more dominant than they are. The attitude taken by members of the English community towards the freed energy of their libido was not only one of excessive repression, but also one of tolerance and even acceptance. It was this latter attitude which has been referred to earlier as a movement towards the inner sources of anarchy, and which will be dealt with below.

Around the very beginning of the modern era, there was in the behaviour of many members of the English community a certain readiness to yield to their instinctual drives, or to their 'id'. They spoke with considerable tolerance, if not approval. about the human need for acquisition and aggression, self-interest, and inherent human inconsistency. It seems that they were inclined not only to accept certain 'human appetites', but also to attach positive values to them. One can even say that there was in the atmosphere of this period a noticeable tendency to build up a pattern of life—a personality structure and a culture—on aggression and destruction, on the anarchic forces of the 'id'. The freeing of the individual from his social ties, the revolt against authority, religious and secular, culminating in the seventeenth-century political revolution, are all symptoms of this tendency. And it should not be forgotten that one of the ideals of the period was the ancient hero, an isolated individual athirst for glory, who looked upon the world merely as a place for his personal adventures. What some sociologists have described as 'the negative character of modern freedom' was in full swing.

But any invasion of the mind by instinctual forces leads to lack of balance and finally to self-destruction. Consequently this attitude of spontaneous surrender had gradually given way to more subtle and elaborate forms of acceptance of the basic libidinal drives of the mind. If one could translate into conscious rational terms a basically unconscious mental process, one would say that people's attitude towards the libidinal drives of their minds became less and less dichotomous and ambivalent, and more and more balanced and constructive. The main problem was not simply that of accepting, or repressing these drives, but rather that of transforming them into constructive forces. It is this creative reaction to the instinctual energy that reveals certain traits that distinguish sharply the personality structure of the modern Englishman from that of medieval man, and to a great extent, from the personality structure characteristic of other modern communities.

The two main ways in which the members of the modern English community transformed their instinctual energies are: *affect displacement* and *rationalization*. The specific meaning attributed here to these closely inter-related terms will gradually become apparent. For the moment it is important that they should be seen as socio-psychological processes rather than simple endopsychic mechanisms.

In the first place, the Englishman of the early modern era

accepted his instinctual drives, and was ready to act upon them, but not before he divested them of their primary emotional significance. He either denied to himself the pleasure derived from the satisfaction of his drives, or minimized it by dissociating it from its original source and projecting it outside himself. The negative feelings connected with these drives such as displeasure, pain, fear, anger, or insecurity were submitted to the same kind of mechanism. There was, on the whole, a constant tendency in the individual to de-emotionalize his behaviour. As a result of this a need was experienced in its conative and cognitive aspects, as an impulse towards action, or as a rational goal, rather than in its emotional aspect as pleasure or pain. The needs for food, aggression and sex were all submitted to this process.

Simple repression or suppression of the instinctual drives would be an inadequate interpretation. It is true that the individual deprives these drives of some of their original qualities, but he does so in order to alleviate his fears of their anarchic character. Indeed, the process is in many ways opposite to repression and suppression. For, the individual finally accepts these drives, and in doing so he builds up a new type of mental balance. In this lies one of the main differences between religious asceticism, as a trait in the personality structure of the medieval man, and secular asceticism which becomes an important trait in the personality structure of the Englishman. The instinctual drives are for the former 'bad', consequently, repressed and projected out on to the objective forces of evil. For the latter, they are emotionally neutral, i.e. natural. There is no 'evil' in food or in sex as such, but there is evil in enjoying and indulging in them. The individual's attitude towards money (money-making, profits, usury) is particularly relevant, money being a social symbol of more than one instinctual drive. As early as the late sixteenth century 'a new spirit' was creeping in: 'What man is so mad to deliver his money out of his own possession for naughte' is a representative opinion of the period. There is nothing medieval about this attitude. The drive towards money-making and profits is neither repressed nor stigmatized. However, the direct emotional experiences derived from it are not accepted, i.e. satisfaction, pleasure, elation, prestige, or even security in a direct form. All this one brushed aside, replaced by inner experiences derived from effort, thrift, diligence and frugality. The drive might be completely de-emotionalized thus, becoming a task or a calling, i.e. a *service* rendered to the community and to God. By this an emotionally-toned self-centred attitude is displaced by an object-centred attitude. Calvin certainly made a strong appeal to this type of man when he preached: 'Whence do the merchant's profits come, except from his own diligence and industry?'

Before passing on to the rationalization of behaviour it is appropriate to mention some traits in the English character whose origin can be connected with affect-displacement. One should start, of course, with the famous English self-control. It is not easy to use self-control as a differential concept among the communities of Western Europe. Differentiation is in this case a matter of degree. It is the value the members of the modern English community put on self-control in their adjustment to life which is important. The same idea is relevant to the Englishman's predilection for understatement, the reserved, distant, and shy attitude characteristic of most members of this community. Finally, one should mention the Englishman's reluctance to show feelings which is often interpreted as lack of feeling. But all this can be summed up by saying that it is in this primary psychic condition described as affect-displacement or affect-dissociation, that one should look for the origin of a new kind of sense of reality characteristic of members of modern English community. This can briefly be described as a disposition in the individual to de-emotionalize his contact with his environment. Thus, adjustment at reality level means adjustment to a perceived environment in which emotionality has been minimized by a system of controls and emphasis.

This can be illustrated in more than one way. Regarding social adjustment for instance, it has often been said that the Englishman has a pronounced inclination and ability to establish relations with others on practical rational levels, i.e. without emotional involvement. The differential value of this trait may be seen particularly through its negative aspect. For recent social anthropological studies have thrown considerable light on the Englishman's difficulty in establishing, and disinclination for, emotional relations with others. Gorer's recent survey makes this point clear.[1] According to this, over 50 per cent of the population

[1] J. Gorer: *Exploring English Character*. London. 1955.

confessed to being shy in their social life. Most of them have a reserved attitude towards their neighbours. 'The typical relationship of the English to their neighbours can probably be best described as distant cordiality.' If they happen to move, most of them take more than four years to make friends round their new home. It is obvious that they cannot easily be emotionally mobilized. They do not believe in and do not experience 'love at first sight'; the average distance of time passing between first acquaintance between two people of opposite sex and their subsequent marriage is three years. The first quality which a man looks for in his future wife is 'a good housekeeper'; the first quality which a woman looks for in her future husband is 'understanding'. 'Love' comes in the fourth and seventh place respectively.

Two traits are particularly relevant in this context, shyness and the sense of humour both frequently found among the members of the English community. Shyness is obviously the inclination of the individual to control and hide his feelings towards others coupled with the unconscious fear that these feelings might be discovered.[1] Sense of humour, a wide topic, must be treated briefly here. However, the difference between the inner mechanism of humour on one side, and that of irony, cynicism and *esprit* on the other, should be noted. The latter can be viewed as symptoms of intolerance and repressing tendencies towards the instinctive impulses in oneself and in others. On the other hand, the mechanism of humour is meant to reduce the emotional tension aroused by such impulses; the impulses as such are tolerated and accepted. 'Reduce the embarrassment, i.e. the emotional tension, and let it go' is the formula of the English sense of humour. In this sense humour can be rightly described as a classic form of affect-displacement.

The individual's contact with his physical environment is no less indicative of the particular sense of reality characteristic of the basic English personality. Here naturally the mechanism of affect-displacement is even more active than in the field of social adjustment. As a result of this the individual's perception of the world becomes excessively de-emotionalized. A series of important psycho-cultural developments are motivated by this

---

[1] Darwin said: 'Thinking what others think of us excites our blushes'. One can also say, 'Thinking what we think of others excites our blushes'.

kind of perception. To start with, Nature becomes in this case an object by itself, independent of, and indifferent to human wishes, aspirations and ideas. The individual's attitude to it tends to be emotionally neutral; it is based on fragmentary de-emotionalized perceptions, i.e. on *facts* and *things* and their formal relations to each other. This basic attitude colours deeply the Englishman's sense of reality for which a thing is more real to the extent that it is more independent from inner factors such as feelings and thoughts. Factualness, hence fragmentariness, is perhaps the highest criterion of reality. 'Hard facts,' a favourite expression with the Englishman, conveys a strong feeling of reality. Needless to say, 'hard facts' are compelling for thought and by implication opposed to its constructive functions. A highly successful young English writer of today conveys this attitude clearly when he says: 'Perhaps there is too much thinking . . . not enough reality; too much chaos.' The contribution made by the English to the empirical scientific notion of reality is unique. This is a reality based on 'facts' floating in a vacuum in which thinking has only a hypothetical function. It is an essential analytical vision of reality.

But the highly active mechanism of affect-displacement in the field of perception implies also that the individual's perception of the world is predominantly controlled by conative elements, i.e. by his basic needs which impinge on his senses. This inhibition of affect causes a more direct contact, and consequently a harder clash between the individual and the external world. This is also reflected in the Englishman's sense of reality. As his perception is basically organized by his impulse to action, reality connotes for him 'resistance' and at the same time 'appeal' for action, that is to say, a 'challenge'. Above all, Nature is—and this shows again a de-emotionalized perceptual field—soulless, non-human; it becomes human only to the extent that it is used and transformed by man's action.

In these primary attitudes, inclination, and feelings lie the origins of a series of well-known traits in the English character such as empiricism, reliance on facts, practical sense, anti-aestheticism, fear of imagination, preference for action or for doing things as against reflection, theorizing, or speculation. There is no need to enlarge on this since these aspects of the English character have for a long time been the subject of a series of studies in cultural anthropology. On the other hand, our present interest is purely psycho-historical.

A point of sociological interest should be clarified at this stage. It might easily be objected that the qualities just mentioned, particularly those described as practical sense, realism, and anti-aestheticism, are more characteristic of the commercial classes than of other members of modern English society. This can in a sense be true. On the other hand, it is not difficult to produce from evidence that these traits are more widespread. Moreover the contention of this study is that they are in one form or another visible in the behaviour of most members of the modern English community, and indeed, in all spheres of life. A certain practical sense, a certain empiricism and realism, and even a certain mistrust of imagination can be seen even in modern English fiction. This is amply revealed by many surveys of people's taste and preferences in this field. There is always a majority who prefer biographical books, i.e. 'slices of life', or stories 'true to life'. Ranke's rule of empirical history, '*Wie es eigentlich gewesen*' seems to govern, if not creation at least enjoyment and interpretation in this field. One exception is lyric poetry, and this is an important one considering that England is the most gifted modern nation in this field.

Rationalization was the other way of coping with the anarchic libidinal forces. As a result of this the individual's diffused instinctual energy was gradually canalized in a definite direction by a process of association with a series of consciously controlled goals, individual and collective, and with certain established social practices. Here again, like affect-displacement, rationalization is a general mental process. It is the degree to which it has determined the English character that is important. The process of rationalization to which the members of the English community were submitted, or submitted themselves, during the second half of the sixteenth and beginning of the seventeenth centuries was unique in its intensity and results.[1]

The first aspect of this is what could broadly be called social conditioning of the individual. There is little need to insist on this

---

[1] The French nation was submitted to disciplinarian training during the reign of Louis XIV. Formal education of the Court, i.e. manners, was the form of this training. But it was in the first instance confined to the aristocracy, and only later on extended to other classes.

point. The expressions 'religious drill', or 'social drill', so characteristic of the late sixteenth century and the beginning of the seventeenth century are significant enough in this respect. There was, during this period a systematic campaign conducted by the state or by the church, or by both, with a view to building up common loyalties and regular patterns of behaviour in the members of the nation. Thus it became the policy of the State to enforce regular attendance at church, '. . . upon pain of punishment by the censure of the church and also upon pain that every person so offending shall forfeit for every such offence twelve pence' (from the Elizabethan Act of Uniformity of 1559). But the spirit lying behind this goes far beyond the struggle for religious conformism. This spirit was adequately expressed by Archbishop Laud in his use of the Aristotelian concept of 'habituation', i.e. the building up of enduring patterns of behaviour in the individual as a result of social conformism. For Laud was conscious of 'the educative influence of regularity and arrangement'.

Now, there is little doubt that this 'drill', religious or secular, was greatly activated by the individual's and the group's needs to cope with strong anarchic tendencies. Only in this way would it be possible to explain, firstly, the development of such practices, secondly, their intensity and thoroughness, and thirdly, the fact that they were accepted by the individual. In other words, the campaign for drill and conformism was a necessary reaction to a religious development rooted in a state of anarchy which was so well expressed by the formula 'free internal choice'. However, a psychogenetic explanation is not enough. There is ample evidence of disciplinarian inclinations in members of the English community long before the beginning of the seventeenth century. Such inclinations were institutionalized in various forms, particularly in the system of education. 'The want of affection in the English for their children is a marked feature,' wrote an Italian traveller round about the beginning of the sixteenth century.[1] It would be easy to prove that the methods of correction, particularly the use of the 'rod' was harsher in English schools than elsewhere. Even in Oxford 'the students led a life almost monastic' and 'their habit was almost the same as that of the Jesuits'.[2] Bearing this in mind, an explanation offers itself for the origins of

[1] Quot. from H. Nicolson: *Good Behaviour*. p. 138.
[2] Paul Hentzner: *Travels in England*. Quot. from D. Wilson. Op. cit. p. 93.

the disciplinarian attitudes characteristic of individuals belonging to the interregnum period. The state of anarchy intensified in these individuals the need for rigid organization of their lives. This determined in them the inclination to select and emphasize those institutions and established patterns of behaviour which could satisfy this need. It is significant here that towards the end of the seventeenth century the French and the Italians changed their disciplinarian attitudes towards their children; after this period it was considered degrading for a boy to submit to corporal punishment. Since there was no such change in England it can be assumed that the English had special need to continue with such disciplinarian practices.

The inner aspect of rationalisation is more revealing for it touches directly upon the individual's need to cope with the anarchy of his instinctual drives. This consisted in the unusual effort made by the individual members of the community to see clear goals in their lives, and to submit their behaviour to a rigorous discipline for the attainment of these goals. 'Conscious united purpose, planned action', 'sustained will effort', are undoubtedly key concepts for the understanding of the behavioural patterns of the period.[1] And, of course, the process was circular: the inner striving of the individual was projected on to social values which were gradually incorporated in a new ethics. This in turn moulded the individual's personality.

No one interested in the social and cultural history of the period can fail to notice the general urge to establish rules of living and to organize life in its smallest detail. This is demonstrated in the first place by the prominence given to the social education of the individual. The part played in this respect by the so-called 'Books of Improvement' can hardly be overemphasized.

[1] The psychogenesis of this pattern of behaviour should not be over-stressed. One has to bear in mind that certain social and economic factors had considerably contributed to the formation of such behaviour. It is well known that commercial and industrial practices normally induce in the individual a more rational attitude in life. As we have seen, such practices developed rapidly in sixteenth-century England. Moreover, some historians of the period speak about nation-wide programmes of labour organization. The Elizabethan 'Statute of Artificers', for instance, aimed at the mobilizing of 'the entire labour resources of the nation', and at a 'programme of full employment' which involved 'the direction of labour in the appropriate callings'. The same Statute established a system of priority among these callings. (Bindoff. Op. cit. p. 200). It is obvious, therefore, that the individual was presented by his society with 'goals' which stimulated his ability for rational organization of life.

There was more than one kind of book, and consequently, more than one way of framing the individual's behaviour within rules and formulae. The famous 'Courtesy Books' of the period were earnestly studied and applied by the members of the upper classes and middle classes alike. Such books were Erasmus' *De Civitate Morum Puerillium* (Trans. in 1532); Castiglione's *The Courtyer* (Trans. 1561); Giovanni della Cass's *Il Galateo* (Trans. 1570); Stephano Guazzo's *Civil Conversation* (Trans. 1681), to mention only a few of them. Close to this came a series of books of behaviour written by Englishmen such as Sir Thomas Elyot's *The Governor* (1531); King James' *Basilikon Doron*; Richard Brathwaite's *The English Gentleman* (1630) and perhaps the most influential of all, *The Complete Gentleman* by Henry Peacham which emphasized 'the cultivation of the qualities that make the gentleman an accomplished versatile personality, as well as a capable servant of the state'.[1]

All this gives only a feeble idea of the depth reached by the process of life organization during that period. The individual was in fact guided, advised and enlightened on all occasions of his life; he was systematically told the 'right ways' of achieving his goals. The range of books of improvement extended to 'manuals of conversation', 'dictionaries of compliments', 'letter-writing', 'practical manuals of rhetoric', 'practical advice for success in courting, wooing and marriage, for personal cleanliness and bed-manners'.[2] An important feature of the period was the collection of proverbs, aphorisms, and similes taken from ancient sages and philosophers as well as from every-day life with a view to presenting the individual with certain ready-made formulae for life. Under the same category should be included a series of 'hand-books' containing professional advice to merchants.[3] The 'didactic' character of poetry and fiction of all sorts which was so obvious during the late sixteenth and the beginning of the seventeenth century, was but another aspect of the same general trend. And last but not least should be mentioned the moral and pietistic literature, and particularly, all those seventeenth-century 'Christian Dictionaries' which not only outlined the ultimate

---

[1] Quot. from L. Wright. Op. cit. p. 127.

[2] Famous ones are: Nicholas Breton's, *A Poste with a madde Packet of Letters*, *The Mirror of Compliments of Cupid's School*. Very popular also was William Vaughan's *Directions of Health*.

[3] John Browne's *The Merchant Avizo* (1591) is a famous one.

ideals of human life but also prescribed detailed rules for the individual's conduct.

Human life was taking the shape of a handbook with a central theme and with a well-organized argument leading to it. The student inclined to make historical analogies might easily be led to use terms such as 'dirigée', 'indoctrination', and even '*Gleichschaltung*'. In a sense he might be right. For there was such a thing as a central doctrine embodied in a specific religious faith and practice, or later on, in a system of *prudential values*, and there was pressure put on the individual to conform to this. But this still does not justify the terms mentioned above. For what seems to be an essential feature of the period can be expressed in one term, 'self-education'. The individual was eager to learn about life in general and to discipline his behaviour in order to improve his condition. Each individual was possessed by the desire to discover 'some North-West Passage' to learning, some short route to the information and culture demanded by the 'complete citizen'. This shows at least that the system of pressures for conformity, and generally speaking, for integration with certain well-established regulations of life came also from within himself. Indeed a strong need for personal status was the main driving force for this thirst for knowledge of approved forms of behaviour.

The drive towards rationalization penetrated deeply into the individual's mind; his disposition to perceive and react to most life situations in the function of practical rational goals grew stronger and stronger. Feelings, emotions, and spontaneous impulses which hampered his rational schemes were displaced, inhibited or repressed. In his *Avizo*, John Browne exhorted the merchant to keep even the prayers 'discreetly short' otherwise too much of his time and mind would be taken away from his business. The rationalization of human relations was perhaps the most marked aspect of this process. The emotional bonds of kinship, of friendship, and even of marriage and love became to a great extent subservient to rational schemes. The same John Browne advises his fellow-men not to 'covet overmuch familiaritie amongst men: for it maketh thee spend much losse of time'.[1] Practical goals started to govern domestic relations between husband and wife also. New attitudes and values were developed which were useful to the efficient conduct of the household. This is shown,

[1] Quote from Wright. p. 162.

as Wright points out, in the change of stress from the value of virginity to that of chastity in marriage. The latter is more important because it assures the stability of the home. The emphasis put on partnership rather than on emotional ties in marriage reveals the same general tendency. Married life was rationalized even in its most intimate aspects, indeed, it became the stronghold of the practice of 'worldly asceticism'. Even those inter-sex relations which are commonly believed to have a pure emotional irrational character were imbued with rational purposes, falling in love and marrying, for instance.[1] What, much later, a Frenchman said on this point expresses this so well: 'An English girl', he writes, 'wants to marry only for love; she creates a romance in her imagination, and this dream is part of her life . . . But in her private romance the English girl is still English, that is to say, positive and practical. She wants to be her husband's helper and useful associate.'[2] Gorer, as has been mentioned, described in similar terms this aspect of life in contemporary England.

The changes which took place during this period in people's attitude towards the poor and beggars should be noted as an extreme example of the rationalization of human relations. Towards the mid-seventeenth century, the idea was crystallized that poverty should be dealt with on sound business principles, i.e. on the basis of the practical principles of work and efficiency. Thus, Parliament passed an act in 1649 providing employment for the poor and the punishment of beggars. The vagrants were offered the choice of working, being whipped, or doing compulsory labour. There remained just one formal sign of an emotional religious attitude towards this social category: poverty and beggary were considered 'sins'. But this was an inversion of the traditional religious attitude, and came as a rational consequence of the promotion of 'work' and 'propriety' to the rank of virtues.

This indicates a peak in the process of rationalization, i.e. the

[1] In the same category comes the increased rationality in the individual's attitude to death. Compare, for instance, the attitude to death imbued with emotional factors, characteristic of the sixteenth-century French—as described by Febvre—with what Thomas Becon says on this point in his *The Sick Man's Salue*. The sick man is told how to make a will, how to exhort his wife and household to love of virtue. He is urged to be generous, to provide property for his children and servant and . . . 'to remember the poor schollers of the University of Oxford and Cambridge'.

[2] H. Taine: *Notes on England*. Trans. by Edward Hyams. Thames and Hudson.

formation in the individual belonging to the English community of a rational attitude towards religion and God. A rational book-keeping God—as shown by Bunyan's visions—urges the individual to keep his own balance-sheet in order. Reciprocal rational expectations rather than emotional appeals govern God-Man relations. Job became the puzzle and the fascination of man. He became the tragic hero of the Christian soul mainly because he gave and did not receive in return. This phenomenon needs no detailed treatment here, as it is the main subject of a series of basic studies on the spirit of the English Reformation.

It is appropriate to say a few words here about the genesis of these two important processes in the formation of the English character, affect-displacement, and rationalization. The hypothesis put forward in this study is that rationalization as well as affect-displacement are enduring response patterns to a state of inner anarchy. Therefore one feels inclined to speak about their genesis in purely psychological terms, and regard them as inner, mainly unconscious, processes or mechanisms, by which an individual copes with the threat to the unity of his personality occasioned by a powerful release of the primitive libidinal energy of his mind. However, in its present usage, the concept of inner anarchy is not meant to cover an independent psychological reality. This study is not concerned with the state of inner anarchy in general, but rather with an historically concrete case of inner anarchy, that experienced with particular intensity by most individuals belonging to the sixteenth-century English community. In this specific case the origins and functions of affect-displacement and rationalization were greatly determined by social and cultural factors. In short, they were mental mechanisms used intensively by a group of individuals in order to cope with a common mental condition created by a specific social and cultural situation.

It would, however, be equally wrong to conclude from this that the origins of rationalization and affect-displacement were ultimately social and cultural, and that they can be identified with specific aspects of the interregnum period. For instance, it has often been suggested that the practical rational attitude to life of the modern Englishman, as well as his wariness of feeling, can be derived from the impact made on his mind by certain practices characteristic of a commercial society, or by the practice of the Calvinist ethics of frugality and temperance. But as soon as Calvinism is mentioned this kind of argument suffers a volte-face. For we say earlier, that in England Calvinism itself was primarily an answer to, or a cultural symbol of a pre-existing psychological condition. In other words, it was not Calvinism that produced inclinations towards rationalization and de-emotionalization of human behaviour, but on the contrary, Calvinism was adopted in order to satisfy such inclination. Thus, the argument can go round and round the circle of socio-psychological interconditioning.

The starting-point of the present investigation into the origin and development of various traits of the English national character was in a complex historical situation in which the English community found itself during the period of the interregnum. Two main ideas must be obvious by now. Firstly, this situation is psycho-social in its origin and character; it is a social and cultural state of radical change and disorganization translated at the psychological level into a state of disorientation and a low degree of integration in the structure of the human personality. Since the two aspects or levels are closely interrelated, any reductionist approach is liable to distortions. Secondly, the starting-point of this study was not an altogether arbitrary one. There is reason for believing that the sixteenth century was for the English community a psycho-historical focus, a situation full of developmental potential. Now, it is against this psycho-cultural background that the present investigation into the origins of affect-displacement and rationalization has been conducted. Naturally, at any stage in the development of these traits, one has to take into account the interplay between socio-cultural and psychological factors. For example, the state of anarchy characteristic of the psycho-historical situation of interregnum had stimulated at the psychological level the processes of rationalization and affect-displacement. But the expression 'at the psychological level' as used here is merely a manner of speech determined by an analytical attitude; in fact these processes cannot be tested in themselves before they have been actualized in a certain social and cultural form. And they were in fact actualized in certain economic practices, in a certain religious belief and ethics, in a certain system of human interrelation, and in many other social and cultural manifestations. The point is that these social and cultural manifestations had a feed-back effect on the processes of rationalization and affect-displacement. It is in this specific sense that commercial practices and Calvinist ethics stimulated a rational, de-emotionalized attitude to life.

This illustrates once more a basic methodological principle of historical psychology which we called earlier the principle of psychosocial cycles. Now a new application of the same principle can be formulated as follows: *no psycho-genesis without a socio-genesis,* and the reverse, *no socio-genesis without a psycho-genesis.* The socio-cultural and psychological conditions of historical development alternate with each other in such a close and complex chain of actions and reactions that neither can be isolated as an independent causal factor. The main concern of the historical psychologist is to find out the rules of this interrelation rather than to contrive patterns of unilinear causation on the lines of a mechanistic explanation. Nothing is more harmful to a true understanding of historical development than a reductionist attitude whether it be religious-spiritual in the manner of Max Weber, economic, in the manner of Marx, or psychological, in the manner of Freud.

FROM MOTIFS TO STRUCTURES

One can go a step further now, and describe in more systematic psychological terms the consequences which the situation outlined so far had for the structure of the individual's personality as well as for the cultural structure of the community.

The individual belonging to the modern English community is basically tolerant towards himself. He not only accepts, indeed attaches, positive values to the instinctual drives. This is not only his first but his basic contact with himself. The external world is for him an unknown resistance. 'Taking one's own chance' and 'looking for one's own interest' is to him the most natural thing in the world.

This basic acceptance of his instinctual drives determines the development and the final structure of the individual's personality; it determines in the first place the function of his super-ego. In order to cope with the destructive character of instinctual forces—or to use an expression coined during the period of interregnum—in order to escape the condition of '*homo homini lupus*', the individual developed two main dispositions which were described here as de-emotionalization and rationalization. By the former he denied to himself part of the satisfaction derived from the gratification of the instinctual drives; by the latter he shaped the manifestation of these drives according to certain socially acceptable patterns of behaviour. This resulted in a considerable amount of control over the instinctual drives, which is in fact the basic function of the super-ego.

But though de-emotionalization and rationalization sometimes take extreme forms, the super-ego characteristic of the Englishman is basically not opposed to his 'id'; its super-individual and ideal character is very feeble. Despite certain appearances to the contrary, the typical relation between these two basic structures of the individual's mind is one of mutual tolerance. Some psycho-cultural phenomena are symptomatic of this relationship. It is, for instance, a fact that modern English culture is the cradle of, as well as the most fertile soil for a series of beliefs and theoretical constructs according to which 'self-interest' coincides with the interests of others or with general interest. There is no need to analyse the cultural articulation of these beliefs. They were an important feature of the cultural climate of the late sixteenth century and of the seventeenth century. It is true that this coincidence is made possible only after a certain formal—not essential—transformation of the 'id'. But despite this it should be made explicit that 'self interest' refers primarily to the individual's 'id'. The mainly economic connotation in which this term was used during the above period is a proof of this. It would therefore be right to conclude that the system of beliefs regarding the coincidence between self-interest and social or general interest reveals a flexible super-ego in a co-operative relation with the 'id'. It should be added that this mental condition constitutes the primary source of the tolerance and understanding of others which the Englishman as an individual possesses in a high degree.

At this point an important question arises: Is not the Englishman strongly repressed? Is he not more repressed than the members of other Western communities? This seems a legitimate question, particularly for an outsider, if the following aspects of the Englishman's behaviour are taken into account: (a) his strong self-control and the inhibition of his affects in particular; (b) his conformism and conventionalism; (c) his legalism; (d) his frugality; (e) his fear of a tyrannical absolute God as expressed in the doctrine of predestination. This is enough to make anyone conclude that, contrary to what we have just been saying the Englishman's super-ego is intolerant, even tyrannical. However, this conclusion is not borne out by a deeper analysis of the characteristic personality structure of the Englishman, as we will quickly see.

It has been shown previously that affect-displacement and de-emotionalization do not imply repression of the individual's instinctive drives. On the contrary they often facilitate the individual's yielding to the 'id'. A series of psycho-cultural symptoms are relevant to this. For instance, the belief that feelings are 'bad' can mean that one can accept the demands of the instinctual drives if one could previously dissociate feelings from them, i.e. if feelings are kept to oneself. But this implies that the more one's feelings can be controlled, the more and the better one can act upon the demands of the 'id'. Thus de-emotionalization turns out to be a form of acceptance of the 'id'. It is this trait that made Max Weber apply the label 'sensualist without a heart' to the personality structure formed by Calvinism and Puritan ethics. Obviously, he referred to an extreme if not ideal type of the personality structure described here.

Though the Englishman's sense of social conformity is great, this results in far less repression than one would believe at first sight. This can be confirmed in two ways. Firstly the individual of the English community has a deep-rooted belief that society does not exist in its own right; it exists only as an abstraction, i.e. as a matter of convention which can at any moment be changed to suit the individual's interests. Secondly, since the early days of the modern era, the individual of the English community has formed the belief that his interests correspond to the interest of his community. 'One who helps himself, helps the nation' or 'individual prosperity leads to communal prosperity' were—and still are—formulae used in this context. It would, therefore, be right to conclude that conformity does not bring repression.

The Englishman's formal legalism, or fondness of the rule of law, is not a symptom of strong repression either. The empirical conception of law characteristic of the English culture should be taken into account here. Though the law might in particular cases be rigidly and severely applied, there is in fact nothing absolute or rigid in the character of the law itself. The fact that in England the law is created *by precedent*, coupled with the famous English hostility to 'written laws' says a lot in corroboration of this. It says at least that the law itself—like society—has no absolute reality, that it is empirical and therefore susceptible to change. This is a sign of a flexible rather than rigid super-ego. The Englishman is a law-abiding individualist; this cliché contains much truth.

There is little to be said, at this point, about the repressing effects of the ethics of frugality embodied in the doctrine and practice of worldly asceticism, or in the Calvinist belief of a tyrannical God.[1] Firstly, the doctrine and the practice of worldly asceticism provide the individual with a system of rules and values which, if conformed to, brings him material prosperity in the first place, i.e. a satisfaction of the libidinal drives of the 'id'. The most important of these rules and values are work, thrift, diligence and prudence. The super-ego based on such rules and values exercises no kind of repression on the 'id', on the contrary, it constitutes an increase in its gratification by a relatively short detour. And one should not forget that worldly asceticism and the super-ego based on it bring not only material prosperity but also salvation. This shows clearly that the belief in an absolutist tyrannical God is not a symptom of repression either. For, the fulfilment of God's command, which is identical with the rule of worldly asceticism, results in material prosperity for the individual. Again, salvation and material progress, that is to say the super-ego and the 'id', go hand in hand.

Keiserling characterizes the Englishman by the word 'instinct'; the Englishman is like a hunting dog; he is the only modern man who displays both as an individual and as a group, the security, directness and determination of instinctual behaviour. In the light of what has been said so far, Keiserling is essentially right. But the matter is much more complex than his terms suggest. For one thing, instinct is, in this case, not a purely biological reality. The reference to animal behaviour even as an analogy has therefore very limited value. As has been previously shown, the amount of deviation and change undergone by instinctual energy in the personality of the Englishman is by any standards

---

[1] What follows in this paragraph refers to a later development of these psycho-cultural traits. As said before, the early Puritans displayed a strong super-ego.

considerable. He rendered this energy more flexible by the process of rationalization; he has even split the primitive structure of the instinct by a systematic dissociation of affect from impulse. It is characteristic of his personality structure—and this relates directly to the changes introduced in his instinctual energy—that he formed a type of conscience, a type of super-ego, which is not on terms of contradiction with his instincts. Therefore, his determination, security, and directness are not of a purely instinctual character; they are structural, i.e. they are derived from his personality as a whole. His conscience and his instincts 'compound matters very amiably'. This is indeed a crucial point in the personality structure of the modern Englishman, and has to be dealt with in more detail.

MEDIEVAL AND ENGLISH PERSONALITY STRUCTURE

Since the Englishman's personality can be described as a prototype of secular personality, there is no better way of pointing out its main differential traits than by comparing it with the basic medieval personality structure. The two points which are particularly relevant here are the system of motivation and the pattern of emotional behaviour.

The motivational system of medieval man involved a basic duality, the voice of God at one level, and that of Satan at the other; spiritual calling on one side, and the temptation of the flesh, on the other; absolute transcendental goals, on the one hand, and worldly appetites on the other. Thus his personality included a basic polarity in the sense that his conscience, or super-ego, was opposed to the structure of his instinctual drives. The coherence and unity of this kind of mental organization was ensured by a series of inner mechanisms and institutionalized patterns of behaviour which made it possible for the individual to make alternating leaps between these two motivational structures. These inner mechanisms and the institutionalized patterns of behaviour were those of repentance, expiation and confession. Consequently the behavioural pattern of medieval man can be described as an oscillating movement between 'fall' and 'redemption', 'sin' and 'virtue', 'evil' and 'good'. A similar behavioural pattern is displayed today by many individuals whose personality has been formed in a Roman Catholic culture; it consists of a zigzag movement between the 'id' and the super-ego, between indulgence and guilt. The degree of inner unity in the medieval personality structure could not be high. The expression 'high-strung personality' which Huizinga applies to late medieval man can be extended to medieval man in general, although, for reasons mentioned elsewhere, the basic polarities characteristic of this personality structure were more clearly visible during the last centuries of the Middle Ages.

There is no duality in the motivational system of the basic English personality. The organization and unity of personality is, in this case, based on a relation of continuity, even of identity, between the motivational structures of the instinctual drives and the super-ego. How was this new development possible? Since the concern of this study as a whole has been to throw light on this question, we should be as brief as possible at this stage.

Firstly, the Reformation in many ways continued and consolidated the drive towards secularization initiated by the Renaissance. Though the psycho-analytical view, according to which Luther had, by the abolition of celibacy, opened the doors of the super-ego to the repressed sexual impulses (as Calvin did for the individual's material appetites) can easily be suspected of dogmatism, it is, nevertheless, true that the Reformation had, on the whole, minimized the conflict between the motivational structure of the instincts and that of the super-ego. This came as a result of a considerable limitation of the sacred authority of the Church. In this way the incompatibility between sacred values and worldly persuasion became less acute in many spheres of human life. The English Reformation contained more of these elements than the Continental Reformations.

Another aspect of the Reformation which expresses even more clearly the development of the characteristic motivational system of the basic English personality structure was the internalizing of the sacred religious symbols which formed the foundation of the medieval super-ego. As a result of the Reformation, God, dogma, Church, and even priesthood became more and more internalized symbols, and as such more liable to the individual's inner choice and personal interpretation. The proof of this—if proof is needed—is the pluralism of faith within the Reformed Church. Naturally, this inner search for and inner contact with God was bound to produce a closer link between God's will and the individual's wishes, between conscience and worldly needs.

There is something in the motivational process of the basic English personality which formally resembles the medieval mystic experience. The process is, in a sense, an inverted 'mystic union'. The medieval mystic opens his soul and lets God come in, undergoing by this both a dissolution of his own personality and a separation from the world, while the Englishman moves himself towards God trying to create God *in himself* and in the world. This secret meeting, taking place in an emotionally tense atmosphere, results not only in a close co-operation but also in a considerable confusion between the voice of God and that of man; the terms of the inner dialogue are often blurred by obscure passions. It is the result of one of these communions that made Angelus Silesius write: 'I know that without me God cannot exist for a moment.' Therefore—one may conclude—ask God to live with myself, rather than ask myself to live with God. This kind of conclusion was very obvious in the behaviour of the German Pietists; for example, as they went round in a closed circle from their own wishes to the wish of God, the circle became smaller and smaller until the two points met. The result was that God often agreed with the individual's wish.[1]

Though the relationship between the motivational system of the English basic personality and that indicated by mystic experience is one of formal parallelism, both involve considerable self-deception. What the individual believes to be the will of God is often his own will in disguise; what he expresses so convincingly in terms of his own duty and conscience may well be a simple personal wish; necessity can easily become virtue. Here lies the psychological root of the often talked-about English hypocrisy. For it is obviously true that the Englishman often— more often than the members of other modern communities— speaks about his interests and drives in terms of conscience, in terms of accepted social values. Sometimes this sounds intriguing in the ears of an outsider. A young woman wishing promotion or simply higher wages would normally go about it by asking for more *responsibility*. It is not done, for instance, for a member of a political party to show to others, or to himself that he

---

[1] H. R. Günther gives a series of convincing examples of this in his 'Psychologie des deutschem Pietismus', in *Personlichkeit und Geshichte*. 1947.

wishes a more important position; what he really wishes is to be 'helpful', or to 'offer his services'. This attitude should not, however, be taken as a simple deliberate disguise of one's own purposes. There is a good deal of truth in the opinion of a contemporary Englishman, a connoisseur in matters of national character, when he writes: 'our seeming hypocrisy arose, not from any desire to deceive others, but from a wish to comfort ourselves, and . . . it was furthered by our infinite capacity for self-deception . . .'[1]

This 'wish to comfort ourselves' has much to do both with the decline of the absolute values which formed the keynote of the medieval super-ego, and with the emergence of the prudential values such as thrift, moderation and work, which form the yeast of the modern Englishman's super-ego. In the rather extremist form characteristic of the early Puritans it can be put: God cannot be against an industrious, thrifty and provident man who works for his own, and at the same time, for God's glory. This can be called simply self-deception, but one has to bear in mind that this term—so often used by modern psychology—cannot easily be applied to the mental structure of individuals and communities who were fighting bitterly for their escape from the external authority of dogmas. The impression, and not only the desire, must have been very strong with these individuals that that which counted most in their actions was their own contact with God, their inner evidence, rather than the repercussions of their actions on others.

As a result of the internalizing process, revelation took its source within the individual who formed the habit of looking for the norms of his action in himself, in a set of inner evidences and convictions as well as internalized conventions. This all formed the substance of his conscience. There is no need to signify the novelty of this mental development. The personality of the Englishman has formed a series of intermediary stages and compromising functions between the super-ego and the 'id'. In this sense conscience has become a larger and more flexible structure which integrates the individual's instincts and values in a new unity. One can call this new unity character, or inner-directed personality, or simply secular conscience. However, terms do not matter. The important thing is that the motivational system, and

[1] Harold Nicolson: 'A Friendly Appraisal.' *The Observer,* June 8, 1958.

consequently, the personality structure of the Englishman displays a higher degree of unity than that of medieval man. This is mainly due to the emergence of a new kind of super-ego.

Though the term reason can be ambiguous, one can nevertheless say that the Englishman's super-ego has an essentially practical rational character, as opposed to an emotional idealist one. This implies that the norms and values which it contains do not have an absolute character; the individual's conformity to them is not carried out by emotional processes, such as fear or love. In the application of its norms the super-ego is deliberative and flexible, i.e. it takes into account the specific instinctual need which motivates the individual's reaction as well as the specific conditions in which the reaction takes place. As a result of this the Englishman displays in his behaviour a sense of unity and gradualness which are completely lacking in the personality of medieval man. Burke's reaction to the French Revolution is highly indicative of this basic trait of the English character. To the revolutionary enthusiasm he opposed the calm spirit of gradualness, to the calling of absolute reason, he opposed the practical wisdom of traditions and 'prejudices' as well as the sense of expediency.

In conclusion let it be said again that the English are the first and the most successful among modern nations to create a mental structure in which conscience and instincts are not fundamentally opposed. Thus they pushed the history of the mind a step forward from its medieval stage. André Gide once said that one of the main features of French civilization consists in an endless dialogue between nature and spirit. This indicates an attitude towards man oscillating between the poles of naturalism and spiritualism. There is nothing less English than this dialogue.

A comparison between the emotional pattern of medieval man and that of the basic English personality leads to a similar conclusion. The same duality and polarity are noticeable in the emotional behaviour of medieval man. The primitive emotions derived directly from the structure of his instinctual drives form one level, while the purified feelings related to the spiritual values of his super-ego form another. As the opposition between the two levels is absolute, the unity of personality is ensured by alternating leaps from one level to another. Thus, in his emotional behaviour medieval man showed a marked tendency to oscillate between the depths of sensuality and the heights of spirituality as his soul became possessed by his 'id', or by his super-ego. 'Possessed' is the right word here, for medieval man could not establish within his soul any compromise between these structures; his choice was to indentify himself either with the one, or with the other. There is little wonder that the striving towards '*coincidentia oppositorum*' had so much obsessed the medieval mystics.

There is a similarity between the emotional structure of medieval man and that of the Englishman: in both cases the primitive emotions are repressed by the super-ego. But the similarity is superficial, for the repressing processes, and particularly the manner in which the repressed emotionality is dealt with differ widely. The super-ego of medieval man accepts emotionality only after submitting it to a process of conversion. This operation is normally carried out by the mechanism of sublimation whose function is to dissociate emotionality from instinct and to project it on to ideal spiritual symbols. Thus love becomes acceptable only as disinterested or desensualised love, only as God inspired love; hatred itself becomes acceptable if projected on to the symbols of evil. In the medieval world enemies were naturally perceived as 'heretics' and friends as men of God. It goes without saying, that what was not dissociated from instincts and sublimized could not be accepted. Consequently the emotionality of medieval man was polarized into absolutely 'bad' and absolutely 'good' feelings.

Medieval man was either an idealist or an emotional primitive: the Englishman is neither. Lack of extremes, unilinearity, smoothness, monotony, and dullness are all terms which can be applied to the Englishman's emotional behaviour. They all suggest a certain amount of repression, as we saw at an earlier stage when dealing with the processes of affect-displacement and rationalization. But in order to understand the emotional behaviour of the Englishman one has to take into account the flexible and basically tolerant character of his super-ego. Owing to this tolerance the primary emotions, although inhibited, are not completely denied by suppression or conversion into ideal values. This can be formulated in a half allegorical manner as follows: Medieval man is either defeated by, or completely defeats his emotions, while the Englishman faces and controls them. Control is the keyword, for the Englishman accepts and displays his emotions as soon, and as long, as he feels that he is above them, that he can 'play them down'. It is most un-English to be overcome by feelings. This amounts to saying that feelings are displayed only to the extent to which they do not threaten the unity of the individual's personality, or as long as they do not distort the character. This can be illustrated in more than one way. Firstly, the Englishman is inclined to display emotionality if his emotions are associated with practical rational goals. For instance, his religiosity is enhanced when God is connected in one way or another with some of his persuasions in life. In more technical terms one can say that the emotional life of the Englishman is mainly manifested as sentiments, i.e. as emotions and feelings organized and controlled by practical rational goals or by social conventions and values. From this point of view the main mechanism by which the repressed emotionality is worked out is not sublimation, as in the case of medieval man, but rationalization. It is interesting to note that it was an Englishman who first spoke about the existence of such an unconscious mechanism.

Expressions such as 'practical rational goals' and 'rationalization' can be misleading. This is why it should be stressed again that 'control' and 'form' are the key terms in the understanding of the emotional behaviour of the Englishman. This sheds light on two emotional aspects of his behaviour, lyric moods and light-heartedness. The origin and nature of the former may become understandable if one takes into account that lyric poetry— for which the Englishman is so outstandingly gifted—is a unique form of expression of the individual's personality as an integrated whole and a value in itself. As such it represents a situation in which the individual exercises his fundamental need for giving form to, and controlling his feelings. The second aspect is more difficult to explain and has seldom been remarked by students in this field. According to a view very popular abroad, the English are gloomy, suffering from spleen and melancholy. The personal view of the writer is that this is a Continental caricature of the Englishman. The truth is that one can see much more cheerfulness among the English than among many other nations. However, this cheerfulness differs in some of its qualities, or rather in one of its dimensions from the cheerfulness of other people. It seems to be more childish, more naïve, more nonchalant in its character. The English are fond of, and often indulge in feelings of light-heartedness. The reason for this seems to be twofold. Firstly, such feelings are a natural compensation and refuge from the strongly practical and rational orientation of their emotionality in general. Secondly—and this is merely stating the obvious—light-heartedness and flippancy, however exuberantly expressed, cannot compel; beneath the thin layer of emotionality lies the impressive solidity of the individual's character and self-control. Thus the emotional behaviour of the Englishman, as opposed to that of medieval man, displays the same evenness and cohesion which are characteristic of other aspects of his personality.

There is nothing that an Englishman dislikes, and perhaps fears, more than feelings that threaten by their intensity the inner unity and control of his personality. It is said, particularly among foreigners, that one can get anything from an Englishman if the appeal is made 'on compassionate grounds'. This may, or may not be the case. What seems to be true is that the Englishman cannot tolerate over-riding feelings in himself or in others. As soon as such a situation is created his reaction is to minimize the pressure, and thus to bring the individual's feelings under the moulding and controlling power of his character. Naturally this deep-seated sense of proportion is often realized by sacrificing richness and intensity in the sphere of sensibility. This is often pointed out as a flaw in the English character. But on the other hand, it can be said that measure, proportion and style in feelings are values in themselves, aesthetic as well as moral values. In their emotional behaviour the English have something comparable to the Greek sense of proportion and harmony.

One point of principle needs clarifying at this stage. According to a commonly accepted view the super-ego is highly emotional; it is the seat of ideal-formation, and as such it is rigid and absolute in its demands upon the individual. The super-ego requires conformity at any cost. It would, therefore, be advisable to introduce here a new term, namely the ego. For, generally speaking, it is the ego that fulfils the functions which have been attributed to the super-ego of the modern Englishman. The ego is flexible, realistic, and rational in the sense given to those terms above. Moreover, the ego is an individualizing structure, i.e. it compromises between the individual's instinctual drives, between the reality of the situation, on one side, and social norms, on the other. Finally the ego is, according to psycho-analysis—an intermediary structure between the 'id' and the super-ego; its function is to socialize the 'id', on the one hand, and to individualize the social norms on the other. These are two adjustive processes strongly present in the personality of the modern Englishman.

With this in mind the personality structure outlined above could be described as an ego-centred or strong ego personality. But this is mainly a matter of terminology. On the other hand, it seems that one of the characteristics of the English personality structure consists precisely in the difficulty to be faced when trying to distinguish clearly between the functions and the status of his ego and those of his super-ego in the usual acceptance of these terms. This difficulty is objectively attested by the belief widespread among members of the modern English community in the coincidence between self-interest and general interest, by their congenial anti-idealistic and anti-spiritualistic attitudes. Would it not be more accurate to say that the Englishman has a personality structure with a strongly individualized super-ego? Nothing can be more significant for this view than the evolution of English political and economic thought during the modern era. This is in many respects one and the same thing with the evolution of the modern liberal mind whose main tenets are: (a) Society is essentially an 'association' based on the individual's needs for survival and security; it therefore implies a deliberative attitude, or at least, provides for the development of such an attitude. (b) Society is a technique, a tool; it provides the mechanism of human welfare and pleasure. As such it is highly historical in the sense that it is moulded and re-moulded according to the needs it has to satisfy, and according to circumstances. In other words, society is a fluid process which has no ideal limit. (c) Society is a consensus based on common interests, and as such has a strong utilitarian hedonistic character. Though this is partly implied in the first two points, it deserves special mention, because it reveals a very close association between society, law, and order, on one side, and the pleasure principle on the other. The basic conviction is that there is a continuity between spontaneity and order, between pleasure and society.

Now, bearing in mind that the super-ego is 'internalized society' the inferences one can make from these points are revealing for the nature of the Englishman's super-ego. Its opposition to the medieval super-ego comes fully to light. While the latter is glued to a permanent ideal world, the former is adjustable to the individual's needs and to the circumstances; while the latter is based on spiritual goals, the former has strong utilitarian hedonistic traits: while the latter aims at salvation, the former aims at survival and self-realization.

A FEW CULTURAL CONSIDERATIONS

Most of what has been said bears directly upon the cultural structure developed by the English community, during the modern era. Some points demand, however, a more explicit treatment.

An individual with a flexible and rational super-ego has an inner-centred personality. On the social plane he is inclined to build up an open social structure. Society is in fact a reality of derivative order. It is a matter of habit, debate and understandings among individuals. In this sense one can say that the basic English personality structure has expressed itself in an individualized democratic society.

The relation between the personality structure described above and the economic system based on private initiative, and free enterprise, on profit-making, and accumulation of capital is obvious. Obvious also is the connection between such a personality structure and the individualist character of secular ethics, or commercial ethics, as it is sometimes called. The same traits of the basic English personality structure, and particularly the relations between conscience and instinct characteristic of it, can explain the preference of the English community for a materialistic outlook on the world in which science is placed at the top of the value system.

The part played by religion in the personality structure described above has been a highly controversial matter for a long time, and particularly since the publication of Max Weber's work, *The Protestant Ethics and the Spirit of Capitalism*. Many traits which have in the present study been attributed to the English personality structure were derived by Weber, in a slightly different form, from the impact of Calvinism upon the English middle classes. De-emotionalization, rationalization, secular conscience, individualism and self-interest are some of these traits. In other words, the personality structure characteristic of the English middle classes—which, according to the present study, influenced the whole nation—was, according to Weber, a religious product.

Weber's thesis aroused strong discussions and protests. A series of studies—Brentano, Sombart, Pirenne, and Robertson— have set out to prove that the spirit of capitalism and the type of man representing it existed before the Reformation. Robertson in particular goes back to the thirteenth century to prove the existence, during that period, of a capitalist economy with all its implied mental attitudes such as competitive spirit, gain-seeking, and rationalization of life. Thus, according to him, the determining relation goes in an opposite direction from that suggested by Weber: it was the spirit of capitalism that determined the adoption and creation of Protestant ethics. Calvinism suited the economic habits of the middle classes.

A psycho-historical approach may, however, throw new light on Weber's view. Firstly, what Weber means by the 'spirit of capitalism' is nearer to what one could describe as integrated personality structure than to a simple economic practice; the 'spirit of capitalism' is a verbal symbol for a type of man whose distinctive character cannot be derived only from a particular kind of economic activity, but rather from the more complex fact that he has formed a conscience, a super-ego, which tolerates, even stimulates this kind of behaviour. Secondly, by the 'spirit of capitalism' Weber also means a society and culture in which the practice of capitalist economy is not only a tolerated form of activity but is stimulated by an adequate system of beliefs, conceptions and values. 'Spirit' means an integrated whole. Now, it seems obvious that if so defined, the 'spirit of capitalism' did not exist before the advent of Calvinism, and of the English Reformation in particular. For, the flourishing capitalist practice in the Italian cities of the Renaissance—Venice, Florence, and Genoa —in Augsburg, Antwerp, and even in sixteenth-century London, was carried out by a limited number of individuals who can best be described as sociological and moral 'islands'. They lived in a society with a system of values which was not their own. Psychologically this is of paramount importance. The personality of these individuals was not integrated. On the contrary, it has a split character, in the sense that the conscience of these individuals, as members of a society based on traditional Christian values, was in permanent conflict with the values lying at the basis of their economic practices. Up to the very end of the Middle Ages, the capitalist groups of various countries had the feeling of leading a 'clandestine' life. They repeatedly showed their eagerness to know—and sometimes to influence—the opinion of the theologians of the time about matters such as the compatibility between money speculation and the canon law.

It is only after the advent of Calvinism that one can speak in the true sense about the spirit of capitalism. For it was during and through the rise and development of this religious movement that a specific psycho-historical process came to maturity. The individuals engaged in commercial practices formed a conscience which not only approved of the values on which such practice was based, but stimulated them. They also formed a society and a civilization based on these values. This is the spirit of capitalism; it is a *Weltanschauung*, or a type of personality and culture integrated round a particular type of economic practice.

Though, in the sense demonstrated above, Weber is essentially right, there are two points of criticism which arise. Firstly, his argument centres round an ideal type of personality characteristic more of the middle classes than of other strata of the English community. Secondly, he often overstresses the part played by religious factors—Puritanism in this case—in the formation of human character. One of the aims of the present study has been to show that the origin of the English character lies in a complex historical situation which in many ways preceded the religious Reformation. The religious movement of Puritanism on which Weber lays such an important stress, is only one stage in the formation of this character. It articulates into a final structure dispositions and trends created before its advent.

INSTEAD OF SUMMARY: LIMITATIONS

As has been said repeatedly, this is a psycho-historical study; its main task is not to describe the English national character, but rather to define an original psycho-historical situation from which some of the main traits of this character can be derived. Its main thesis is that a psychological phenomenon cannot fully be understood except in a historical perspective; the mind is what it is because of what it was. Psychology should aim at being a historical science as well as a positive experimental one.

But apart from its limited task, and the specific thesis it sets out to prove, this study suffers from other important limitations. The most important are:

(a) *Sociological*. It can be said that the character structure outlined in the foregoing pages fits the middle classes rather than the modern English nation as a whole. This is to a certain extent true. There is, however, one point, which if taken into account might considerably minimize the importance of such an objection. From the seventeenth century onwards this character structure has been extended in various degrees to all classes. This is a historical fact, and there is little need to resort to any of the well-known 'dominant class' theories in order to explain it. After all, there is much to be said about the middle-class character of the modern English nation.

(b) *Historical*. The character structure described above has a restricted historical application. For instance, it does not apply, or only in a limited sense, to the twentieth-century English community. It has, however, to be said that this study is concerned with the historical origins of this character structure. It would, nevertheless, be important to see the historical evolution of the main traits included in this structure. In the opinion of the writer this structure has, on the whole, been preserved, and even intensified up to the Victorian period.

(c) *Psychological and Moral*. Perhaps too much stress has been put in this study on the unity of the personality structure defining the English character; too much stress has been put, for instance, on the strength of secular conscience, and the tolerant attitude towards the instinctual drives. There are grounds for believing that in some ways the traditional Christian conscience was not altogether dissolved. Consequently the individual often shows the tendency to act according to the transcendental values of Christianity. In this case, he no longer sees his final salvation as a result of the same effort towards material prosperity. The presence of the old traditional super-ego seems to be a fact, and it indicates a potential defection in the character structure described above.

It must be said, however, that as far as the English character structure is concerned this basic defection has seldom come out as moral polarity or duality. This duality has become more obvious after the transplantation of this character structure to America. This seems to be an interesting case of cultural diffraction. But even there, one cannot speak about a divided structure, Christian and commercial morality co-exist.

(d) *Methodological*. The personality structure which I have developed in this study, defines the English national character as, admittedly, an *ideal type*. The only thing that could be said here on this point is that *ideal* is not the equivalent of *unreal*. The traits which have been attributed to the English national character may not be visible in the behaviour of all individuals, and at any time in their life. They, nevertheless, constitute constant trends, aspirations and values to which each individual tends, consciously or unconsciously to adjust his personality. They are general vectors in the psycho-social field.

INDEX

Index

Insecurity, 45, 46; generalised, 48; and messianic feelings, 50, 51, 67; and social unrest, 151–2
Introjection, 75
Interregnum, period in England, 154

Jaeger, W., 69, 71, 72, 87, 96 n., 102, 141
James I, King of England, 196
Jonson, 174

Kallinos, 78, 81, 83
Katharsis, 89, 100
Keiserling, Count, 204
Kempis, Thomas, 185 n.
King Lear, 170–2
Kitto, H. D. F., 142
Kyd, 174

Lamprecht, 12
Laud, Archbishop, 194
Lassaigne J., 33 n.
Law, attitude to, in Greece, 104; and punishment, 106
Leach, A., 157 n.
Lévy-Bruhl, 7
Lewin, K., 2
Louis XIV, 193 n.
Lucianic, *Lucianique,* 61, 160, 161 n.
Luther, 152, 153, 206
Lykurgos, 104
Lyons, silk workers' rising, 48

Machiavelli, 163, 164, 187
Magic, mentality, in Greece, 77, 100, 112, 113; in sixteenth century France, 23–4
Manichean, 54, 64
Marguerite de Navarre, 22
Marlowe, 174
Marston, 174
Marx, 56, 137, 201
Masculinity-Femininity, in sixteenth-century England, 166, 167
McDougall, W., 14
Medea, Euripides' play, 88
Medieval Man, ambivalent feelings of, 59–63; personality of, 162, 205–6; self-awareness of, 76; emotionality of, 209–10
Menander, 73, 123–5, 138
Meyerson, J., 77 n.
Middle Classes, in Greece, 90; in England, 149, 153, 180, 181, 184; and Puritanism, 185; and English character, 193, 217
Mimnermos of Kolophon, 81
Misch, G., 72 n., 78 n., 139, 141
Modern Man, 142–4, 168
Moira, 82
Monism, 119, 134
Monotheism, 134, 139
Monnerot, J., 48, 49
Murray, G., 123

Myers, A. R., 185
Myths, secular, 49

Nazism, 16
Nicolson, H., 194, 208
Nietzsche, 143
Nihilism, 56
Nomoi, 104, 105

Odyssey, 83 n., 122
Open society, 70
Orphic cults, 53, 100
Oresteia, 86
Orestes, Euripides' play, 88
Ossian, 52

Paros, battle of, 79
Participation, *mistique,* 77
Paston Family, 166 n.
Pathos, 165
Peacham, H., 196
Perception, 20 ff; definition of, 20; developmental aspects of, 31; historical aspects of, 21, 31, 39–42; and the Renaissance, 26, 27, 35, 40; and repression, 40; and science, 25–9, 35, 37, 38; and the self, 29, 30, 34, 35; and space representation, 35–8; and system of beliefs, 24–6, 36, 37; and inner security, 26–31; in sixteenth century France, 22–4; and techniques, 38, 42
Pericles, 89, 92, 135, 136
Personality, definition of, 129–30; historical character of, 6, 130, 132, 140–2; and religion, 134, 135; formation of, in Greece, 73, 74; formation of, in England, 180 ff.
Phryne, 138
Piaget, J., 7, 36, 105, 111
Pilgrims' Progress, 64
Pindar, 79
Pirenne, H., 215
Plato, 103, 107, 123
Pluralism, ethic, 110, 111
Polarity, cultural, 63; mental, 142, 143
Political naturalism, 186–7
Popper, K., 85 n.
Polybius, 70, 127, 138
Polytheism, 134
Praxiteles, 138
Pre-individualistic, civilizations, 71–3, 76, 117
Pre-Socratics, 84 n., 85, 113, 115
Primitive Man, 77
Projection, 75
Psycho-genesis, 81
Psycho-historical, focus, 10, 102, 200
Psycho-social, cycles, 14–16, 162, 181, 200, 201; model of explanation, 65
Ptolemy, 50